The Prophet of Harvard Law

AMERICAN POLITICAL THOUGHT

Jeremy D. Bailey and Susan McWilliams Brandt
Series Editors

Wilson Carey McWilliams and Lance Banning
Founding Editors

The Prophet of Harvard Law

JAMES BRADLEY THAYER AND HIS LEGAL LEGACY

Andrew Porwancher, Jake Mazeitis,
Taylor Jipp, Austin Coffey

 University Press of Kansas

Published by the University Press of Kansas (Lawrence, Kansas 66045), which
was organized by the Kansas Board of Regents and is operated and funded by
Emporia State University, Fort Hays State University, Kansas State University,
Pittsburg State University, the University of Kansas, and Wichita State
University.

Library of Congress Cataloging-in-Publication Data

Names: Porwancher, Andrew, author. | Mazeitis, Jake, author. | Jipp, Taylor,
   author. | Coffey, Austin, author.
Title: The prophet of Harvard Law : James Bradley Thayer and his legal legacy /
   Andrew Porwancher, Jake Mazeitis, Taylor Jipp, Austin Coffey.
Description: Lawrence, Kansas : University Press of Kansas, 2022. | Series:
   American political thought | Includes index.
Identifiers: LCCN 2021061655
   ISBN 9780700633593 (cloth)
   ISBN 9780700633609 (ebook)
Subjects: LCSH: Thayer, James Bradley, 1831–1902—Influence. | Law
   teachers—Massachusetts—Cambridge—Biography. | Harvard Law
   School—History—19th century.
Classification: LCC KF368.T45 P67 2022 | DDC 340.071/17444 [B 23'eng'20220]
   —dc30
LC record available at https://lccn.loc.gov/2021061655.

British Library Cataloguing-in-Publication Data is available.

Printed in the United States of America

10 9 8 7 6 5 4 3 2 1

The paper used in this publication is acid free and meets the minimum
requirements of the American National Standard for Permanence of Paper for
Printed Library Materials Z39.48-1992.

To John Hansen

It is usually assumed in the law that a man, even of pre-eminent ability, must close his career upon the bench, if he is to perpetuate his name. It must be admitted that a lawyer who has not done this can leave no conspicuous and tangible proof of his learning. But if a man's work is more important than the world's knowledge of that work, and if a man's life is more important than an emblazoned monument after his death, then it is true that Professor Thayer did a work and lived a life which achieved the best results. . . . More important than the existence of innumerable printed decisions is the service which he has rendered to thousands of men who are to-day practicing the law throughout all the States of this country. While these men live his influence will be felt, and through their instruction of others his influence will be perpetuated.

—Charles Sherman Haight, "James Bradley Thayer," *Columbia Law Review* 2 (1902): 240

Contents

List of Figures, ix

Preface, xi

Acknowledgments, xiii

Introduction, *1*

1 Thayer's Origins, *9*

2 Thayer's Scholarship, *28*

3 Thayer's Protégé: Oliver Wendell Holmes Jr., *62*

4 Thayer's Students: Louis Brandeis, John Henry Wigmore, Roscoe Pound, and Learned Hand, *88*

5 Thayer's Heir: Felix Frankfurter, *125*

Conclusion, *141*

Notes, 145

Index, 177

Figures

James Bradley Thayer, 1852, *12*
Dane Hall, circa 1850, *15*
James Bradley Thayer, circa 1874, *21*
James Bradley Thayer, circa 1885, *33*
Oliver Wendell Holmes Jr., 1867, *63*
Louis Brandeis, circa 1876, *89*
John Henry Wigmore, 1887, *99*
Roscoe Pound, circa 1904, *107*
Learned Hand, 1893, *114*
Felix Frankfurter, circa 1910, *127*

Preface

When I arrived more than a decade ago as a new faculty member at the University of Oklahoma, I was immediately struck by the high caliber of our best undergraduate students. I have long thought that many of them, with some guidance, would be capable of producing publishable work. Finally, in 2019, I decided to test that theory. I asked three recent alumni of my department whether they had any interest in working alongside me on a new book, not as research assistants but as full-fledged coauthors. The subject of the monograph, I explained, was the understudied legacy of a nineteenth-century legal scholar. Happily, they all agreed to participate. The relationship between authorship and topic—a book *by* a professor and his former students *about* a professor and his former students—was perhaps too on the nose. But we proceeded apace regardless. Whatever merit there may be in the pages that follow is owed in large part to their talents and efforts.

I am hardly alone in recognizing the considerable abilities of my coauthors. Jake Mazeitis is currently enrolled at Yale Law School. Taylor Jipp is pursuing graduate study at the University of Cambridge. Austin Coffey became a Luce Scholar and then research associate at Kissinger Associates. Given all their individual accomplishments, I am grateful to have my own name attached to our collective endeavor.

Andrew Porwancher
Norman, OK

Acknowledgments

We would first like to thank the team at the University Press of Kansas for helping to bring this book to fruition. David Congdon is a thoughtful editor who stewarded the project through the publication process with diligence and insight. Thanks as well to all those involved in the production, publicity, and design.

We are indebted to the archivists and librarians at the Harvard Law School Library Historical and Special Collections, Houghton Library at Harvard University, and McCormick Library of Special Collections and University Archives at Northwestern University. Many thanks to the University of Missouri Press for permitting the reproduction of select passages from *John Henry Wigmore and the Rules of Evidence: The Hidden Origins of Modern Law* (from pages 3, 8, 9–10, 22, 37–47, 52, 56–57, 70–73, 80, 137–138). The Institute for the American Constitutional Heritage and the Department of Classics and Letters at the University of Oklahoma supported the completion of this project. Cassie DeGroot offered invaluable research assistance.

While we are obliged to the foregoing persons for their aid, any errors of fact or interpretation rest with the authors alone.

Finally, we wish to thank a longtime member of the Department of Classics and Letters, John Hansen, who outpaces even James Bradley Thayer in his selfless devotion to students. It is to him that we dedicate this book.

Andrew Porwancher
Norman, OK

Jake Mazeitis
New Haven, CT

Taylor Jipp
Cambridge, UK

Austin Coffey
New York, NY

Introduction

The snowstorm was punishing, even by the standards of a New England winter, but the students remained undeterred. They gathered by the hundreds outside his home. Forming an honor guard, they escorted his casket through the streets of Cambridge. Bells began to toll as the procession passed under Johnston Gate into Harvard Yard. The cortege then reached Appleton Chapel in the heart of campus. Just a week prior, the students had been in class learning at the feet of the legendary professor who had mentored three decades of aspiring lawyers. Now, unexpectedly, they found themselves partaking in the funeral rites of James Bradley Thayer.[1]

If Thayer's death in 1902 marked the end of his era for Harvard Law, it was merely the beginning of his legacy for American law. His circle of protégés had not yet reached their greatest heights. Thayer's name is largely forgotten today, but those who carried on his legal philosophy are certainly not: Oliver Wendell Holmes Jr., Louis Brandeis, and Learned Hand, to name only a few. For sixty years following Thayer's burial, one or more of his acolytes sat on the US Supreme Court, while others became preeminent appellate judges and law school deans across the country. From these lofty perches, they reshaped the law in Thayer's image.

His life stretched the last seven decades of the nineteenth century, and in many respects, his journey embodied America's own. In an era of rapid urbanization, he moved from a rural village in western Massachusetts to the growing metropolis of Boston-Cambridge. Amid a transportation revolution, Thayer worked as a young reporter covering the expansion of railroads in the West. At a time when Harvard Law became the forerunner of modern professional education, he belonged to its small but nimble faculty that pioneered innovations. The case method of instruction, full-time research faculty, three-year degrees, alumni committees, law reviews, comprehensive libraries, greater meritocracy—the elemental features of today's law schools were launched during Thayer's era, and he played a critical role in their realization.

But it was not merely legal training that required updating. The law itself had grown increasingly out of touch with the modern age. Over the span of Thayer's lifetime, he saw the world of candlelight give way to electricity, horse-drawn carriages yield to locomotives, and countryside farms lose ground to cityside factories. Against the backdrop of these seismic changes, Thayer advanced a jurisprudence to meet the moment.

In Thayer's philosophy of the law—which would come to be known as "legal realism"—legal principles are not categorical maxims but at best flexible guidelines with all manner of exceptions.[2] Common-law doctrines do not exist in the ether as some embodiment of eternal justice; they are man-made and historically contingent.[3] Far from autonomous, law is deeply woven into the broader fabric of society.[4] The value of legal doctrine ought to be appraised by its real-world consequences rather than its consonance with abstract principle.[5] Lived experience, not hollow logic, must determine its trajectory.[6] Expedience and practicality are reason enough to establish, discard, or legitimize a given rule.[7] The federal and state constitutions are living documents to be flexibly interpreted in accordance with modern demands.[8] Thayer often defined his ideas as a rejection of formalism—a model of law wherein objective judges discover universal and timeless principles, which they then apply with syllogistic precision to achieve rectitude of decision and uniformity of result.[9] He saw the world as far too complex for such a facile approach.

Thayer's view of judicial discretion was his most important contribution to legal realism. He maintained that the resolution of disputes in court requires that judges make and not merely interpret policy. Legislating from the bench is unavoidable. While judges may prefer to make false pretenses to self-restraint and obscure their legislative role, it is far better for them to candidly concede this reality. Such an acknowledgment, however, does not justify unfettered judicial activism. To the contrary, only by forthrightly recognizing the inevitability of judicial legislation can its scope be appropriately circumscribed. The bench must take special pains to exercise restraint when considering the constitutionality of statutes.[10]

Legal realism dominated American law in the twentieth century—and did so largely thanks to the outsized influence of Thayer's protégés. Holmes came under Thayer's tutelage long before gaining renown as, arguably, the most important justice of his day. Brandeis and Hand were star students who further popularized Thayer's ideas on the bench. Two of the most important law school deans, Roscoe Pound and John Henry Wigmore, had also been Thayer's pupils. And a host of other significant jurists, most notably Felix Frankfurter, came of age after Thayer's passing but self-consciously fashioned themselves Thayerites.

This constellation of judges and scholars was so effective at promoting a realist agenda that their insights are now considered commonplace truisms. But before assuming their places on the bench and in the academy, they were young men in their intellectually formative years—and it was then that Thayer left his indelible mark. In the eyes of many of his followers, Thayer was no mere mentor. He was a quasi-religious figure bequeathing to them revealed truths. Wigmore referred to Thayer as his "master and father-confessor" and counted himself among Thayer's faithful "disciples."[11] Hand described Thayer as a "prophet."[12] Frankfurter exalted Thayer's theory of judicial restraint as his "Alpha and Omega," invoking the two Greek letters that together refer to God in the book of Revelation.[13] If Holmes was the father of realism, Thayer was the godfather.

That a single scholar who taught at only one institution could leave such an enduring imprint on American law vividly underscores the hierarchical nature of legal progress. Elite judges, lawyers, and professors have long wielded power highly disproportionate to their numbers. The pyramidal nature of the court system requires it, as precedent is handed down from on high. And while the work of prestigious scholars is not likewise binding on their lesser-known peers, academic stars nonetheless catalyze trends that pervade their fields of study. Only in a world where a small handful of thought leaders in the courthouse and ivory tower set the national pace for rulings and research—and who shared a single mentor—was it even possible for someone like Thayer to exert such a far-reaching impact.

Although his list of publications is hardly extensive, it is a testament to Thayer's personal relationships that what little he did write always commanded a sympathetic audience. The best example of Thayer's minimal output enjoying vast reach is his iconic study "The Origin and Scope of the American Doctrine of Constitutional Law." Appearing in the *Harvard Law Review* in 1893, "Origin and Scope" has been referred to by one twenty-first-century scholar as "probably the most influential article about constitutional law ever written."[14] The twenty-eight-page essay explored the proper bounds of judicial review. Drawing on legal doctrine, historical investigation, and political philosophy, Thayer forcefully argued that the bench must afford legislation a presumption of constitutionality. The question, then, is not whether a presiding judge believes that a given statute comports with the constitution but whether anyone rationally could. If so, the law must stand. As Thayer famously put it, the courts "can only disregard the Act when those who have the right to make laws have not merely made a mistake, but have made a very clear one—so clear that it is not open to rational question."[15] His theory applied to American courts, legislatures, and constitutions, regardless of whether they were federal or state.

Thayer's desire to sharply limit judicial review rested on his most fundamental belief about American democracy. For him, the foundational principle of democracy is self-government. In a republic, that principle finds its ultimate expression through the people choosing representatives to pass the laws that govern their lives. Legislators, sure enough, will sometimes enact misguided statutes. But a grave danger lies in reliance upon an activist judiciary to undo the people's will. The proper forum to remedy legislative mistakes is not the courtroom but the ballot box. If we resort to an unelected bench to save democracy, it is already lost.

Thayer's theory of judicial restraint became a lodestar for a generation of progressives because it was perfectly suited to the exigencies of the era. Industrial capitalism was then generating extraordinary wealth for a select few. It also exacted a brutal toll on innumerable laborers who toiled long hours in dangerous jobs for little pay. Lawmakers in statehouses and Congress, responsive to the outcry of the voting masses, passed sweeping legislation to mitigate the excesses of capitalism. Judges were generally slower than legislators to comprehend novel industrial realities, and in a number of high-profile cases they struck down new regulations. Reformers decried an activist bench that enacted its own policy preferences in place of those codified by the people's representatives. Thayer's canonical "Origin and Scope" article provided these progressives with a legal, philosophical, and historical basis on which to mount a defense of their legislative achievements against judicial interference.

Thayer's jurisprudence reveals the arbitrariness of our current ideological spectrum in the law. Today many people conflate judicial restraint with conservatives and living constitutionalism with liberals; originalists pride themselves on privileging the former and rejecting the latter. But to Thayer, judicial deference to legislatures was in perfect harmony with an adaptive mode of constitutional interpretation. He believed that in a modernizing America, federal and state lawmakers should see their governing constitutions as flexible charters that empowered them to robustly address modern needs. And it was the role of judges to stand back and let them. If that required rejecting the original intent of the framers, so be it.

While Thayer the scholar championed a vision of American law that would resonate in the twentieth century, Thayer the gentleman was rooted in the nineteenth. He was heir to neither family fortune nor lofty lineage, yet Thayer always felt at home amid the elite "Boston Brahmins" (a term coined by Dr. Oliver Wendell Holmes Sr., father of his future protégé). Thayer's undergraduate education, legal training, and professorship all took place at Harvard, the epicenter of Brahmin life. He belonged to various literary and social clubs that were de rigueur for patrician Bostonians. And Thayer was often praised for exhibiting genteel values: honor, moderation, affability. His gentility was not merely a matter of temperament or taste—it informed his intellectual orientation as well. Thayer held fast to the ideal of a well-rounded gentleman-scholar who knew something of everything. Even as Thayer recognized and advocated the specialization that a modern economy demanded, he never abandoned generalism. In many respects, then, Thayer was an intermediary figure who bridged the antebellum world of his birth and the Progressive Era of his death.[16]

This book comes with caveats. It should not be read to imply that Thayer was the sole influence upon his mentees; people are complex and their intellectual debts many. In the pages that follow, we seek to make a contribution, not a substitution.

Another qualification: Thayer was not quite the radical that some of his devotees liked to imagine. Although they described him as "subversive" and "heretical," in truth Thayer was more of an innovator than an iconoclast. Other voices in the late nineteenth century promoted legal realism.[17] To concede, however, that Thayer was not wholly singular for his era is hardly to suggest that he was mainstream. Contemporaries recognized his work as provocative. "Origin and Scope" struck some as "peculiar" and even "unpalatable."[18] And Thayer truly *was* unique in one respect—no other professor in American history shaped more giants of legal realism. His endowed chair at Harvard Law afforded him stature and credibility. It also granted him direct access to future leaders of the bar, bench, and academy. Thayer brought to his vocation a commitment to mentorship that allowed him to capitalize on that access and thereby proliferate his legal philosophy.

To be sure, not every tenet that would become associated with the legal realist movement found expression in Thayer's thought. He did not urge the bench to apply balancing tests as a means of reconciling competing values, doctrines, and policy concerns.[19] Nor did Thayer anticipate the call for social scientific data to supplant legal precedent.[20] And the realist exhortation to reorient law around the collective rather than the individual never materialized in Thayer's writings.[21] These ideas came into vogue after his lifetime. That Thayer advanced most, but not all, of the realist agenda lends itself to a disclaimer. Legal realism was not a monolithic movement, as a number of historians have rightfully cautioned.[22] Not every realist subscribed to every tenet associated with realism, and realists disagreed among themselves on any number of issues. It would, moreover, be reductive to assume that realism covers the totality of Thayer's thought.[23] Still, the term *legal realism* is useful as a semantic tool for our purposes because it allows us to describe a largely shared vision for American law that united Thayer and his acolytes.

Another caveat is in order regarding the jurisprudential terrain that Thayer occupied. He and his band of realist disciples often juxtaposed their approach with legal formalism. In their eyes, formalists were engaged in a comforting fantasy that ignored the hard realities of law. Formalism provided the façade of a dispassionate judiciary neutrally applying impartial principles, a myth that masked how a biased bench inscribed its prejudices into law—or so the realists claimed. For all the realists' hand-wringing about formalism, such a reductive jurisprudence hardly prevailed in the Gilded Age and the Progressive Era. While true that a conservative judiciary sometimes impeded progressive legislation, the bench's often sluggish recalibration of the law to modern times did not equate to a mythical formalist agenda. And although some contemporaries of Thayer's advanced formalism, they were not dominant. The legal system that the realists sought to tame was characterized not so much by formalism as by the dearth of any organizing philosophy. Formalism was more of a straw man against which realists railed than a reigning jurisprudence in Thayer's age.[24]

An additional comment about our vernacular is warranted. A Thayer admirer coined the term *legal realism* in 1930, decades after Thayer's death.[25] Though the nomenclature postdates Thayer, the jurisprudential values that *legal realism* denotes were very much at play in his philosophy, so we use the term freely. We find comparable utility in other anachronistic terms such as *judicial review, originalism, living constitutionalism,* and *judicial activism.*[26] These idioms may not have appeared during Thayer's era either, but the concepts they denote certainly did.

Finally, this book—though biographical in certain respects—makes no claims to be a full-fledged biography. Our focus, instead, is on the development of Thayer's thought and his influence. Details of his life merit comment insofar as they are relevant to these topics. But a comprehensive biographical study lies beyond our ambit here. We also depart from the structural conventions of biography; our interest in Thayer's impact upon others has led us to privilege interpersonal relationships over pure chronology as an organizing principle, particularly in the latter half of the book.

Scholars in recent decades have published articles, many of them excellent, on various aspects of Thayer's jurisprudence, but no one has attempted a book about Thayer and his legacy. This is the first. Each of his disciples discussed in this volume—Holmes, Brandeis, Wigmore, Hand, Pound, and Frankfurter—has inspired at least one book-length treatment and often more. And yet Thayer, who shaped all these figures, has never before received comparable consideration.[27]

This omission is not an arbitrary oversight. It is, rather, symptomatic of a bias in the field of legal history. Service on the bench is usually a prerequisite for a book about a given legal figure. Unsurprisingly so, as a judicial appointment affords high visibility and concrete power. And to the extent that legal scholars of past generations are deemed worthy of attention, that honor is typically reserved for those whose corpus of writing is so extensive as to beggar the imagination. Wigmore was prolific enough that his scholarship, when lined on a shelf, stretches an astounding eighteen feet. Even he was outmatched by Pound; a bibliography of the latter's books and articles runs fifty-four pages. But long before judges don their robes or scholars their gowns, they are mere law students on the brink of adulthood. In this formative phase, before patterns of thought become entrenched, a mentor can make a mark that lasts forever after.

Thayer never wielded the gavel or produced dozens of tomes, but his influence was profound. Indeed, he left a heavy imprint on his followers precisely *because* he left such a faint one on the historical record. Time is a finite resource—hours that Thayer might have spent building his research profile or seeking a judicial nomination he invested in others. Be it his students, colleagues, or alumni, Thayer perennially subjugated his needs to theirs. As a colleague of his recalled, "Instead of concentrating his energies on attaining fame and fortune for himself, he preferred to pause by the wayside in order to render unpaid service to his friends."[28] Once those who had been graced with his guidance passed away, Thayer faded in the collective memory. His story gestures toward the neglected import of legal educators to the history of law writ large.

Not long after Thayer's death, a former student named Charles Haight predicted that his professor's contributions were just the kind to elude detection by future generations. Haight lamented that "a man, even of preeminent ability, must close his career upon the bench, if he is to perpetuate his name." The annals of case law simply failed to register the significance of someone like Thayer. Haight continued, "But if a man's work is more important than the world's knowledge of that work, and if a man's life is more important than an emblazoned monument after his death, then it is true that Professor Thayer did a work and lived a life which achieved the best results."[29] We could muse on Thayer's obscurity relative to his more prominent protégés, but that would miss the point—their landmark opinions, visionary dissents, and pathbreaking publications *were* Thayer's legacy. And thanks to their efforts, the core insights of legal realism not only became commonplace in their era but continue to define ours. Realist values today are ubiquitous. One current scholar observes that the phrase "we are *all* realists now" is "so often said that it has become a cliché to call it a 'cliché.'"[30] And if indeed we are all realists, then the legal world we inhabit is, in no small part, a world of Thayer's making.

1. Thayer's Origins

James Bradley Thayer came into the world "in the midst of a tremendous snow storm" on January 15, 1831, as he later recorded. He was the third of four children born to Abijah and Susan Thayer in the small village of Haverhill, Massachusetts, on the border with New Hampshire some sixty miles north of Boston.[1] James Bradley would inherit from his father a penchant for the printed word and passion for social reform. Abijah was the young editor of the *Essex Gazette*, named for the county where it was published. Deeply committed to several moral causes of the day, Abijah served as secretary for both the Haverhill Temperance Society and the Haverhill Anti-Slavery Society, and he frequently ran advertisements for both groups in his newspaper.[2] Abijah's newspaper expressed a Whiggish view, but his partisan leanings never hardened into ideological zeal. After a newspaper in Salem accused him of susceptibility to "the current of illiberal nationalism," Abijah responded that the *Essex Gazette* sought to studiously "avoid the gulph of democratic despotism on the one hand, as well as 'the current of illiberal nationalism' on the other." He insisted, "We have lost all relish for political *ultraism* of any sort."[3] That same skepticism of rigid ideology would later characterize his gifted son's approach to the law.

As a teenager, James Bradley and his family lived in Northampton in western Massachusetts. There, he became a beneficiary of the generosity of a town matriarch, Anne Lyman. The wife and later widow of a reputable judge, Mrs. Lyman was beloved "for her many wise and kindly deeds," as a contemporary recounted. She was a veritable institution in Northampton with a well-earned reputation for helping local youth.[4] So widely adored was Mrs. Lyman that when her daughter later produced a memoir of her life, luminaries from Ralph Waldo Emerson to Thayer himself contributed remembrances.[5]

Thayer anticipated enrolling at nearby Amherst College, but Mrs. Lyman wanted him to attend Harvard.[6] And so, in 1848, the seventeen-year-old Thayer joined the freshman class in Cambridge. Mrs. Lyman was mindful of every detail, from funding Thayer's tuition to outfitting his room with furniture to making him shirts.[7] He thus experienced firsthand the outsized impact the generosity of an older person can have upon a younger one on the cusp of adulthood. It was a lesson Thayer would never forget.

The town of Cambridge still bore the signs of a quaint village. The roads were unpaved, uncurbed, and poorly maintained—though one advantage of streets made of dirt and grass was their suitability for grazing livestock. While the local government provided for schools and an almshouse, there was no sewer system or waste management. No police force yet existed; in a town with little crime, the constable proved sufficient to preserve law and order. Cambridge also lacked a hospital, a public library, and parks.[8]

Yet for all the indications that Cambridge kept a foot in its bucolic past, markers of progress soon surfaced. The population was expanding steadily. In 1852 the town began planning the construction of sewers, and two new utilities—the Cambridge Gas Company and Cambridge Water Works—swung into action. The lifeblood of Cambridge was, of course, Harvard. Most Cambridge residents either worked directly for the university or were somehow involved with catering to the needs of its student body. And the presence of Harvard meant that Cambridge was home to some of the era's greatest minds.[9] The town paper, the *Cambridge Chronicle*, gives a fair hint of the intellectual milieu of the community. During Thayer's freshman year, a townsman placed a notice in the newspaper about a lost cow he had found, and he used the opportunity to display his poetic flair: "Found! Found! Quite gone astray, / A large *red Cow*; claim her who may. / 'E. Robins' burned upon her horn, / Points home, or else the place where born."[10]

Cambridge also afforded Thayer close proximity to one of the nation's great urban centers. Every hour, a stagecoach ushered passengers from Cambridge across the Charles River on a toll bridge to Boston.[11] The city offered a dynamic change of pace from Thayer's boyhood days in rural Massachusetts. His move from Northampton to the greater Boston region was reflective of national migration patterns, as the proportion of Americans living in cities nearly doubled between the time of Thayer's birth and his college days at Harvard.[12]

Boston was undertaking public works projects that the more provincial Cambridge had not yet initiated. While Cambridge residents were still fetching water from wells, Boston began piping fresh water some twenty-five miles from a reservoir outside the city to the Common downtown. Thanks to a thriving textile industry, Boston had become not just a commercial entrepôt but also a manufacturing hub. Prosperity flowed disproportionately to members of the Brahmin class, who built lavish houses, joined exclusive clubs, and patronized cultural institutions. Although Thayer was not born into a Brahmin family, he would find himself increasingly aligned with these patrician Bostonians. Far less affluent were the throngs of immigrant laborers who had fled famine in Ireland. This surge of immigration, combined with the annexation of some surrounding towns into Boston, led to a population boom in the mid-nineteenth century that made the city the third largest in the country. Population and economic growth entailed costs as well as benefits— slums, crime, and poverty were all elements of Boston life. Suburbs like Cambridge were thus highly appealing to those who could afford a leafier existence, especially after the midcentury development of railways and streetcars that provided easy transport between Boston and outlying communities.[13] The modernization playing out before Thayer's eyes undoubtedly informed the jurisprudence he would ultimately adopt, which stressed a flexible approach to constitutional interpretation that accounted for changing social conditions.

Thayer had an impressive college career, adored as he was by classmates and faculty alike. Harvard linked scions of the Boston establishment with boys like Thayer and his childhood friend Chauncey Wright, who otherwise had no direct ties to the city's elite circles. His modest background notwithstanding, Thayer "formed a nucleus around which centered the best literary interests and good fellowship of the class," according to James Parker Hall, who later studied under Thayer and in time became a friend.[14] Thayer had wide-ranging intellectual tastes and excelled in his studies; he graduated ninth out of eighty-eight students, despite working part time during the semester. On the inside cover of a notebook from his college days, he inscribed a quotation from the English man of letters Matthew Arnold, who lauded the elevation of "character above everything else."[15] Those who would come to know Thayer only posthumously through his writings would praise him for his intellect, but those who knew Thayer the person spoke with equal esteem for his character.[16]

Thayer's most memorable collegiate moment was also his last. His fellow students had selected him as class orator, an honor that filled him "with the greatest pride," he confessed.[17] On June 25, 1852, as Thayer was set to address his classmates and professors, the weather seemed inauspicious. Cambridge's skies were filled with "lowering clouds threatening rain," wrote the class secretary. But shortly thereafter "the thunder bolts forged by Vulcan were carefully

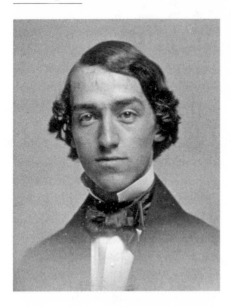

James Bradley Thayer at the time of his graduation from Harvard College in 1852. (Harvard University Archives)

laid on the shelf for another occasion," and Thayer gave his speech in the college chapel undistracted by any storm.[18]

Thayer reminded the audience that they were fortunate to live in an era that allowed them to enjoy "many of the most benevolent and peculiar ideas of the age" and "the improvements which civilization has wrought in the world."[19] His appreciation of the present, however, did not imply a disregard for the past. He reproached those "who, in professed conformity to the spirit of the times, would abandon studies consecrated by the admiration of many centuries—a delight and a storehouse of instruction to every age."[20] With respect for progress and tradition alike, Thayer would prove something of a mediating figure between the horse-and-buggy world of his youth and the modern society of his golden years.

As a recent Harvard graduate with debts to pay off, Thayer moved to the small town of Milton, Massachusetts, some ten miles south of Boston. There he began teaching full time at a school where he had worked during his winter breaks from college and where his older brother William was already employed as an educator. Mrs. Lyman, happily, had also moved to Milton, and both brothers boarded with her for a while.[21] Thayer did not consider himself an especially talented teacher, later recalling that he worked "laboriously, but, I fear, with only indifferent success."[22] If, however, the subsequent adulation of his law students is any indication, Thayer was in fact exceptionally gifted at the front of a classroom and his foregoing evaluation was unduly self-effacing.

Perhaps it was his ungenerous assessment of his pedagogy that led Thayer to take a leave from teaching in 1853 and spend several months traveling around the West, where he earned money as a journalist. That exploration brought Thayer into contact with the railroad system, one of the dominant structures of a modernizing America. The story of the nineteenth century is one of increasing communication, travel, interdependency, and mass markets —and railroads played a critical, if messy, role in accelerating these developments.[23] Reporting on the expansion of railroads in western cities ranging from Detroit to Denver, Thayer saw firsthand the possibilities and pitfalls of this transit revolution. He was enthusiastic about the railways' potential effects on tourism, predicting, for instance, that more people would be able to visit Niagara Falls while heading west. But Thayer also admonished railroad planners who relied too heavily on mathematical abstractions divorced from reality; their "estimates are always overrun, for all the invincible logic of those who make them and their beautifully-drawn pictures of success."[24] Throughout his life, he would remain wary of the human tendency to find comfort in facile logic without due regard for real-world consequences, a lesson that he would apply not just to locomotive trains but also to legal texts.

Thayer returned from this journalistic expedition to his classroom in Milton, where daily teaching kept alive his engagement with classical civilization.[25] His affection for the study of antiquity was of a piece with the archetype of the gentleman-scholar in an era when that ideal still enjoyed cachet. He also put his literary acumen to use by contributing to a collection of essays that appeared in 1854, when Thayer was twenty-three. His chapter overviewed the life of the American lawyer and congressman Fisher Ames.[26] It was well written and well organized but at times excessively erudite; one short page managed to reference Plato, Shakespeare, and Homer.[27] That may explain Thayer's later judgment that the essay "was the work of an industrious but puerile hand."[28]

His experience working on the Ames piece perhaps first piqued Thayer's interest in the law, for there he wrote that the legal profession "breathes unusual dignity into its servants, especially the young ones." He then complicated that sanguine picture of the profession by observing, "in its various duties, the giving of counsel, the questioning of witnesses, and the frequent display of capacity before courts and juries, the seeds of vanity find propitious soil and start into rank growth."[29] Thayer was reverential enough toward the law to eventually dedicate his career to its study yet discerning enough to spend that career critiquing its shortcomings.

It took Thayer a couple of years to settle on the law as a profession—his Unitarianism was strong enough that he seriously considered pursuing theology—but having made his choice, Thayer moved quickly.[30] He returned to Cambridge in 1854 to enroll at Harvard Law School. Thayer also continued his relationship with Mrs. Lyman, who had moved from Milton to Cambridge by the spring of 1853.[31] Thayer reliably visited her for Sunday tea, even as her mind began to deteriorate. Her kindness endured past her mental acuity. As Thayer recalled, "It was often sad to notice the signs of her failing powers," but "her old hearty welcome never once failed."[32] Mrs. Lyman reciprocated his fondness, speaking to her daughter of that "always good young man, who never forgot me at any time, but came every Sunday evening to take tea with me, when he might have gone to pleasanter places."[33] Thayer was keenly grateful for all she had done, and he would forever repay that debt indirectly by extending the same spirit of altruism to a younger generation.

At the time that Thayer applied to Harvard Law, neither a bachelor's degree nor an entrance examination were prerequisites for admission. However, if an applicant was "not a graduate of some college, [he] must be at least nineteen years of age, and produce testimonials of good moral character," as stipulated in the law school's catalog.[34] Thayer easily passed that threshold—his undergraduate diploma had been minted just two years prior, and barring that, he could have produced abundant testimony of his probity. He would later play a critical role in raising and formalizing the school's admission standards.

This era at the law school was characterized by a text and recitation method of instruction. Students in class would regurgitate materials they had either heard in a professor's lecture or read in a legal treatise. Though more participatory than the exclusively "lecture and copy" technique that preceded it, the pedagogy was still rather rote—more drill than dialogue.[35] "Professor Parker [is] the very dullest lecturer I have ever heard," Thayer bemoaned. "It is his aim to give you the law, and he does it, but in such an inanimate, monotonous, ill-digested, indifferent manner that one is lucky if he can fasten his attention."[36] The school had yet to undergo the thoroughgoing professionalization that would define it in the latter decades of the nineteenth century. Harvard Law students at midcentury exercised considerable freedom in structuring their education. At a time when graduation from law school was not a requirement for becoming an attorney, students chose which classes to

DANE LAW-SCHOOL. CAMBRIDGE,MASS.

Dane Hall, circa 1850. This building housed Harvard Law School from 1832 to 1883 and was Thayer's academic home as a law student and later as a professor. (Harvard Law School Library, Historical and Special Collections)

take according to their whims. No course required previous knowledge gained from any other. Many students learned what they wanted and then dropped out to launch their legal careers sans degree.[37]

Thayer throve in law school. He graduated first in his class in 1856, and his thesis on the law of eminent domain won first prize in the annual essay contest.[38] The competition was designed to ensure that prizes were awarded impartially. Each student anonymously submitted his essay with a motto or pseudonym on it; an accompanying sealed envelope had the same motto or pseudonym on the outside and the author's true identity enclosed within.[39] Thayer must have been elated when he took first prize, not only for the accolades but also for the cash award of $60 (around $1,800 today)—no negligible sum for someone who had to work his way through both his degrees. Contest rules mandated that no essay was to "exceed in length the amount of thirty pages, as large as the 16th page of the first volume of Greenleaf's Evidence," which was the dominant treatise for that branch of law.[40] While Thayer as a student could not exceed Greenleaf in page size, Thayer as a professor would try to exceed Greenleaf in rigor.

His winning thesis indicates that he was already developing his theory of judicial restraint, which was to be his most enduring contribution to constitutional law. The thesis conceded that the judiciary has an obligation to strike down an exercise of eminent domain if the legislature spuriously invokes a "public exigency" as a mere pretext that, in reality, "has no existence." But, Thayer insisted, the latitude that the bench owes to the legislature is vast. "If there be room to say that any public advantage is to be gained by the appropriation of private property," then the legislature's will must prevail. "The judiciary may not substitute their discretion for that of the legislature," he declared.[41] Here, at the age of twenty-five, he was previewing the argument that he would articulate in fuller form nearly forty years later in his career-defining article "The Origin and Scope of the American Doctrine of Constitutional Law."

Thayer passed the Suffolk bar in December 1856 and then worked for six months in the office of a Cambridge lawyer.[42] When that association ended, he became a partner in a Boston firm headed by William J. Hubbard.[43] He was still in debt and would remain so until at least 1858, but he was unfazed by his financial liabilities, for he had "prospects of success, excellent friends, and good courage," as Thayer put it.[44]

Despite his humble origins, Thayer became increasingly aligned with the Boston Brahmins.[45] Thayer and the company he kept were very much gentleman-scholars. Nowhere was this dynamic more evident, and nowhere was Thayer's playful side more apparent, than in the Septem Club. The name paid homage to its seven founders, each of whom would go on to achieve prominence in fields ranging from architecture to journalism. Their ranks included Thayer, Wright, and several other friends from their undergraduate days at Harvard.[46]

The Septem Club first met in 1856 for the purpose of promoting among its members both learning and leisure "in such proportion as might at any time seem desirable," according to the club's journal.[47] Thayer was elected

"Perpetual Secretary" at the club's inception, and the whimsical minutes in Thayer's hand suggest that, much to his credit, he took himself less seriously than he did his legal work.[48]

The club did not produce as much scholarship as initially intended, but Thayer's writings outside of club life advanced unabated. Between the chapter on Fisher Ames, his lively accounts of the West, and his award-winning thesis, he had begun to build a profile that would expand over time with more numerous and more varied publications. Thayer's commentary appeared in the *Evening Post, North American Review*, and *Atlantic Monthly*. And he maintained sufficient skill in Greek and Latin to review new translations of Virgil and Plutarch.[49] In so doing, Thayer was following the advice he had given to his classmates in his college graduation speech several years earlier: heed the wisdom of the past.

Thayer's daily life also consisted, naturally, of work at his law practice.[50] He certainly had the intellectual aptitude for law, but he was too nuanced a thinker to fully flourish amid the adversarial rough-and-tumble of the legal arena. "Though respected and successful in practice, Mr. Thayer was perhaps not enough of a partisan ever to take the highest rank as a lawyer," Hall observed perceptively. "He was perhaps too judicially-minded, and saw the merits of opposing views too clearly for this."[51] The very resistance to one-sided polemics that made Thayer poorly suited to litigation would make him perfectly suited to academia.

Upon Hubbard's death in 1864, Thayer succeeded him as master of chancery, a legal official who administered the process by which parties in civil and criminal cases assured their bonds and bail.[52] He also formed a new law practice of his own with two other partners.[53] They handled legal matters for both the government and corporations, with Thayer notably representing the Northern Pacific Railroad Company. The firm dealt with wills and estates for smaller clients.[54]

Thayer's personal life was likewise in transition in the 1860s. He married Sophia Ripley, who, in contrast to her husband, had been born into the Brahmin elite.[55] Her uncle was the legendary Ralph Waldo Emerson—arguably the most famous intellectual in nineteenth-century America—and Thayer's integration into the family would eventually lead to a friendship with Emerson himself. The earliest letter between them is a request from Thayer to Emerson on June 15, 1861, at the dawn of the Civil War. Given Emerson's stature and connection to US senator Charles Sumner, Thayer asked Emerson to lean on

Sumner for a favor involving a relative's prospects in the army. The relative was a lieutenant in a local Massachusetts company but—Thayer explained to Emerson—should that company be subsumed into the national army, he would "drop into the ranks" and become a mere private owing to military policy. Although this pending demotion "does not in the least disturb him or shake his resolution," Thayer wrote, "some of his friends would regret it very much," in part "because he has qualities that fit him for something better."[56] Emerson was amenable to helping, and the lieutenant wound up keeping his rank. Thayer's willingness to spend his social capital not for his own advancement but for the betterment of someone else would become a defining feature of his long career.[57]

Thayer was soon managing a good deal of Emerson's finances, and Emerson began requesting that Thayer visit Concord for both camaraderie and counsel. Letters from Thayer across the 1860s included checks for Emerson to deposit, advice on stocks to purchase, discussions of poetry, and an extended account of how Emerson could publish his works in both England and America while preserving copyright in each country.[58] Emerson was especially appreciative of the financial guidance, telling Thayer, "I am highly gratified . . . & much your debtor for it, & pray you to proceed as you propose in all particulars."[59] It was also in the 1860s that Thayer and his wife began to spend Thanksgivings with the Emersons in Concord.[60]

In many respects, Thayer personified the transition between the generalism that Emerson celebrated and the specialization that would increasingly define modern society. Amid revolutions in transportation, communication, and industry, America became ever more complex. That astounding complexity accelerated the division of labor and increased the premium on expertise. Emerson's writings extolled just the opposite. In his canonical essay "Self-Reliance," he celebrated the ideal of "a sturdy lad" from rural New England who "tries all the professions . . . and always, like a cat, falls on his feet," as distinct from the "city dolls" of Boston or New York who specialize in one profession.[61] Thayer certainly fit the Emersonian mold: he claimed roots in small-town Massachusetts and worked a diverse array of jobs from silkworm farming and physician assisting to school teaching and newspaper reporting. Yet Thayer's career was ultimately defined by the sustained cultivation of expertise in one domain over a period of decades. Though he never shed his Emersonian passion for wide-ranging interests, Thayer's emphasis on specialization had more in common with his legal protégés in the twentieth century than with Emerson. It is a noteworthy irony that the author of "Self-Reliance" seemingly had no qualms about his dependence on Thayer's financial and legal expertise, perhaps a tacit concession from Emerson that even *he* had to reconcile himself to modern exigencies—if not in theory then at least in practice.

In a palpable indication of Thayer's role in professional specialization, he ranked among the founders of the American Social Science Association (ASSA) in 1865 and served as chairman of its jurisprudence committee.[62] The ASSA—consisting of economists, sociologists, lawyers, and historians—sought to use its members' specialized skills and knowledge to redress societal problems. In time, the constituent disciplines broke off into their own discrete organizations, such as the American Historical Association and American Political Science Association. Still, the ASSA marked an important step in the direction of professionalized disciplines and technocratic management.[63] Thayer was there for the ferment. He would later find other opportunities to help lead the professionalization of legal academia.

The Septem Club—after a break occasioned by the marriages of several members—resumed in the mid-1860s. This second life for the club was marked by the arrival of a new participant who would become especially important to Thayer's career: Charles William Eliot. When Eliot joined the club in 1865, he was a professor of chemistry at the recently opened Massachusetts Institute of Technology. Having previously studied and taught at Harvard, Eliot would soon return to his alma mater for a forty-year tenure as its president. He transformed Harvard into a modern research university.

Three years after assuming the presidency of Harvard, Eliot offered Thayer a position as the Boylston Chair in Rhetoric in 1872.[64] Thayer declined, in no small part because of the pay cut the position would entail.[65] Undeterred, Eliot approached Thayer in 1873 with another proposition: the Royall Chair in Law. It paid better than the Boylston Chair, if not quite as well as Thayer's law practice. He accepted.[66] And so in the fall of 1874 the forty-three-year-old Thayer, Sophia, and their four children moved from Milton to Cambridge, and he began the career that would justify all the graces he had ever received.

When Thayer returned to Harvard in 1874, the university as a whole was in a period of flux that was not soon to end. Eliot, who assumed the presidency of the institution five years prior, wasted no time making changes. Harvard had found in Eliot a leader who could shepherd the university into modernity with a combination of pragmatism, fortitude, and wile. He still stands as perhaps the most influential figure in the history of American higher education.[67] Eliot emphasized research, foregrounded the scientific method, and increased the requirements for Harvard's professional schools.[68] A crucial component of his success was his willingness to challenge orthodoxy.[69]

One of Eliot's most fateful decisions was hiring Christopher Columbus Langdell to serve as dean of Harvard Law School in 1870.[70] Langdell grew up under dark circumstances—by the age of ten, he was impoverished and nearly orphaned. His unlikely rise to the upper echelons of Boston society is a testament to his single-minded perseverance.[71] But that very drive would prove double-edged as he ascended the Harvard hierarchy; if Eliot ruffled feathers at Harvard, Langdell shaved the birds entirely.

Langdell's irreverence and industry were both essential for the ambitious project he had in mind. He sought to reimagine the school with new emphases on research faculty, analytical pedagogy, meritocracy, fundraising, and alumni relations. The task of reform was challenging, as Langdell was neither a gentleman nor a gentle person. He may have rubbed shoulders with the Boston Brahmins, but he lacked their temperament and polish. His steadfast convictions often came across as obstinance. Rarely if ever did Langdell rely on consensus building as he stewarded the school.[72] Although he provoked ire from others, he was successful in reinventing Harvard Law. Professional education across the United States ultimately followed Langdell's lead. He served at Harvard Law from 1870 to 1900—the first twenty-five years as dean and the last five as a regular faculty member—and so it was Langdell's revolution in legal education that formed the backdrop to Thayer's own lengthy tenure at the institution.[73]

The two men had first crossed paths as undergraduates at Harvard. Langdell's college roommate was Thayer's oldest friend, Chauncey Wright. Thayer and Langdell also belonged to the same literary society on campus. Later, in adulthood, both joined the Septem Club. Despite their shared social circle, Thayer counted among those faculty members who found the dean trying.[74] Tensions arose not just because of Langdell's occasional brusqueness but also because of serious disagreements about pedagogy and policies at Harvard Law.

Langdell was the first law professor in the country to consistently employ the case method, and it was a serious innovation. In this approach, students

James Bradley Thayer around the time he took up the Royall Chair at Harvard Law in 1874. (Harvard Law School Library, Historical and Special Collections)

would discuss actual cases rather than only absorb textbooks and lectures that gave surveys of the law's various branches. Hypothetical fact patterns forced students to hone their aptitude for analysis instead of mere memorization. Although the case method that Langdell pioneered would come to dominate legal pedagogy in the fullness of time, it occasioned discord in the early days of his deanship.[75]

Thayer was not an advocate initially. Shortly after accepting his position at Harvard, Thayer confessed in his diary, "I cannot think as Langdell does about his method." He was concerned that the case method might leave students lost amid the law's granular details and thereby sacrifice a more comprehensive command of the subject. "It is wise to give [a student] as quickly as possible the outfit of a general and cursory view of the whole field of law," he asserted. Thayer worried that students would otherwise be "at the disadvantage of having the great body of legal knowledge an unknown wilderness."[76]

Thayer delivered his first lecture as the Royall Chair in October 1874. In what was a Harvard Law tradition, he framed it more as an inaugural speech for incoming students than as an academic lecture on a specific topic. Thayer seized the opportunity to define his personal philosophy of law. He held forth that the law is a branch of "knowledge arranged, classified, methodized—knowledge which is referred to principles, so that you can reason upon it, infer and deduce."[77] Legal historians have often depicted efforts to classify law and induce governing principles as twin pillars of formal legal thought.[78] But for Thayer, his foregoing description of the law was not incompatible with the tenets of legal realism—and he made this much clear with the remainder of his address.[79]

He told the students that legal doctrines are not unbending axioms but rather general guidelines replete with exceptions. "Legal rules are complex and many-sided, and vary evermore with the *intuitus*," Thayer explained. "They are often a stumbling block," and a practitioner must "apply them with circumspection."[80] Ever the historian, he emphasized that common-law doctrines did not derive from some metaphysical ideal of true justice—they were the result of historical forces. Thayer urged students to "trace back the doctrine to its source and note its ultimate foundation, its history and its modifications; see where it first started, in what shape, and in reference to what it was first announced."[81] He touted a historical approach to making sense of legislative statutes as well. "I have seen a point of law upon the language of a statute argued with full and ingenious yet ignorant elaboration, as if the statute were a piece of wholly new work, when it was only a patch set upon the old law," he shared.[82] Precisely because law is a historical outgrowth, and historical processes are forever unfolding in real time, there can be no static legal maxims. As Thayer put it, "human affairs are not going to begin for the first time now to stand still."[83] His emphasis on looking to the past as a means to master the present would inform his pedagogy and publications for the rest of his long academic career.

Closely related to Thayer's notion of law as historically contingent was his conception of law as socially constructed. Judges did not discover eternal principles and then simply apply them. Rather, as he explained to his pupils in his inaugural lecture, "the law is made by grown men; it arises and grows out of their necessities and experience in actual life, and is from year to year changed and corrected."[84] Thayer's description of law as purely man-made marked a departure from his stance a generation earlier when he had been a student at Harvard Law; his prize-winning essay had described eminent domain as dependent upon "the Deity itself."[85] Now, as a professor, he eschewed claims to authority on religious grounds. Thayer derisively quoted the Mormon leader Brigham Young—Thayer had once seen Young sermonize during a trip to Utah[86]—who griped that lawyers would do well to pursue other professions instead of "trying to take the property of others . . . through litigation." Thayer shot back that Young's own pretenses to power were based on "pretended revelation," and he chafed at any "attempt to establish political authority on a supernatural basis."[87] While Thayer's personal Unitarian faith never faded, he nevertheless insisted on separating God from the gavel. In so doing, he anticipated the secularization of knowledge that would increasingly define academia in the decades to come.[88]

Another prominent realist tenet in Thayer's first address was the interdependence of law and society. Solely through their presence in the world, his students had been engaging with the law—whether they fully appreciated it or not—long before they set foot in a Harvard Law classroom. Thayer observed that the "happy peculiarity of the law [is] to be concerned about those practical affairs, motives, and actions of men with which [you] are already familiar."[89] The mutuality of law and society means that other disciplines are essential tools in legal training, for the law "cannot be thoroughly investigated without running into psychology and logic."[90] Indeed, any field of study that concerns human behavior is germane. "To a lawyer no knowledge can come amiss which relates to *men*, and especially to what concerns them in the minuter activities of their daily life," Thayer assured his listeners.[91]

Still, Thayer was candid with his audience that the modern era demanded they cultivate expertise. "You must face, squarely, the fact that you have entered upon new studies and that your main strength must now be applied to them," he affirmed.[92] Thayer pithily reconciled the competing demands of generalism and specialism: "be as good lawyers as you can, but you have no right to be *merely* lawyers." He warned, "You will be poor lawyers, or at any rate, *poorer lawyers than you would otherwise be,* if you are not also trained by other culture to the habits of liberal-minded and public-spirited men."[93] Thayer hoped to hang on to some vestige of antebellum generalism while paying heed to the specialism that modernity required. That dual desire explains what attracted him to the proverb "he is a well-educated man who knows a good deal of something and a little of everything," which he once recorded for himself in his diary.[94]

Thayer's speech also included admonitions about the importance of healthy routines. He cautioned the students that they would "surely lose ground and fall behind" if they failed to implement a regimen of "physical exercise," "sound, sufficient sleep," "healthful food and drink," and "proper intervals of rest, social enjoyment, and relaxation."[95] It was this kind of paternalistic concern for his students' well-being that would make Thayer a beloved professor.

Cognizant that not all faculty at Harvard Law employed identical approaches to legal pedagogy, Thayer offered students some practical advice on surviving their course of study: "You will greatly err if you do not loyally adopt and follow in the case of each instructor the method which he shall point out in his own department."[96] Thayer surely had Langdell, with his novel case method, in mind. Had Thayer joined the faculty just a few years later, the foregoing speech would never have happened, as Langdell terminated the tradition of the welcome address for incoming students, most likely because he viewed the custom as a genteel relic.[97]

Thayer bore witness to a series of institutional developments that made Harvard Law a trailblazer in professional education. Some of these changes preceded Thayer's arrival. Langdell had already initiated a transition to sequential education. The conventional hodgepodge of courses that could be taken in any order was replaced by a set of first-year courses that laid the foundation for subsequent electives. The dean also emphasized the importance and growth of the law library.[98] But Langdell had only just begun, and Thayer was on the scene for the most substantial overhauls. For a time, Thayer was one of only four full-time law professors (including the dean), a number small enough to generate considerable progress if the faculty members were united but considerable friction if they were not. Thayer largely approved of Langdell's reform agenda and helped bring it to fruition. Much of Thayer's energy throughout his career would be directed toward fundraising, cultivating alumni relations, raising the research profile, and expanding the law library—all elements that made Harvard Law the forerunner of modern professional education.

However, the dean and the professor did not always agree on how to fulfill some of their shared ideals. Langdell, for instance, preferred that a bachelor's degree become prerequisite for admission to Harvard Law, but Thayer was concerned that such a narrow path would exclude worthy applicants.[99] The distinction between Langdell and Thayer went beyond admissions policy to temperament and style. Thayer was regarded as an affable gentleman. A colleague suggested that few people anywhere could match Thayer "as a conversationalist," for he always had "the right word and right turn given to each phrase; with no appearance of effort; no display of learning."[100] Langdell did not elicit such genteel descriptions.[101] Even in disagreements with the dean, Thayer showed a gentleman's magnanimity. As Thayer told President Eliot, in front of Langdell, "Whatever criticisms I may make, I do it with the very great-est respect for him, and whatever I desire to have done or undone, I would not have him otherwise than just as he is."[102]

Although Thayer was arguably the law school's most esteemed educator, he did not believe that teaching came easily to him. A former student recollected that Thayer "found teaching very hard at first, and there were certain streets in Cambridge through which he afterwards hated to go because he had been used to walk[ing] there disheartened in this early time."[103] This commentary recalls Thayer's postcollegiate days teaching in Milton, when he had also been critical of his pedagogical abilities. In both circumstances, his self-deprecation was probably unduly harsh. A student-turned-colleague asserted that Thayer's pupils learned more than just law from him: "Something at least of the accu-rate and careful habits of mind, the patience in wearisome investigation, the absolute intellectual sincerity, the never-failing kindness and courtesy, which distinguished the teacher, must have borne fruit in the minds and hearts of the pupils."[104] Thayer, perhaps subconsciously, was particularly attentive to the most promising students in his classes, surely seeing something of his younger self in them. A colleague observed, "the brilliant, the mediocre, and the dull cannot always get nourishment from the same food," and although Thayer was "infinitely patient with the poorly gifted," it was nevertheless "to the better men in his classes that Professor Thayer's teaching was chiefly addressed."[105]

Often it was only after they entered legal practice that erstwhile students came to fully appreciate the depth of their debt to Thayer. Students in the class-room craved clear-cut answers, but Thayer, to their frustration, insisted that the law is rife with exceptions, disclaimers, and contradictions. As one former student recollected, "We sometimes complained of [a] lack of definiteness on Professor Thayer's part. But now that we have been in practice all this time, we find that what he said stands by us better than what was said by anybody else."[106] Thayer's powerful effect on the students was not lost on his colleagues. Fellow professor James Barr Ames remarked that, for Thayer, teaching was not just about imparting a domain of knowledge; it was an exercise in men-torship. "No one can measure his great influence upon the thousands of his pupils," Ames declared. "They had a profound respect for his character and ability . . . his quick sympathy, his unfailing readiness to assist the learner, out of the class-room as well as in it, and his attractive personality, gave him an exceptionally strong hold upon the affections of the young men."[107] Whether by unconscious intuition or intentional design, Thayer embodied the truism that great teaching is about not just intellectual content but also personal connection.

Although he expressed reservations about Langdell's case method in the classroom, in practice, Thayer's approach was not entirely divergent from the dean's. Central to the Langdellian method was the posing of questions that required students to apply the law. Thayer likewise informed his criminal law class, "I shall ask you questions pretty frequently." For instance, he offered his pupils a hypothetical fact pattern in which a defendant was charged with a crime on US Navy property in Charlestown, Massachusetts, raising the question of whether the matter was federal or state. Thayer inquired, "Can he be punished by both jurisdictions? By whichever one gets him first? By only one, which?" And just as Langdell's method made cases the prime fodder for class discussion, Thayer also required students to read cases. However, it would go too far to suggest that Thayer, at least in his initial years as a professor, was thoroughly mirroring Langdell's novel pedagogy. Thayer's courses were more didactic than Langdell's. And while Thayer still relied heavily on conventional legal treatises, the dean had forged a new genre of legal literature to work hand in glove with his case method: the casebook.[108]

Langdell published the first casebook, *Cases on Contracts*, in the early 1870s.[109] It differed from a traditional treatise in several respects. Not all contemporary treatises even used cases, and those that did included cases only to instantiate a given legal principle under discussion. Langdell's casebook, by contrast, made cases paramount. He eschewed editorial comment in favor of having readers inductively determine governing principles from the raw material of legal precedent. *Cases on Contracts* also ordered cases chronologically—not thematically, as a treatise would—which underscored the notion that the law is fluid rather than fixed. As soon as Langdell published his casebook, he began to use it in his contracts course.[110] Eventually, Thayer would produce casebooks of his own, indicating that he moved ever closer to the case method over time.

Thayer was an enthusiastic participant in student moot courts early in his professorial tenure. Every Friday afternoon, two pairs of students would face off and litigate a case; professors took turns adjudicating. Thayer encouraged students to partake "most faithfully" in these exercises because "they give you the opportunity to apply your knowledge and to try your hand at the actual work of the profession." He was apparently quite faithful himself, as indicated by the copious notes he penned during the moot courts over which he presided.[111]

By the dawn of the 1880s, Thayer must have marveled at the extraordinary journey that took him from an economically unstable upbringing in rural Massachusetts to a named chair on the faculty of Harvard Law. A variety of factors played a role in his meteoric rise—the beneficence of a widow who made his Harvard education possible, an opportune marriage into an elite family, and Charles William Eliot's membership in the Septem Club. But it was Thayer's congenital brilliance more than anything else that accounts for his success. And now that Thayer finally felt more secure in the classroom, he directed that brilliance to a new endeavor: the research, writing, and publication of legal scholarship.

2. Thayer's Scholarship

James Bradley Thayer published relatively little compared with other giants of the legal profession. One colleague, Jeremiah Smith, asked after Thayer's death, "Why was not more work completed in all these years and given to the world; why were not his wider plans of book-making fully carried out?" Smith offered several reasons for Thayer's limited output. For one, Thayer suffered from a perfectionist streak; he would not submit a given manuscript to his publisher until every detail met his own exacting standards. Also, friends and colleagues routinely leaned on Thayer for assistance with their publications, and he was all too willing to deprioritize his scholarship to enhance theirs. "He repeatedly, we might almost say daily, turned aside from his own work to render assistance to other writers," Smith recalled. And most importantly, his students were his overriding concern. As Smith put it simply, "He made teaching his first object." Even as an experienced educator, Thayer exhaustively prepared for each class period.[1] Yet what little he *did* publish was of the highest quality and eagerly absorbed by an ever-expanding circle of admirers who had been the beneficiaries of his generosity. As a consequence, the impact of Thayer's writings far exceeded their volume, and they became the principal means by which he promoted legal realism beyond the four walls of his classroom.

Thayer's first scholarly article while a professor at Harvard, "Bedingfield's Case.—Declarations as a Part of the *Res Gesta*," appeared in three installments between late 1880 and early 1881 in the pages of the *American Law Review*. Here, Thayer made his initial foray into the law of evidence and advanced his core belief that legal flaws require legislative corrections, free from interference by judges.

In the Bedingfield case, an assailant attacked a woman named Eliza Rudd in her home, cutting her throat. She came outside to the yard and told two of her assistants that Harry Bedingfield was the culprit. Rudd died minutes later.[2] Testimony from the assistants about Rudd's statement would be considered hearsay for the purpose of proving the statement's accuracy, and hearsay is generally inadmissible in court. However, there are exceptions to the hearsay rule, including a doctrine known as *res gesta*. Under res gesta, a hearsay statement is regarded as credible, and thus admissible, if it is a spontaneous exclamation made in the heat of the moment during an event (in contrast to a statement made after an event, by which point the speaker may have had time to contrive a fabrication).[3]

Whether res gesta applied to Bedingfield's case hinged on whether Rudd's statement was considered concurrent with, or subsequent to, the attack. Had she cried out, "Don't, Harry!" while the alleged murderer was cutting her throat, then plainly hearsay testimony about the statement would be admissible under res gesta. But in this case, there was a lapse of time, albeit brief, between the assault and the statement. The presiding judge held that Rudd's statement was insufficiently concurrent to fall under res gesta and therefore any hearsay testimony intending to establish the truth of that statement was inadmissible. The decision prompted a furor in the legal community.[4]

Thayer considered the merits of both sides of the argument in an article comprising eighty highly technical pages. With his characteristic emphasis on history, he conducted a thoroughgoing genealogy of germane cases and treatise commentaries. Thayer determined that the term *res gesta* lacked any rigorous meaning, and perhaps any meaning at all, in its present usage. "Judges, text-writers, and students have found themselves sadly embarrassed by the growing and intolerable vagueness of the expression," he lamented.[5] Amid the welter of perspectives on res gesta, Thayer saw one solution that could provide clarity and coherence: statutory reform. "It is much to be wished," he concluded, "that wise legislation should come in to revise the whole law of hearsay, with a view to simplify it and to admit many things that cannot now . . . be received."[6] This conviction—that the legislature, not the judiciary, should remedy problematic laws—would become a cornerstone of Thayer's jurisprudence writ large.

His Bedingfield article also stressed that the purpose of evidence law is to discover not truth as such but rather truth insofar as it is useful for the administration of justice. The law of evidence would look "peculiarly absurd" to those who conceived of it as "a system elaborated for the mere discovery of truth," observed Thayer. Conversely, to others who rightly understood that res gesta, and indeed evidence law on the whole, is merely "subsidiary to the distribution of justice . . . it may present a very different aspect." Given that a jury of one's peers constitutes an "untrained tribunal," an article of evidence could be rendered inadmissible, despite its relevance, because of its tendency to distort the views of lay jurors and thereby subvert the ends of justice.[7] This insight would lie near the heart of Thayer's celebrated treatise on evidence that was still years in the offing.

If evidence law was one half of Thayer's expertise, constitutional law was the other, and he opted for a mainstream publication to first espouse his position on the latter. Thayer published an article in the *Nation* in 1884 entitled "Constitutionality of Legislation: The Precise Question for a Court." There he laid the groundwork for his theory of judicial restraint. He suggested that the judiciary must afford legislative statutes a presumption of constitutionality; if any plausible claim to constitutionality exists, the law must stand. Thayer described the question "Is the law a constitutional one?" as "dangerous" because it could tempt a court to move away from its "precise judicial function, that, namely, of determining whether the Legislature has transgressed the limits of reasonable interpretation."[8] According to Thayer, his perspective was hardly novel. Abundant precedent was on his side (even if that precedent had all too often been ignored): "It is quite uniformly laid down that courts should not declare laws unconstitutional unless it is a very plain case, and it is put as strongly as this, viz., that the matter must be plain beyond a reasonable doubt."[9] In other words, the very same burden that a prosecutor must meet in a criminal trial also applies to a judge considering whether to void a statute.

Given the strength of the presumption of constitutionality owed to legislation, Thayer advised the following: when the interpretation of a constitution, state or federal, does "fairly admit of two opinions," the legislature "is not to be deprived of its choice between them." A majority in the legislature may belong to "the liberal school" of constitutional construction, while a majority on the court subscribes to "the strict school," but it is "not a judicial question whether the strict or the liberal theory be the sounder."[10] Instead, the judicial question is whether the legislature acted upon *any* rational theory of constitutional interpretation in passing the law. Thus, a judge could easily think a statute unconstitutional according to his own jurisprudence but still uphold the law as a valid exercise of legislative authority.

Part of Thayer's concern was that judicial overreach bred legislative laziness. If lawmakers know that the bench will eagerly intervene, then they feel as though they have a free hand to err. "It seems plain that our constitutional system has tended to bereave our legislatures of their feeling of responsibility," he griped. Thayer noted that a "common saying" among lawmakers contemplating the passage of a constitutionally dubious bill was, "Oh, the courts will set that right." Legislators dramatically overestimated the judiciary's responsibility to ensure the constitutionality of statutes. Thayer did not merely want courts to take a step back but legislatures to take one forward. His article in the *Nation* was concise, filling just about a page. Nearly a decade later, his celebrated "Origin and Scope" article would offer a far more detailed elaboration of his argument, but all the critical elements of his theory of judicial restraint were present at this earlier stage.[11]

Thayer was not the only commentator in the 1880s to warn about the dangers of judicial review. The year before Thayer's article came out in the *Nation*, a former politician named Robert Street gave a contentious address on the topic at the annual meeting of the American Bar Association. Street took a far more radical stance than Thayer—he outright rejected the notion that the judiciary can nullify legislation. "There is no power in the courts to annul an act of Congress," Street asserted bluntly. In his view, a court could find a statute unconstitutional and refuse to apply it in a case at hand, but such a judicial conclusion should not bind the legislature or executive. The statute should remain operative for those latter branches of government. Street derided the practice of judicial review as a "gross delusion" that threatens to "bar the progress of our civilization" because it prevents Congress from freely adapting policy to "the requirements of constantly changing conditions."[12] It is little surprise that Street, who had recently served in the Texas state legislature, was not fond of a doctrine permitting appointed judges to impose their will on elected officials.

Street's explosive speech made a strong impression on a young lawyer named William Meigs. Feeling "emboldened," Meigs decided to expound on Street's ideas in an 1885 article in the *American Law Review*. There he seconded the position that courts, while free to ignore statutes that they deemed unconstitutional, could not void legislative acts for coordinate branches of government. Meigs disparaged judicial review as "almost an absurdity" that found favor because the "funguslike idea of the omnipotency of courts" had spread insidiously throughout the body politic. He lamented that the doctrine inculcated in the citizenry an overly expansive sense of judges' authority. The striking down of legislation "necessarily has a tendency to exaggerate in the minds of people the power of courts in the matter of interpretation." Meigs conceded that he and Street were iconoclastic but nevertheless insisted that the principle of judicial review was "utterly wrong."[13]

There is much that bound Thayer to Street and Meigs. They all shared a concern that the bench was apt to overreach. Like Street, Thayer's desire to constrain the bench dovetailed with his preference for a living constitution (although Thayer would not elucidate the harmony between judicial restraint and living constitutionalism until his 1893 article "Origin and Scope"). Like Meigs, Thayer feared that the very exercise of judicial activism served to persuade Americans of its rectitude. These commonalities notwithstanding, Thayer cut a decidedly different figure from the likes of Street or Meigs. The professor wanted to shrink the scope of judicial review, not eliminate the practice entirely. It was the relatively moderate Thayer, rather than the renegade Street or Meigs, who would emerge as the more influential voice on the subject of judicial review. Reformers would find in Thayer's theory of judicial restraint a palatable approach that promised to amend, not upend, American law.[14]

Thayer soon found occasion to argue for the limits of judicial authority in another realm: advisory opinions. His cousin, the former chief justice of Rhode Island, tapped Thayer to address a constitutional conundrum.[15] Rhode Island's General Assembly had been considering whether it possessed the authority to call a convention to rewrite the state constitution. The upper house of the legislature asked the state supreme court to issue an advisory opinion on the matter's legality. Advisory opinions differ from typical judicial opinions. The former are solicited prior to a contemplated action by a coordinate branch; the latter arise afterward and only in the event of a legal dispute in which a party seeks redress in court for an alleged injury. The Rhode Island Supreme Court, in the end, did agree to deliver an advisory opinion to the General Assembly and held that the state constitution could be changed only by amendment, not by convention.[16]

Thayer's essay on the subject appeared in 1885. It did not address the wisdom of that particular advisory opinion but rather whether advisory opinions in general are binding. "What is the legal quality of such opinions?" he queried. "Are they authoritative declarations or merely advisory?" As a proponent of judicial deference to legislatures, Thayer naturally took the position that advisory opinions are just that: advisory, with no legal force. He surveyed the only four states that even allowed advisory opinions and happily found that the legal precedents in three—Massachusetts, New Hampshire, and Rhode

James Bradley Thayer, circa 1885.
(Harvard Law School Library,
Historical and Special Collections)

Island—clearly indicated that advisory opinions are nothing more than suggestive. But in the fourth state, the Maine Supreme Court had recently held that advisory opinions are compulsory. Thayer was displeased. "This strange doctrine was laid down with no citation of authority, no reference to any line of reasoning upon which it could be supported, and no recognition of the history and the law bearing upon the topic in hand," he lamented. Thayer predicted that Maine would reverse its anomalous precedent (and he lived just long enough to see his prediction borne out in 1901). His worries were not limited to Maine. Even in jurisdictions where precedent made plain that advisory opinions were not binding, many people erroneously believed otherwise. Thayer urged, "It is of grave importance that the notion of their binding quality should be dispelled."[17]

The 1880s saw Thayer move closer to the Langdellian model of pedagogy. In a course on sales law, he assigned students Langdell's casebook on the subject. And Thayer opted to forgo traditional treatises in his evidence course. But he was not yet a full convert to the case method; treatises continued to appear in at least some of Thayer's classes. Back in 1874 he had expressed concerns about the case method's ability to give students a comprehensive understanding of a subject, and even though he was becoming more Langdellian with time, Thayer continued to fret that he could not do justice to the breadth of a branch of law within the allotted class period. "For this great subject, we have but one hour a week," he told his criminal law and procedure students in 1884. "What shall we do? Shall we skim it all? . . . Or shall we do some thoroughly and skim the rest? I shall try to do the last. It will be very imperfectly done, but we will do it as best . . . we can."[18] And their best, they did. It was only at the end of a semester that Thayer's students could appreciate the vast scope of material they had learned under his tutelage in a few short months. As a former student reminisced, "Few, if any, realized the compactness of the instruction or the breadth of the ground actually covered until a course had been completed."[19]

Thayer continued to develop his scholarly profile in the latter part of the decade. In 1887 he published an article in the *Harvard Law Review* titled "Legal Tender" that discussed the constitutional limitations thereof. The piece reflected his ongoing concern that both legislators and the public tended to confound constitutionality with prudence. For Thayer, a legitimate exercise of power by some arm of the state could be both constitutional *and* foolish. As he put it, "The question whether Congress has the power to make paper a good tender in the payment of debts, and the question whether under any given circumstances it is wise or right that Congress should use it, are very different things."[20]

The essay was typical of Thayer's scholarship, in that it was both historical and current. He began with the Constitutional Convention. The framers did not speak with a single voice about paper currency. Ultimately, they opted to say nothing on the topic in the Constitution. Most of the delegates believed that by omitting language about paper currency they had de facto prohibited Congress from issuing it. Their premise was that the Constitution created a government of limited powers, and thus Congress could not exercise any authority not expressly enumerated in its text. But Thayer was no devotee of originalism. He saw the Constitution as a flexible instrument that could accommodate modern exigencies; accordingly, he did not feel bound by the framers' intent. "In the debates of the Convention, so far as we know anything about them, the majority of the speakers thought that they were prohibiting bills of credit and paper money" through the Constitution's silence. Thayer minced no words on the matter: "They were wrong."[21] Despite what the framers thought in 1787, the subsequent century of American history had demonstrated the merit of an alternative view—namely, that the absence of an "express grant of power" is not, in practice, a "prohibition of the power."[22] Thayer's rejection of originalism went hand in hand with his conviction that the Constitution was open to multiple legitimate interpretations.

The late 1880s and early 1890s were productive years for Thayer. He published several articles focused largely on the field of evidence. They ranged from the historical development of the jury to the meaning of "burden of proof." As we will see, he would later integrate these articles into his most ambitious scholarly endeavor—his *Preliminary Treatise* on evidence. Thayer was also at work on his first casebook, *Select Cases on Evidence at the Common Law*, which appeared in the summer of 1892. A sprawling 1,238 pages, the casebook contained excerpts from countless judicial decisions covering every aspect of the rules of evidence.[23] No scholar had ever before produced a casebook on this branch of law.[24]

Thayer certainly still lectured in class, but his decision to publish this casebook signaled a more thorough embrace of the Langdellian case method as part of his pedagogy. With respect to the classroom interplay between a professor and his students, Thayer explained in the preface, "My experience confirms that of others who have found, in dealing with our system of law, that the best preparation for these exercises is got from the study of well-selected cases." By invoking "others," Thayer deprived Langdell of the pleasure of being credited by name. Thayer continued, "As for methods of teaching—that is another matter. . . . Every teacher has his own methods, determined by his personal gifts or lack of gifts,—methods as incommunicable as his temperament, his looks, or his manners."[25] To be sure, pedagogy bears some relationship to personality, but Thayer here overstated the matter. Ineffable charisma is not in itself a method. The case method, in contrast, was an identifiable mode of instruction that existed apart from—even if it could be enhanced by—a professor's idiosyncratic persona. There was nothing especially "incommunicable" about inductive reasoning through Socratic dialogue. Perhaps Thayer accentuated the role of personality in order to downplay, consciously or otherwise, his pedagogical debt to a dean who had vexed him more than once.

In any event, the volume was well received. The *Harvard Law Review* predicted that "the book will be of great use to practising lawyers as well as to students."[26] Meanwhile, the *American Law Review* suggested that anyone on the bench or bar seeking a survey of the "whole field of the law of evidence will do well to take this book as a guide." The reviewer quibbled that "the very small type" was "a trial to weary editorial eyes" but still allowed that the "young eyes of pupils" might fare better.[27] Thayer would publish a second edition within a decade.[28]

In August 1893 Thayer delivered an address at the World's Fair that would prove his single most important contribution to constitutional law.[29] It soon appeared both in pamphlet form and in the pages of the *Harvard Law Review* under the title "The Origin and Scope of the American Doctrine of Constitutional Law." Here was Thayer's full-throated exposition of his theory of judicial restraint that he had sketched a decade earlier in the *Nation*. Once again, he considered those instances, be they federal or state, when the judiciary ponders whether to declare a statute unconstitutional. He argued that in the exercise of judicial review, courts must extend to a legislative act a presumption of constitutionality. The outcome should hinge not on whether a judge personally believes a given statute to be constitutional but on whether anyone rationally could. If there exists any plausible argument in favor of the act's constitutionality, it must be upheld. In Thayer's words, a court "can only disregard the Act when those who have the right to make laws have not merely made a mistake, but have made a very clear one—so clear that it is not open to rational question."[30]

Thayer analogized a presumption of constitutionality for legislative acts to the standard of proof in a criminal trial. A jury's verdict of "not guilty" does not establish a defendant's innocence; it only means that the evidence against the defendant leaves room for reasonable doubt about his guilt. By Thayer's lights, the same logic should apply to judicial review. Upholding an act does not necessarily signal that the law is constitutional. Judges do not thereby lend the legislation the imprimatur of "their own opinion of the true construction of the constitution." The decision to uphold legislation means "merely" that the act is "not unconstitutional beyond a reasonable doubt."[31]

To explicate his point, Thayer borrowed a thought experiment from a former chief justice of the Michigan Supreme Court. Imagine that a legislator, enjoying wide discretion, votes against a bill on the grounds that he finds it repugnant to the constitution. That same bill nevertheless passes into law, and that same dissenting legislator is then appointed to the bench, where he is tasked with assessing the act's constitutionality. Now operating with a far narrower remit in his judicial capacity, he is obliged to uphold the act—despite his own misgivings—because others can rationally argue in favor of its harmony with the constitution.[32]

To afford legislation a presumption of constitutionality is to afford the legislature a presumption of decency, in Thayer's view. "Virtue, sense, and competent knowledge are always to be attributed to that body" by the bench. "The conduct of public affairs must always go forward upon conventions and assumptions of that sort." Here, Thayer was not Pollyannaish about legislators. He recognized that, in reality, they were all too often disappointing—"indocile, thoughtless, reckless, incompetent"—but he also knew that republican government cannot function on the premise that lawmakers are imbeciles in need of perennial correction by appointed judges. "Our theory of government assumes" that legislators are "competent, well-instructed, sagacious, attentive, intent only on public ends." The very notion of "a self-governing people" requires that the representatives chosen by the people enjoy considerable license to make laws. Relying on appointed judges to save democracy from elected legislators is a paradox, for it devastates the foundational principle of democracy: self-rule.[33]

Thayer offered a number of other justifications for his doctrine. For one, lawmakers are the first arbiters of a statute's constitutionality as they consider whether a bill conforms to the constitution before passing it (at least in theory). Courts, in contrast, do not weigh in on pending legislation. They rule only if and when a statute occasions a legal dispute. Because legislators *always* have to consider an act's constitutionality and courts do so only sporadically and after the fact, the judiciary ought to give the legislature due deference. As Thayer wrote, "It is plain that where a power so momentous as this primary authority to interpret is given, the actual determinations of the body to whom it is intrusted are entitled to a corresponding respect." Had the American people—in enacting the state and federal constitutions—desired the bench to be the principal umpire of constitutionality, those constitutions would have provided for preemptive judicial review of proposed bills. "The judiciary may well reflect that if they had been regarded by the people as the chief protection against legislative violation of the constitution, they would not have been allowed merely this incidental and postponed control," Thayer surmised. "They would have been let in . . . to a revision of the laws before they began to operate." (As a caveat, he acknowledged that in a handful of jurisdictions courts sometimes did offer advisory opinions on pending legislation, but he was quick to minimize this function as extrajudicial and thus nonbinding.)[34]

Another basis for Thayer's doctrine was related to the courts' prerogative of having the last word in legal disputes. The judiciary's decisions are not reviewable by the other branches of government. Precisely because judges are so robustly empowered—Thayer reasoned—the bench ought not expand its authority even further by substituting its opinion on policy for that of the legislature. "The ultimate arbiter of what is rational and permissible is indeed always the courts, so far as litigated cases bring the question before them," he recognized. "This leaves to our courts a great and stately jurisdiction. It will only imperil the whole of it if it is sought to give them more. They must not step into the shoes of the law-maker."[35] Finality in its rulings was power enough for an unelected branch.

Thayer inveighed against judges who used the superficial logic of formalism to ignore legitimate considerations that influenced a legislature's decision to pass a given bill into law. Judges claimed, in formalistic fashion, to measure a statute against the constitution, and if one conflicted with the other, they privileged the supreme law over a mere legislative act. Courts speciously characterized this exercise of "construing two writings and comparing one with another" as an "ordinary and humble judicial duty." In a rebuttal typical of legal realism, Thayer suggested that this facile logic served to obscure—behind a false veneer of judicial humility—an unjustifiable neglect of the legislature's valid concerns. As Thayer put it, "Instead of taking them [lawmakers' considerations] into account and allowing for them as furnishing possible grounds of legislative action, there takes place a pedantic and academic treatment of the texts of the constitution and the laws." He lamented that "this petty method" results in "many specimens" of ill-conceived judicial decisions that "are found only too easily to-day."[36]

But judges are not exclusively to blame for their creep onto legislative turf, according to Thayer. Legislators are all too willing to cede ground to an overzealous bench. Elected representatives often fail to give weight to the constitutionality of a bill before passing it into law, knowing that an eager judiciary will happily intervene to remedy their misdeeds. And even when legislators do consider the "mere legality" of a statute, they erroneously assume that whatever survives challenge in the courts is a good law. This conflation of a statute's legality with its merit has a "tendency to drive out questions of justice and right," questions that *should* preoccupy lawmakers. The citizenry needs to better understand the "limits of judicial power; so that responsibility may be brought sharply home where it belongs"—that is, to the people and their legislators.[37]

The presumption of constitutionality that Thayer championed was useful in an era of rapid modernization. Novel societal problems required novel statutory solutions, and reformers wanted the bench to give lawmakers a wide berth in their efforts to update the legal code. As Thayer described the presumption of constitutionality, "This rule recognizes that, having regard to the great, complex, ever-unfolding exigencies of government, much which will seem unconstitutional to one man, or body of men, may reasonably not seem so to another." In a complicated world where "the constitution often admits of different interpretations," it was incumbent on the judiciary to conclude that "whatever choice is rational is constitutional."[38] It is altogether fitting that Thayer's pioneering article, attuned as it was to modern times, had been first delivered as a paper at a World's Fair featuring the wonders of a new age.

Although Thayer's doctrine was well suited to his era, this did not mean that a presumption of constitutionality was newfangled. On the contrary, his approach had a rich tradition dating back to the early decades of the republic, and Thayer was keen to highlight the ample precedent for his position. "I am not stating a new doctrine," he explained, "but attempting to restate more exactly and truly an admitted one."[39] A historian always, Thayer dedicated substantial space in his article to an exploration of the doctrine's past. He noted that judicial review had not been expressly promulgated in the early state constitutions or the national one, and as a consequence, the very legitimacy of judicial review had been debated in the early republic. Among its proponents, Thayer observed, were giants of American law—Alexander Hamilton and John Marshall among them—who found judicial review to be inherent, albeit implicit, in constitutional governance. Thayer's interest was not in repudiating judicial review wholesale but in sharply circumscribing its limits. To that end, Thayer quoted delegates to the Constitutional Convention, state court judges from the founding generation, and Marshall himself, all of whom stressed that the judiciary owed legislative statutes a presumption of constitutionality.[40]

Thayer, with his characteristic intellectual honesty, acknowledged that some jurists in the early republic preferred far greater discretion from the bench in its exercise of judicial review. He reasoned that the very existence of these voices of dissent against the presumption of constitutionality counterintuitively underscored the doctrine's validity. "A rule thus powerfully attacked and thus explicitly maintained, must be treated as having been deliberately meant, both as regards its substance and its form," Thayer concluded.[41]

Upon the appearance of "Origin and Scope," Thayer's contemporaries immediately recognized its significance. With legislatures passing statutes to address the challenges of modern life and judges striking some of them down, the proper scope of judicial review was a question of paramount importance. Thayer had now provided a key contribution to a reform movement searching for a jurisprudence that could meet the demands of an industrializing America.

Thayer gave copies of his article to the Boston Public Library and helped oversee its sale as an octavo pamphlet by his publisher—Little, Brown—for twenty-five cents (around $7.50 today).[42] He also mailed it to a number of legal luminaries, who responded with approbation. A recent nominee to the US Supreme Court wrote back, "I entirely concur in your views which seem to me very clear and forcible." A former judge—who had served on both the Iowa Supreme Court and a federal appellate court—offered, "Not perfunctorily, but most heartily, do I thank you for a copy of your essay." Meanwhile, the chief justice of the Michigan Supreme Court sent Thayer a paper with some of his own thoughts and assured him, "You will find in it nothing that is not entirely in harmony with what you have written." Nor was interest limited to judges and lawyers. The chair of the History Department at the University of Chicago was eager for a lengthier exploration of the topic: "I learn to my great satisfaction that you propose to elaborate the important question more fully and publish the results of your ever thorough researches in book form."[43] (No such book was forthcoming.)

In addition to the personal correspondence sent to Thayer, a number of legal periodicals and law reviews extolled "Origin and Scope." *Law Book News* deemed the article "valuable and interesting."[44] The *Yale Law Journal* lauded it as "very vigorous" and added, "To all citizens who desire to elevate the standard of our legislatures, this paper is valuable for its suggestiveness."[45] Notably, Thayer's article won the approval of William Meigs, who, as a young lawyer in the 1880s, had defended the subversive position that there is no justification at all for judicial review. Now, in a law review essay, Meigs walked himself back to occupy Thayer's less uncompromising ground. Like Thayer, Meigs argued that the judiciary's role as the final arbiter of constitutionality entails "far-reaching power [that] should be carefully guarded and should not be abused." This meant that courts ought to uphold legislation "unless it is plainly in violation of the constitution." He made favorable reference to Thayer's essay: "A well-known writer has examined this subject quite recently . . . where special emphasis is thrown upon the scrupulous care with which the power in question should be exercised." It remains unclear why Meigs adopted Thayer's test now. Perhaps he found Thayer's reasoning persuasive enough to disabuse him of his iconoclasm, or maybe Meigs was simply aging out of his youthful dalliance with extremism. It is also conceivable that Meigs realized he had a better chance at reining in judicial activism if he tempered his views and traded on the credibility of a well-regarded Harvard professor. Possibly a combination of these factors was at play.[46]

Other outlets offered more substantial, and more nuanced, commentary. The *American Law Register and Review*—later renamed the *University of Pennsylvania Law Review*—published an editorial note indicating that Thayer's theory of judicial restraint was not mainstream. "Because of the peculiar position taken, [it is] of exceptional interest," the *Register and Review* remarked. It granted that "Origin and Scope" was of "great value" but took considerable issue with Thayer's presumption of constitutionality. The *Register and Review* inferred that Thayer wanted his rule of presumption to apply universally to all legislation and therefore insisted, "If this criterion of interpretation is sound it must be good in all cases." In other words, Thayer's theory was meritorious only if it always produced sound results. This was, arguably, an unfair bar to clear. While true that Thayer's article did not enumerate exceptions to his theory, he did—consistent with legal realism—generally reject categorical maxims. The *Register and Review* was therefore projecting onto Thayer's theory a sclerotic quality that was ungenerous, given Thayer's own aversion to axiomatic thinking.

In any event, the *Register and Review* raised an issue that would bedevil Thayer's protégés: his theory of judicial restraint, if applied unsparingly, could result in the bench sustaining legislation that encroached on fundamental liberties. To avoid this outcome, the *Register and Review* called for a two-tiered doctrine that employed Thayerian deference in most instances but allowed for heightened judicial scrutiny when tyrannical majorities tried to crush minority rights. "However unwise, however foolish, if it is a question of the exercise of a power of government, those powers should be construed in no narrow spirit"—that is, the presumption of constitutionality should hold—"but, if, on the other hand, it is a question of the rights of individuals . . . no pains, it seems to us, should be spared to protect the individual as [*sic*] against the legislature."[47]

This was a farsighted approach that, we will see, many Thayer devotees would adopt as they wrestled with the constitutionality of legislation restricting speech. Other Thayerites, however, would find no constitutional basis for the judiciary to act as the guarantor of countermajoritarian liberties. Thayer himself did not live long enough to see the landmark free speech cases of the late Progressive Era, which brought to the fore the tension between majority rule and civil liberty.[48] If he had, perhaps Thayer would have carved out an exception to the general rule he advanced in "Origin and Scope." Perhaps not. Ultimately, it would be left to his mentees to confront the difficult reality that democratic majorities sometimes erode individual rights.

Thayer had printed his prequel to "Origin and Scope" in the *Nation* back in 1884, so it was fitting that this magazine would thoughtfully engage his ideas now that he had finally published his full-throated elaboration of that prior piece. The *Nation* found "Origin and Scope" uniquely intriguing. "Neither the *Harvard Law Review*, nor any of our legal periodicals, has given us for a long time a more interesting study of a vital subject than Prof. Thayer's," the review declared. The *Nation* was largely sympathetic to Thayer, endorsing his view that the public was overly reliant on the judiciary and that lawmakers lazily conflated the constitutionality of a legislative act with its wisdom. "Prof. Thayer shows in a few brief but forcible paragraphs" that judicial review must "be kept rigorously within judicial limits." The magazine predicted that some readers would bristle at Thayer's article. "To many good citizens, the views of Prof. Thayer . . . will be unpalatable food for thought." And in fact, some of it was unpalatable to the *Nation*. The magazine criticized Thayer for not adequately addressing the proper judicial standard when a state passes legislation impinging on the federal government. "Will this easy-going rule do when State authority collides with the supreme law of the land?" the review asked.[49]

Thayer had indeed discussed that issue in "Origin and Scope." For state legislation that did *not* impede the national government, Thayer contended that the usual presumption of constitutionality should apply. But when the question arises whether a state legislature has infringed upon the authority of the national government, the federal judiciary—according to Thayer—has a special obligation to protect all three federal branches from encroachment by a legally inferior body. In those cases, federal courts ought to strike down state legislation more readily than they would congressional statutes. Thayer did not flesh out with specificity the appropriate standard of review; he suggested merely that "the limit is at a different point."[50] For the *Nation*, his discussion of the foregoing issue was insufficient: "Thayer treats this question too briefly." And the magazine pointed out that Thayer had failed to address another matter of import—namely, "where an act of Congress trenches upon the constitutional rights of States." The *Nation* also raised doubts about Thayer's history of the doctrine of judicial review, which he claimed had roots in the era of British colonial rule. "As to the origin of the American doctrine, we are not now prepared to controvert the views of Prof. Thayer, and yet are not altogether willing to assent to them," the magazine announced.[51]

If the *Nation* was ambivalent about Thayer's historical analysis, the British periodical the *Law Journal* was not: Thayer's rendition of history was "fanciful and inconclusive, and the essayist makes no attempt to substantiate it." Still, the *Law Journal* found much merit in "Origin and Scope" and assured readers that it was "extremely interesting and valuable."[52] That this periodical wrote about Thayer's article at all was an indication of his international reach. French and Australian commentators also took note of his much-discussed essay.[53]

In all, "Origin and Scope" elicited immediate attention from the legal profession and no small measure of praise, but it did not receive uniform plaudits. It took time for Thayer's article to become a classic in the annals of American legal history. His protégés, who were naturally the most receptive to his teachings on judicial deference, had not yet reached their privileged perches on the bench and in the academy. Eventually, they would inscribe his theory of restraint into canonical judicial opinions and influential works of scholarship. But in the mid-1890s the impact of "Origin and Scope" was yet to be fully realized.

Two years after Thayer's slender and striking publication on judicial review, he produced a casebook on constitutional law.[54] Like his evidence casebook, it was the first of its kind on the subject.[55] Critics commended his curation of cases. *Political Science Quarterly* remarked that "the selections and quotations are made with excellent judgment and rare discrimination."[56] Meanwhile, the *American Law Register and Review* lauded the casebook's comprehensiveness, finding within its pages "all the principal cases dealing with the Constitution of the United States."[57] Yet reviewers also lamented the absence of Thayer's authorial voice. The *American Historical Review*, in its inaugural issue, acknowledged that when writing "as a law teacher for law students," one must maintain "a certain reserve" so that students are free to draw their own inferences from the raw material, but this was a regrettable omission for "the general reader," who wants to hear more from the erudite scholar in his own words. "Whatever Professor Thayer says is well said, and few know as well the full uses of the lessons of history."[58]

In 1895 Thayer journeyed to Detroit to deliver to the American Bar Association conference what would become one of his more influential lectures. He began the address by describing Detroit as a "beautiful city, a novel and strange place to many of us." But it could not have been too strange to Thayer, who had spent time there reporting on the growth of the railways in the Midwest. His lecture, "The Teaching of English Law at Universities," referred to both English and American universities, and by way of comparison, he commended the efficacy of law schools in the United States. "We, in America, have carried legal education much farther than it has gone in England," he asserted. To convince his listeners that his perspective was not merely American chauvinism, Thayer observed, "The more enlightened members of our profession in England have keenly felt the backward state of things there."[59]

Thayer's overall intention, however, was not to cultivate complacency but to urge the further development of legal education in America. While society at large could plainly see the value of expertise in the natural sciences or engineering, the utility of legal expertise was not obvious to the general public. "Men do not now need to be told what it is that has given them the steam-engine, the telegraph, the telephone," he acknowledged. "But as regards our law, those who press the importance of thorough and scientific study are not yet exempt from the duty of pointing out the use of it and its necessity."[60]

Thayer reasoned that for law to rank as a discipline of the highest order, law schools had to institute a number of reforms. For one, faculties had to comprise professors dedicated exclusively to academia, not practitioners who taught as a hobby. "You cannot have a learned faculty of law unless, like other faculties, they give their lives to their work," he proclaimed. Law professors must not limit themselves to classroom instruction but must also produce original scholarship. Research would lead to the "clearing away of ambiguities, of false theories, of outworn and unintelligible phraseology. . . . The publishing of these results by competent persons is one of the chief benefits which we may expect from the thorough and scientific teaching of law at the universities." Consistent with the division of labor in modern society, Thayer stressed the importance of specialization for faculty members. "Instead of allotting to a man the whole of the common law, or half a dozen disconnected subjects at once, it means giving him a far more limited field," he recommended. Scholarly endeavors required, of course, books—and so "generous libraries shall be collected at the Universities suited to all the ordinary necessities of careful legal research." The varied aspects of a modern law school all cost money; fundraising would therefore be critical. "Our law schools must be endowed as our colleges are endowed."[61]

Full-time faculty, specialized research, expanded libraries, increased endowments—Thayer was prescribing for the legal academy writ large developments that had already taken root at Harvard Law. Whatever differences of opinion or style existed between Langdell and Thayer, the two men shared the same prescient vision for legal academia. And so did others. One Harvard Law student recollected that, after the speech's publication, Thayer received an "extraordinary number of approving letters from judges, teachers and lawyers throughout the English-speaking world, including the Lord Chancellor and the Lord Chief-Justice of England."[62]

Among those in attendance at the American Bar Association meeting in Detroit was future US president William Howard Taft. The year after that conference, Taft helped found a law school at the University of Cincinnati. Surely with Thayer's speech on legal pedagogy in mind, he solicited guidance from Thayer on this new academic undertaking. Taft self-deprecatingly joked that he and four colleagues in Ohio, all of whom "are reputed to be lawyers," were "given complete control of the department and told to work out our own salvation." Taft listed five subjects they considered requiring as first-year courses and wrote to Thayer with "the hope that you will be willing to comment on the wisdom of our selection."[63] Surprisingly, Thayer advised cutting his beloved subject of evidence law from the initial year of study. Taft replied, "We have stricken out of the first year's course evidence and have put in, in accordance with your suggestion, criminal law." Taft's final words on the subject were heavy with gratitude: "We should not have ventured to trouble you gentlemen of Harvard at all, if we had not felt that you were greatly interested in promoting the cause of legal education throughout the country."[64] Taft and his colleagues in Cincinnati were typical of legal educators nationwide who looked to Harvard Law as a model worthy of emulation.

Still, progress at Harvard Law had its limits. Its student body remained exclusively male even in the latter years of Thayer's tenure, even though thirty-eight other law schools were coeducational.[65] Alongside gender bias, Harvard Law earned a reputation for anti-Catholic prejudice, discriminating against applicants who had received their undergraduate degrees from Catholic institutions. Racial diversity was also slow in coming. By the end of Thayer's career, the law school in its entire history had enrolled nine Black students, four Latinos, a solitary Native American, and not one Asian American.[66]

Thayer's canon of scholarship included a mix of law review articles, published speeches, and casebooks for students. But the surest path to enduring influence in his era was an original legal treatise, and Thayer produced precisely one in his long academic career: *A Preliminary Treatise on Evidence at the Common Law*. It was a bid to redress a branch of law that was in abject disarray and in dire need of modernization. Over the course of the nineteenth century, evidence law had expanded into a disorienting litany of antiquated and often contradictory rules. A protégé of Thayer's denounced it "as the most disordered, ill-defined, and little understood topic in the whole range of the common law."[67]

At the time that Thayer was preparing his *Preliminary Treatise* for publication, evidence law was dominated by an outdated treatise produced more than a half century earlier by a previous occupant of the Royall Chair at Harvard Law: Simon Greenleaf. He published the first edition of *A Treatise on the Law of Evidence* (hereafter referred to as *Greenleaf*) in 1842.[68] Prior to the appearance of *Greenleaf*, legal practitioners in the United States had relied on treatises by English jurists.[69] Because much English precedent was not applicable to US jurisdictions, *Greenleaf* tapped into a latent demand among American lawyers for a reference work all their own.

By the mid-1890s, *Greenleaf* had been through fifteen revisions over five decades, the first seven by Simon Greenleaf himself before his death and the subsequent iterations by various eminent judges and Greenleaf's grandson. These editors added annotations for recent cases but did not substantively reshape evidence doctrine to address changing needs. As a result, *Greenleaf* grew increasingly anachronistic.[70]

"Variance" was one instance of a *Greenleaf* doctrine that had grown out of touch with legal practice by the end of the nineteenth century. According to the rule, judges should not admit evidence that was at "variance" with "the essential elements of the legal proposition in the controversy." Greenleaf explained that evidence of intent was irrelevant in tort cases and therefore inadmissible under the variance doctrine. "For removing earth from the defendant's land," Greenleaf offered by way of example, "whereby the foundation of the plaintiff's house was injured, the allegation of bad intent in the defendant is not necessary to be proved, for the cause of action is perfect, independent of the intention." In the decades after Greenleaf's death, rapid industrialization gave rise to novel torts that were ill suited to inherited legal doctrine. Courts came to see intent as a relevant, if not quite determinative, aspect of tort law.[71] Testimonial disqualification because of interest was another *Greenleaf* doctrine inconsonant with modern legal practice. This rule held that a judge could bar from the stand a witness possessing some vested interest in the trial's outcome. The state of New York had repealed disqualification by interest in 1848, a move soon emulated by every other American jurisdiction.[72]

Not only had much of *Greenleaf* become obsolete by the century's end, but the legal profession now considered several topics in the treatise to lie outside the ambit of evidence law. Consider, for instance, the statute of frauds, a seventeenth-century English law adopted in the United States that required parties to finalize certain kinds of agreements in writing. The statute of frauds had migrated from the procedural law of evidence in Greenleaf's day to the substantive law of contracts in Thayer's own.[73]

In 1882 one commentator in the *American Law Review* complained, "Our present law of evidence—made up as it is of case law, modified by numerous statutory amendments made at different times, many of them based upon theories entirely inconsistent with each other, and some upon no theory at all—is a system of patch-work."[74] Thayer himself condemned the rules of evidence as "a great degree ill-apprehended, ill-stated, ill-digested," little more than a confused mass.[75] Latter-day historian Tal Golan similarly concludes, "The law of evidence had turned . . . into a highly complicated and technical domain, sagging to the point of collapse under the burden of its own distinctions, exceptions, and exclusionary duties."[76] By the 1890s, the field was ready for the Greenleaf of a new generation to fundamentally reshape the unruly mishmash of evidence rules—and Thayer endeavored to pick up the gauntlet.

A work of both history and theory, his *Preliminary Treatise* was "preliminary" in that it was the first installment of what was intended to be a grander enterprise. Thayer hoped to ultimately translate insights from this initial, and quite academic, work into a full-fledged treatise for practitioners that would overhaul the increasingly outmoded rules of evidence. As he explained it, the time was "ripe for the hand of the jurist" to undertake a "full historical examination of the subject," culminating, eventually, in a "restatement of the existing law and with suggestions for the course of its future development."[77]

The *Preliminary Treatise* did not appear all at once. Thayer released the first four chapters in 1896 with the subtitle *Part I. Development of Trial by Jury.* Then, in 1898, his publisher—Little, Brown—produced two versions of an expanded *Preliminary Treatise*: one edition with chapters 5 through 12, and another that combined all twelve chapters into a single comprehensive book spanning 636 pages.[78] The early chapters covered the history of the English trial system from which America derived its own, and the remainder of the treatise was largely concerned with exposing substantive law that masqueraded as evidence law. With respect to the latter topic, Thayer lamented in the treatise, "It is discreditable to a learned profession to allow the subject to lie in the jumble that now characterizes it in this respect."[79]

The *Preliminary Treatise* reflected many of legal realism's central tenets. Thayer, for instance, expressly privileged experience over logic. He commented that "the law of evidence is the creature of experience rather than logic," a clear echo of Oliver Wendell Holmes Jr.'s famous aphorism (discussed in chapter 3) that "the life of the law has not been logic: it has been experience." In that spirit, Thayer railed against the incursion of abstract logic on legal doctrine. The opening pages of the *Preliminary Treatise* stated that the law of evidence "is not concerned with nice definitions, or the exacter academic operations of the logical faculty. It is attending to practical ends." Thayer lamented that "a bastard sort of technicality has thus sprung up, and a crop of fanciful reasons for anomalies destitute of reason, which baffle and disgust a healthy mind." On the subject of the parol evidence rule—which proscribed evidence that contravened the terms of a contract—Thayer criticized the "mere rules of procedure, and reason, and logic which overloads it." The notion that logic can overload an area of law reflects the typical realist concern that a fetish for logical form comes at the expense of common sense.[80]

The *Preliminary Treatise* chastised the judiciary for obscuring the realities of law behind a façade of logic. Thayer dismissed as pure fantasy the expectation that formalistic modes of judicial analysis would result in the uniform application of the law. "Judges, and whole benches of them," he observed, "may decide such questions differently, while perfectly agreeing on the rule of law and keeping within it." In the same vein, Thayer criticized judges who spuriously denied that they legislated from the bench. That kind of judicial activism was "not quite in harmony with the general attitude of the common-law courts and their humble phraseology in disclaiming the office of legislation." But in actuality, the need to adjudicate amid "ever-changing combinations of fact" forced the bench to "constantly legislate." Rather than hide behind a false veneer of self-abnegation, "it is best that this be openly done" by judges.[81] In Thayer's view, courts had to countenance the hard realities of legal practice rather than seek refuge behind the comforting fictions of legal theory.

Thayer's treatise maintained that experience could guide the law in more prudent directions where ill-conceived logic had led it astray. In a broad sense, the entire *Preliminary Treatise*, with its emphasis on legal history, embodied his faith in experience as a tool to shape doctrine.[82] More specifically, Thayer noted that courts often applied "reasonableness" as a standard for behavior, and he directed the legal system to rely on "its fund of general experience" to determine the boundaries of that ambiguous term. Similarly, the interpretation of documents "may depend on no legal rule, but only on the rules, principles, or usages of language and grammar, as applied by sense and experience." Thayer also noted that juries often had to "estimate damages and to act upon expert testimony" by "bringing into play that general fund of experience and knowledge" from which "they must in all cases draw."[83]

The *Preliminary Treatise*, in true realist fashion, was wary of universal axioms. To be sure, Thayer did maintain that "certain great principles" should govern evidence law, but he saw these principles as flexible guidelines rather than categorical dictates. Absolutes were quixotic. The law of evidence, Thayer insisted, could never achieve "exact results; it deals with probabilities and not with certainties; it works in an atmosphere, and not in a vacuum; it has to allow for friction, for accident and mischance." He praised the "more elastic procedure of the English courts," which offered a contrast to the rigidity of their American counterparts.[84]

Thayer's belief that law was woven into the broader social fabric was another realist theme of his treatise. For example, he situated in the context of monarchical authority the transition from legal practice premised on supernatural beliefs to more rational methods. "Where royal power was vigorous," Thayer recounted, "it required safer and directer ways of settling those matters of fact on which its revenues depended than the rude, superstitious, one-sided methods which were followed in the popular courts." He further indicated his belief in the interdependence of law and society when he expressed optimism that the communications revolution of his own era would facilitate the rapid expansion of "enlightened modes of proof" at trial. Though he acknowledged the endurance of antiquated legal conventions, Thayer still posited, "Perhaps it will be otherwise as the superior and elect minds of our race come to find an audience among the men of their own day—a thing more and more happening as swift means of communication make all men neighbors."[85] Having lived through the advent of both the telegraph and telephone, he understood the relative isolation of an earlier age.

The *Preliminary Treatise* reflected Thayer's conception of legal categories as constructed rather than innate. He treated classification as a contingent and somewhat arbitrary enterprise. For instance, Thayer rejected any natural distinction between "law" and "fact." This dichotomy was particularly relevant to the rules of evidence because, in jury trials, law was the domain of the judge, while fact (generally) rested with the jury. Thayer recognized that the classification of "law" versus "fact" was historically fluid. He described how, in cases of negligence, courts had once considered the question of whether "one conformed to the standard of the prudent and reasonable man" to be a legal rather than factual inquiry. Yet in his own day, reported Thayer, such a determination was now "clearly recognized as a question of fact for a jury."[86]

Practicality was also a realist motif in Thayer's treatise. "The peculiar character and scope of legal reasoning," Thayer contended, "is determined by its purely practical aims and the necessities of its procedure and machinery." Pragmatism alone was reason enough to justify a given means of conducting trial procedure. On the topic of litigation, he wrote, "It must shape itself to various other exigencies of a practical kind" to preempt unduly long trials or unending rounds of rebuttal. The doctrines constituting the law of evidence all "spring from the practical aims of a court of justice and the practical conditions of its work." Thayer praised the jury system for elevating "easily applied principles of practical sense." In determining which party shouldered the burden of proof, Thayer announced, "Now, and at all times, the tests of justice and practical convenience are legitimate ones." For him, a just legal system was necessarily a pragmatic one.[87]

The *Preliminary Treatise* frequently evaluated evidence rules based on their effects rather than their internal logic. Thayer applied this outcome-based approach to the interpretation of documents. Although language "shall have its natural and proper meaning" ordinarily, he insisted that courts sometimes should "make words bear other meanings than the usual and proper ones, in order to avoid absurd or unreasonable results." Elsewhere, Thayer dismissed the semantics of a specific rule of evidence and highlighted its consequences. As he put it, "The important question in any particular instance is what is the effect and operation of the rule, not what its name is." Thayer was similarly results oriented in discussing litigation at large. "It must adjust its processes to general ends, so as generally to promote justice, and to discourage evil, to maintain long-established rights, and the existing governmental order," he argued. The various realist tenets that Thayer employed throughout his treatise were ones his cohort of disciples would advocate for decades to come.[88]

In its rebuke of judicial activism, the *Preliminary Treatise* accorded with Thayer's "Origin and Scope" article. His treatise was explicit about the need for restraint from the bench in the domain of substantive law (even as he called on the bench to exercise more agency with respect to procedural law). In Thayer's words, "It would never do to submit to the free control of the judges, through rules of court, the great mass of substantive law that now lies disguised under the name of the law of evidence."[89] He was especially keen to discriminate between substantive law and procedural law because only a proper distinction between the two would allow judges to rightly determine which circumstances merited their deference and which their discretion.

The *Preliminary Treatise* offered some hint of its sequel—a tome that would restate and reform the disorderly rules of evidence. Thayer delineated general principles governing the work ahead of him. Evidence doctrine ought to be "simple," "not too rigid," and never "impracticable." It should serve as a prophylactic against the trickery that was all too common among trial lawyers. And in the interest of swift justice, after a judge in a court of original jurisdiction has ruled on the admissibility of evidence, only in the rarest of circumstances should a higher court overturn any such ruling.[90]

The *Preliminary Treatise* was immediately met with emphatic acclaim. The *American Historical Review* celebrated it as "one of the most valuable contributions to English constitutional and legal history published in this country."[91] Meanwhile, the *Virginia Law Register* found Thayer's methods "masterly" and his conclusions of "absorbing interest." It greeted the treatise as a canonical work, "the most important contribution to the *rationale* of the law of evidence that has ever been made."[92] The *Western Reserve Law Journal* went further, suggesting that the *Preliminary Treatise* was a superlative addition not merely to evidence law but also to American law writ large—and to English law as well. "It is one of the greatest legal treatises ever written in this country or in England," its reviewer declared.[93] A number of reviews stressed the value of the *Preliminary Treatise* to nonlegal scholars. *Political Science Quarterly*, for instance, stated that it would be of "interest not to lawyers alone, but to all students of institutional history."[94]

Reviewers were particularly grateful that the book was not just erudite in its substance but lively in its prose. As the *Harvard Law Review* observed, many knowledgeable scholars produced books that were "dry bones and dust for the general reader, and a terror to the struggling student." Against this grim backdrop, general readers and struggling students who opened Thayer's treatise would "have to thank him for making his work not only thorough and accurate, but also lucid and interesting."[95] The *Yale Law Journal* appreciated that the clarity of Thayer's ideas went hand in hand with the clarity of his language: "the book seems one long plea for such clearer thinking and writing." The journal then sounded a soft note of caution. Because the *Preliminary Treatise* offered a critique as much as a description of evidence law, it was best left in the hands of experienced practitioners rather than novices who were simply trying to get their bearings on the subject. The journal predicted that Thayer's book would be "an inspiration and a stimulus" to "older lawyers and judges" but "might prove a source of danger to a beginner who was seeking the law of evidence as it is now conceived."[96]

It is a testament to Thayer's transatlantic reach that his treatise garnered favorable opinions from England's foremost legal historians: Sir Frederick Pollock, the Corpus Professor of Jurisprudence at Oxford, and F. W. Maitland, the Downing Professor of the Laws of England at Cambridge. Together Pollock and Maitland had published one of the most influential works of legal scholarship ever produced, *The History of English Law before the Time of Edward I*, which appeared in 1895. That iconic book had commended Thayer's *Harvard Law Review* articles on the history of the jury trial in England, remarking, "Lately Mr J. B. Thayer has published . . . three articles so full and excellent that we shall make our own sketch very brief." Then, in an allusion to the still-in-progress *Preliminary Treatise*, Pollock and Maitland added, "We are glad to hear that Mr Thayer is about to publish his papers in a collected form."[97] It is little surprise, then, that when Thayer's book finally came out, it was lauded individually by Pollock and Maitland, each of whom wrote his own review. In the pages of the *English Historical Review*, Maitland gushed that "nowhere else could the student of institutions find so complete, so truthful, or so lively an account" of the development of evidence law in English history.[98] Pollock, for his part, extolled the book's relentlessness. "It goes to the root of the subject more thoroughly, we venture to say, than any other textbook in existence," he wrote in the *Law Quarterly Review*.[99]

A number of journals commented that the *Preliminary Treatise* made it impossible for the legal profession to ignore the benighted condition of evidence law any longer. According to the *Harvard Law Review*, Thayer revealed that "our rules of evidence are neither logical nor wholly reasonable."[100] The *American Law Review* credited Thayer for his exhaustiveness in exposing the scope of the problem. "Now we have a completed picture," its review read, "in which upon a single canvas the whole dark and intricate course of the jury is for the first time fully spread out."[101] If the *Preliminary Treatise* had uncovered the darkness, then it would be the task of Thayer's sequel to provide the light.

Reviewers highly anticipated the arrival of this subsequent tome that would tame the unruly law of evidence. "Having cleared the ground of this mass of spurious undergrowth," wrote the *Harvard Law Review*, "the author is ready to treat of [*sic*] the law of evidence proper, and the preliminary gives good promise for the further work."[102] The *Virginia Law Register* was similarly enthused about the prospect of a treatise by Thayer for use in the courtroom: "We trust that nothing will prevent the realization of the 'good hope' he expresses of supplementing the present volume before long by another."[103] Good hope indeed—Thayer was already nearing seventy when he published the complete edition of the *Preliminary Treatise*. It remained to be seen whether his health would cooperate with his ambitions.

The kind of legal realism that characterized the *Preliminary Treatise* and Thayer's other writings was not entirely unique to him. Other voices from his generation promoted tenets of realist jurisprudence. Among them was James C. Carter, who had attended Harvard College with Thayer. Carter became a lawyer with a penchant for publishing legal theory on the side.[104] In a pair of law review articles in 1890, Carter defended core elements of legal realism. He argued in favor of practicality as a governing principle of law. "The judge, the lawyer, the jurist of whatever name . . . is constantly employed in the contemplation of what is fit, useful, convenient," Carter asserted. He saw law as inextricably bound up in the larger society and called on the legal practitioner to accommodate the law to a quickly changing world: "Sympathizing with every advancing movement made by society, catching the spirit which animates its progress, it is [the lawyer's] aim to keep jurisprudence abreast with other social tendencies."[105] Carter believed that because societal transformation required the law to "be *adapted* to human affairs," legal principles had to be dynamic rather than immutable. He scoffed, "It is folly to suppose that unbending rules can be made beforehand, and men be disciplined to learn them and adapt the business of life to them."[106]

Fifteen years later, Harvard Law invited Carter to give a lecture series wherein he planned to develop additional realist themes. He unexpectedly passed away before he could deliver the lectures, but they soon appeared in book form. In this posthumous publication, Carter rejected the conceit that law claimed metaphysical provenance. He explored that idea in the context of a hypothetical fact pattern wherein a panel of judges ruled against an insurance underwriter in a fraud case. The "notion of right and wrong" used by the panel to resolve the case "did not come from on High. It was not sought for in the Scriptures, or in any book on ethics." Rather, the bench rendered its decision based on real-world outcomes. As Carter put it, "The judges considering whether the act was right or wrong applied to it the method universally adopted by all men; they judged it by its *consequences*."[107] The need for law to evolve with its social context, a rejection of supernaturally derived axioms, due regard for the actual effects of legal decisions—so much of Thayer's agenda was Carter's as well. In fact, Thayer dedicated the *Preliminary Treatise* to Carter.

Another realist theme voiced by some of Thayer's contemporaries was the recognition that judges, despite their protests to the contrary, legislated from the bench. John F. Dillon was a pedigreed proponent of this view.[108] Born the same year as Thayer, Dillon served as a justice on the Iowa Supreme Court and then as a judge on a federal appeals court. Following Dillon's retirement from the bench, Yale Law School invited him in the early 1890s to take up the prestigious Storrs Lectureship, which brought eminent jurists to New Haven for an academic year to deliver a lecture series. Dillon used his platform at Yale to refute the notion that judges merely applied the law. "It was long a favorite fiction that the judges did not make, but only declared, the law," he lamented. "But it is no longer denied, nor can it be, that the judges in the process of the interpretation of statutes . . . are actually, though indirectly, engaged in legislating." Like Thayer, Dillon held that countenancing the reality of judicial legislation did not license the bench to do whatever it pleased. Although the "work of indirect judicial legislation" could "never be entirely abrogated," nevertheless, Dillon insisted that "this function of the judges may be limited, and it ought to be."[109] Comparable ideas were propounded by the esteemed constitutional theorist A. V. Dicey, who held the Vinerian Chair at Oxford. In the fall of 1898 Dicey gave a lecture series at Harvard Law that connected the notion of judicial legislation to the integrated nature of law and society. He observed, "The Courts of the judges, when acting as legislators, are of course influenced by the beliefs and feelings of their time, and are guided to a considerable extent by the dominant current of public opinion."[110] Although these lectures were not published until after Thayer's death, Thayer was almost certainly in attendance when Dicey delivered them in person at Harvard.

There is debate among scholars today about the prevalence of legal realist views in the late nineteenth century.[111] Dillon illustrates the complexities of pinning down the jurisprudential zeitgeist of that era. Although he was candid about the unavoidability of judicial legislation, Dillon departed from realism by clinging to a metaphysical notion of law. For instance, in the Storrs Lectures, he celebrated the Fifth Amendment to the US Constitution for its "language which shone resplendent with the light of universal justice."[112] William G. Hammond—law dean at Washington University in St. Louis—was another figure of that era whose embrace of realism was only partial. On the one hand, he forthrightly acknowledged in realist fashion that the archetypal judge offers merely a "superficial consistency and certainty of the law, and hides from careless eyes its utter lack of definiteness and precision."[113] On the other, Hammond held fast to the idea that a "Divine order" informed "fixed principles of jural as well as moral right."[114] Dillon and Hammond alike espoused a transcendental basis for law, a view that distinguished them from Thayer. It appears, then, that Thayer's realism was relatively full throated for his day. Although Thayer's acolytes would later go too far in describing him as "subversive" and even "heretical," the fact that they felt compelled to use these adjectives at all suggests that Thayer was not simply parroting a uniformly accepted jurisprudence of the time.

Thayer's commitment to legal education extended beyond Cambridge. In 1900 he cofounded the Association of American Law Schools (AALS) and was selected its first president.[115] Of the thirty-five schools initially invited to join, thirty-two quickly did. Through its conferences, the AALS offered a forum for scholars to discuss the law and techniques of legal pedagogy.[116] Professional associations such as the AALS were key tools in the modernization of professions. They developed standards, debated professional issues, and represented the interests of their respective fields to society at large.[117] The very premise that universities rather than law offices should be the focal point for legal training was a modern idea and not yet commonplace;[118] at the time of the AALS's founding, most attorneys still did not attend law school.[119] Thayer's service as the association's inaugural president thus indicates not only the esteem with which his peers held him but also his leading role in the professionalization of legal academia.

Around that same time, current events prompted Thayer to offer his most comprehensive defense of living constitutionalism. America was in the throes of a brutal war for control of the Philippines. That conflict occasioned a debate in the United States about the constitutionality of territorial conquest. Thayer's essay "Our New Possessions," in the *Harvard Law Review*, advanced the claim that the Constitution raised no bar to America's seizing and governing territories anywhere in the world. He saw the Constitution's "shortness" and "silence" as its greatest virtues, for those qualities had freed successive generations throughout American history to tailor the meaning of that document to "the purposes of a great, developing nation"—purposes that now included imperial expansion in Southeast Asia. The framers' keen insight was that they lacked foresight, Thayer explained, so they avoided being overly prescriptive when drafting the nation's fundamental law in 1787. It was their humility that accounted for the Constitution's longevity. Thayer proclaimed, "As it survives fierce controversies from age to age, it is forever silently bearing witness to the wisdom that went into its composition, by showing itself suited to the purposes of a great people under circumstances that no one of its makers could have foreseen."[120]

This take on living constitutionalism differed in some key respects from Thayer's stand on the subject in his 1887 article "Legal Tender." There, he noted that the Constitution said nothing about Congress's authority to print paper money, an omission that a number of framers believed to be a de facto prohibition of the practice. Thayer maintained that the framers erred in treating constitutional silence as a limit on congressional power, and he celebrated that American courts had not confined themselves to the framers' view. Now, in his article about the Philippines, Thayer recast constitutional silence as a deliberate license that the framers had bequeathed to later generations to adapt the Constitution to changing conditions. No longer did Thayer reject original intent, for living constitutionalism *was* the original intent. Although these two articles were inconsistent, they were united by a shared faith in a dynamic approach to constitutional interpretation.

Thayer's affinity for living constitutionalism was surely informed by his firsthand experience with the strikingly rapid modernization of American society over his lifetime. When he arrived in Cambridge as a college freshman, the town lacked gas, electricity, water infrastructure, trains, sewers, parks, or a hospital. But this once provincial college town now boasted all these amenities.[121] Thayer's jurisprudence was attuned to the unforeseeable exigencies of the future, and his protégés would find in his teachings the tools they needed to address the challenges of the twentieth century.

Thayer turned his attention to the only biography he would ever author. Titled simply *John Marshall*, the book appeared in 1901 to coincide with the centennial anniversary of Marshall's ascension to the chief justiceship of the US Supreme Court. Thayer had recently produced an article on Marshall for the *Atlantic Monthly* and delivered a speech on the chief justice to a joint audience from Harvard Law and the Boston Bar Association. He now drew from those materials to fashion a slender volume of 157 pages with a conspicuously large font.[122]

Thayer's selection of Marshall as a subject of study seems curious at first glance. After all, it was Marshall who made judicial review a cornerstone of American jurisprudence, and Thayer's abiding anxiety was the bench's eagerness to invalidate legislative statutes. Marshall articulated the doctrine of judicial review in *Marbury v. Madison* (1803), arguably the most important Supreme Court case in US history. Writing for the majority, Marshall deduced that the Constitution, though silent on the question of judicial review, implicitly gives the judiciary the prerogative to strike down legislation. "It is emphatically the province and duty of the Judicial Department to say what the law is," Marshall declared as he anointed the judiciary the final arbiter of constitutionality.[123]

Perhaps Thayer wrote about Marshall precisely because it allowed him to sound the alarm about judicial review. Although his biography of Marshall did not go so far as to claim that the chief justice had decided *Marbury* wrongly, still, Thayer criticized Marshall's opinion. Thayer derided the portion of *Marbury* that discussed judicial review, calling it "short and dry" and adding, "this treatment is much to be regretted." The brevity of Marshall's commentary on the doctrine left it open to future abuse, in Thayer's view. Marshall failed to contemplate the "grave and far-reaching considerations" that attend the judiciary's power to nullify legislative acts. "If the subject had been deeply considered and fully expounded" by Marshall, then his *Marbury* opinion would have taken pains to mark the proper limits of judicial review. Thayer realized that his unsympathetic assessment of *Marbury* bucked the conventional wisdom in the legal community. "It is not uncommon to speak of the reasoning in Marbury *v.* Madison . . . with the greatest praise," he acknowledged. Nevertheless, he insisted that the opinion was, in fact, not "entitled to rank with Marshall's greatest work."[124]

Thayer revived an argument from "Origin and Scope" in his critique of Marshall. As he had in 1893, Thayer once more maintained that judges cannot shoulder the sole burden for an act's constitutionality because there are matters of state that never reach the courts. The bench, for instance, does not have the opportunity to rule on a given statute if it fails to occasion litigation. Nor does the bench adjudicate so-called political questions, even when they raise constitutional issues; only the political branches—never the judiciary—can resolve such questions. It is thus imperative for legislators (and executives, for that matter) to scrutinize the constitutionality of their own actions. "All the departments, and not merely the judges, are sworn to support the Constitution," Thayer reminded readers.[125]

Following his discussion of *Marbury*, Thayer included in the middle of the biography an entire chapter that largely eschewed commentary on John Marshall in favor of an elaboration of Thayer's own theory of judicial restraint. Here again, Thayer renewed a line of reasoning pursued in "Origin and Scope." He condemned the abuse of judicial review as a catalyst for malign tendencies that undermined democracy. When courts "too promptly and easily proceed to set aside legislative acts," they unwittingly engender two insidious habits among lawmakers. The first is that legislators feel unencumbered by "consideration of constitutional constraints," since they see such consideration as a judicial responsibility. The other is that elected representatives falsely conflate the merit of legislation with its ability to withstand judicial scrutiny. In Thayer's words, lawmakers "insensibly fall into a habit of assuming that whatever they can constitutionally do they may do—as if honor and fair dealing and common honesty were not relevant to their inquiries." The lackluster quality of legislatures, in turn, leads citizens to grow "careless" in casting ballots. Voters reconcile themselves to electing "unfit persons" who end up passing "foolish and bad laws." The bench then intervenes to undo the damage wrought by mediocre legislators. This cycle reinforces the public's sense that there is virtue in judicial activism.[126]

For Thayer, this dynamic posed a serious threat to the very principle of representative democracy. When the "correction of legislative mistakes comes from the outside"—that is, from the judiciary—there arises a "serious evil." Citizens no longer hold themselves and their elected representatives accountable. The point of democracy is for the people, through their chosen lawmakers, to rule. Judicial activism undermines this central purpose; it serves to "dwarf the political capacity of the people, and to deaden its sense of moral responsibility." To trust unelected judges to save democracy from itself is to tacitly concede that the ideal of self-governance has already been abandoned. Thayer reasoned that if the judiciary's zeal to void legislation was the first domino in this regrettable chain of events, then by the same logic, the bench was uniquely positioned to reverse this state of affairs. "By adhering rigidly to its own duty," he predicted, "the court will help, as nothing else can, to fix the spot where responsibility lies." Only then can an electorate—reinvigorated with a sense of its own civic obligation—look to the polling station rather than the courtroom to rectify legislative errors.[127]

Thayer happily noted that even Marshall, in the fullness of time, came to warn against the overuse of judicial review. Fully three decades after *Marbury*, the storied chief justice cautioned at the twilight of his long tenure on the bench, "No questions can be brought before a judicial tribunal of greater delicacy than those which involve the constitutionality of a legislative act." Marshall urged courts to always seek reasons to uphold statutes, declaring, "A just respect for the legislature requires that the obligation of its laws should not be unnecessarily and wantonly assailed."[128] Thayer included this quotation in a chapter that otherwise offered scant mention of Marshall. It suggests much about Thayer's conception of history as a discipline that he shoehorned into a biography a protracted meditation on judicial review. As dedicated as he was to the study of the past, Thayer was no mere antiquarian. His historical investigations were always undertaken with an eye toward diagnosing current problems and prescribing future remedies.

Upon publication of the biography, the *Harvard Law Review* marveled, "It is not often that a man accomplishes so many things in one little book as Prof. Thayer has done in this one." Thayer managed to walk the fine line of scholarly dispassion. On the one hand, he avoided the "partiality to which biographers are so prone" by "point[ing] out a few indiscretions and errors" on the part of the normally lionized Marshall. On the other, Thayer was not overly critical. If anything, the book left readers "more than ever convinced of the substantial basis of Marshall's fame" and "filled with a new admiration for the sweetness, simplicity and strength of his personal character." The reviewer also appreciated Thayer's utilitarian approach to history, concluding that the biography's "practical suggestions" would "merit the careful consideration of all who have to do with the making or the interpretation of our laws."[129]

Described by a contemporary as "tall, straight, spare, and ascetically beautiful," Thayer remained relatively active through 1900.[130] The first sign of his enervation appeared in 1901, when the seventy-year-old Thayer confessed to a colleague, "fast walking and mountain climbing are for others now."[131] But his mental acuity remained sharp. As that year's fall semester drew near, he sketched out a scholarly agenda as demanding as ever, while conceding that he could not escape the ultimate fate of all mortals:

Sep. 15.

For next year.

Have a single plan to be put through. Without that the small, everyday matters eat up all the time. They easily may, for they can be done either well enough, or *perfectly.*

That plan must be the 2nd volume of Evidence.

For the year following, a small Vol. on Const. Law.

For the time following that, the works, writings, and life of Marshall—*and then an End.*[132]

With the phrase "either well enough, or *perfectly,*" Thayer admitted to himself that if he continued to indulge his lifelong perfectionist streak, he would never publish all he desired. A fellow Harvard Law professor, John Gray, noted, "Mr. Thayer was fastidious . . . in passing upon his own work. To discover or verify a fact which might make his material more complete, to arrange and rearrange that material so that its expression might be more perspicuous, no time or trouble seemed to him too great." That, in Gray's eyes, was the principal reason why Thayer's corpus was slim but stellar. As Gray put it, Thayer's writings collectively "cut no great figure" but nevertheless stood out because "their quality is high."[133]

At the time that Thayer listed his scholarly ambitions on the eve of the fall semester in 1901, he plainly anticipated having several years ahead of him. But fate would grant him not even one. On February 14, 1902, after sitting down to dinner, Thayer's heart stopped.[134]

Poignantly, Thayer had a reputation for delivering beautiful and fitting tributes to the deceased. When a friend of Thayer's was asked to deliver a eulogy for the beloved scholar, he instinctively thought: "Why Thayer would be the man for that."[135] A colleague similarly reflected, "He was the one to whom we all turned when memorials and epitaphs were to be written. We all feel to-day that the lips are silent which alone could pay a worthy tribute to such a man."[136]

The homage that spoke loudest was not of words. Befitting a New Englander born in the midst of a snowstorm, Thayer's funeral was conducted during a blizzard. No fewer than five hundred law students braved the weather to form an honor guard that accompanied his coffin on its journey from his home to the chapel on the Harvard campus.[137] Those students would soon take their places as leaders of the bench, bar, and legal academy, just as twenty-seven years' worth of Thayer's students already had. The lessons he taught them, they would never forget. His life was over; his legacy would echo through courthouses and classrooms for generations to come.

3. Thayer's Protégé:
Oliver Wendell Holmes Jr.

Oliver Wendell Holmes Jr. was born in Boston, Massachusetts, on March 8, 1841, to Amelia Lee Jackson and Oliver Wendell Holmes Sr., a celebrated author and future dean of Harvard Medical School. Holmes Jr. grew up witness to a nation in turmoil, graduating from Harvard University in 1861 at the dawn of the Civil War and enlisting in the Union army. He served for three years and narrowly evaded death more than once. After returning home to Boston, Holmes completed his law degree at Harvard in 1866.[1] Another decade would pass, however, before James Bradley Thayer became the Royall Chair in Law at the same institution, meaning that Holmes was never a student of the esteemed scholar.[2]

Fortunately for Holmes, Thayer did not wait for his entry into academia to begin mentoring. In fact, after Holmes joined Thayer's law firm—Chandler, Shattuck, & Thayer—in 1866 as a legal apprentice, Thayer became an important advocate for the recent Harvard Law graduate, affording Holmes opportunities seldom available to junior legal staff.[3] The two men were natural friends, industrious and scholarly Boston Brahmins who would both become major catalysts for realism in American law.[4]

They began to collaborate immediately upon Holmes's employment at the firm. Indeed, on Holmes's very first day, he was tasked with research for a case that Thayer was set to argue involving the postmortem disposition of an estate. Holmes toiled in the recesses of the courthouse library, writing abstracts of relevant precedents; Thayer went on to win the case before the Massachusetts Supreme Judicial Court.[5] The young lawyer initially cultivated a strong affection for a different partner at the firm, George Otis Shattuck, later recalling Shattuck as a "dear and honored friend." Holmes described him as a "sweeping, all-compelling force" in the courtroom and admired Shattuck's oratorical powers and remarkable energy.[6] Despite his effusive praise for that particular attorney, Holmes did not follow in Shattuck's litigious footsteps. Rather, it was the thoughtful and professorial Thayer who ultimately captured Holmes's attention and gave the apprentice his first taste of scholarly acclaim by asking him to coedit the twelfth edition of Kent's *Commentaries on American Law.*

Oliver Wendell Holmes Jr. in 1867, shortly after he began working for Thayer. (Harvard Law School Library, Historical and Special Collections)

Kent's *Commentaries* was first published in 1826 by the legendary James Kent shortly after he resigned the New York chancellorship, the seniormost legal office in the state. His compendium of American law was based on a lecture series he had given decades earlier when serving as the first professor of law at Columbia in the 1790s. The four-volume work ranged in topic from property and contracts to real estate and commercial law.[7] Kent's treatise was both influential and profitable from its inception (the elusive dream of all scholars), filling a need for a clear and concise overview of American jurisprudence. Fourteen editions appeared over the course of the nineteenth century. One reviewer gushed that it was "not only the standard, but the only authority."[8]

Kent's grandson, James Kent Jr., implored Thayer to produce the twelfth edition of *Commentaries* in 1869, a request betokening Thayer's reputation as a legal thinker.[9] Thayer agreed to Kent's offer, but he had a number of conditions. "I understand that you wish me to consider myself responsible for the undertaking and I do so," Thayer wrote to Kent in a letter that was part acceptance and part contract. "But at the same time it is to be understood that

Mr. Holmes is associated with me and that our names are to appear jointly as the editors in the preface—which I am to write if I desire to." Thayer went on to outline the various particularities of an arrangement that he would find acceptable. For example, the treatise had been perennially updated in successive editions with new material, and Thayer required that he and Holmes be free to edit anything beyond James Kent's original text and notes. Thayer indicated that they would attempt to complete the work in the two-year period Kent desired but asked for some "grace" should more time be needed. They would finish the book in the allotted period if "it can be done by such diligence as any fair person would call reasonable." Thayer would rather have a well-researched edition of *Commentaries* tied to his name than a rushed one.[10] Not until 1873 would Holmes submit the final draft, two years after Kent's original deadline.

Thayer's decision to involve Holmes in this project undoubtedly arose not only because of their workplace proximity but also because of Holmes's pertinent experience summarizing case law for the *American Law Review*. Holmes had first joined the journal's staff while still working at Thayer's firm and became its editor around the time he left the firm in 1870. For each of the journal's quarterly issues, Holmes read, compiled, and condensed important state supreme court decisions throughout the country into a "digest"—tasks closely mirroring the updates that Thayer and Holmes would be making to *Commentaries*.[11] The *Central Law Journal* would later point to Holmes's time with the *American Law Review* as a reason for his success as editor of *Commentaries*, observing that his "editorial management of one of the leading law journals of the country had well prepared him for work of this character."[12] Holmes embraced the endeavor as a vocation. Although he was nominally in private practice with his brother, Edward, Holmes had little time for any labor beyond the treatise.[13] Holmes wrote to Thayer in 1872 that he had "given up all my time to Kent's Commentaries," particularly in the past year, when he had "hardly touched any other business." And he needed more time yet to complete the last of the four-volume set.[14] Holmes, who would later gain renown for his concise judicial decisions, was quite verbose in this early stage of his career. He went far beyond providing simple updates to the text of *Commentaries*, adding in the margins dozens of small historical and legal essays concerning various topics. Holmes also rewrote entire footnotes to add clarity and introduce new legal concepts. Eager and ambitious, he saw fit to publish longer articles in the *American Law Review* to which he directed readers of *Commentaries*. In so doing, he recast a project many viewed as routine and custodial as a platform for his superlative analytic abilities.

When Holmes sent Kent a copy of the finished manuscript near the end of 1873, Kent wrote an angry letter to Thayer inquiring why Thayer's name was not accorded "first place," meaning listed as one of the work's editors—a status Holmes had reserved solely for himself.[15] Holmes's self-serving stunt apparently elicited a more muted reaction from Thayer. The professor's response to Kent is lost to history, but we can glean a sense of its contents based on Kent's subsequent reply, which praised Thayer's self-effacing restraint. Thayer was "a saint, I [an] ordinary mortal," Kent exclaimed.[16] The book named Thayer only in the acknowledgments section, where Holmes recognized that Thayer "has read all that I have written, and has given it the benefit of his scholarly and intelligent criticisms."[17] It was Holmes, claiming sole editorship, who received the accolades for this particularly insightful edition of *Commentaries*, with some going so far as to liken him to that legal oracle of old, chancellor James Kent himself. As the *Albany Law Journal* raved, Holmes "has infused into his labor something of the pride and love which animated the venerable Chancellor, and throughout the volume we see marks of intellectual comprehension and ability which render the new work akin to the old."[18] Given the esteem with which the legal community still held Chancellor Kent, this was high praise indeed. The *Central Law Journal* took its adoration a step further, insisting that "no previous edition equals this in the style in which it is published."[19] Thayer, originally tapped to serve as lead editor, was little more than an afterthought.

This is not to say that Holmes's ideas expressed in Kent's *Commentaries* were free of Thayer's influence. On the contrary, as Holmes noted, Thayer had read his work in its entirety and offered feedback, which meant the two jurists engaged in extended dialogue regarding a vast body of American law. The period during which Holmes produced the manuscript was significantly longer than his tenure as a law student. In other words, as a function of time and one-on-one interaction, Thayer had greater opportunity than Holmes's law professors to shape the future judge. And the exchange of legal ideas between the two men had only just begun.

Following the successful publication of Kent's *Commentaries* in 1873, Holmes reunited with his old boss George Shattuck and joined his firm, which now took the name Shattuck, Holmes, & Monroe.[20] Though Thayer and Holmes were neither working in the same office nor collaborating on the treatise any longer, their correspondence continued. In July 1879 Thayer wrote to Holmes praising him for a pair of articles in the *American Law Review*—one titled "Possession" and the other "Common Carriers and the Common Law."[21] Thayer encouraged the young scholar to continue publishing, sharing that the articles "seem to me of the greatest value" and that Holmes could "do nothing more honorable to yourself or more serviceable to our calling than to add other such to the list." Although Thayer then offered a couple critiques of "Possession," he emphasized his conviction that Holmes's scholarship merited attention at Harvard Law, expressing "the wish that our fellows at Cambridge should be attracted to the reading of these admirable papers."[22] It appears that Thayer was already laying the foundation for an eventual campaign to bring Holmes to the Harvard Law faculty.

A year later, in the fall of 1880, the Lowell Institute in Boston invited Holmes to deliver its prestigious annual lecture series.[23] Holmes hoped to develop "a general view of the Common Law" and seized the opportunity to test his ideas in front of an audience.[24] He labored for a year preparing the set of a dozen lectures, giving each one to a large crowd without the aid of notes.[25] Thayer was, of course, in attendance,[26] and he hailed the lectures in a letter to Holmes as a "triumphant success" and "beautiful performance."[27]

Although Holmes had edited Kent's *Commentaries* to wide acclaim, he would have to take on the more formidable ordeal of writing his own treatise to join the pantheon of iconic legal thinkers. The Lowell Lectures provided the impetus Holmes needed to initiate that daunting endeavor. As he acknowledged, "I should hardly have attempted the task of writing a connected treatise at the present time, had it not been for the invitation to deliver a course of Lectures at the Lowell Institute in Boston."[28] Shortly after his final lecture, Holmes started to turn his lecture materials into what would become *The Common Law* (1881), one of the most cited law books ever produced. And he did so with Thayer's help.

In a letter congratulating Holmes on the Lowell Lectures, Thayer offered "with pleasure" to provide a second pair of eyes to edit Holmes's treatise in progress.[29] Two days later, Thayer passed along "some marks" for Holmes's "Trespass + Negligence" chapter, along with the promise to read two articles that Holmes was adapting for inclusion in the book.[30] When *The Common Law* debuted, Holmes left a signed copy at his publisher's office for Thayer, a gesture that Thayer appreciated. "It is very kind of you, having so many friends whom you must wish to remember, to remember me also," he told Holmes. "I congratulate you most warmly on getting the book fairly into its covers."[31]

The opening passage of *The Common Law* is perhaps the most famous in any American book on law, and it helped set the terms for legal realism for generations to come. Here appeared Holmes's timeless maxim: "The life of the law has not been logic: it has been experience." He called for analysis that penetrated the veneer of syllogistic logic expressed in judicial decisions and reached the substratum of practicalities, policies, and prejudices that discreetly informed legal doctrine. In Holmes's words, "The felt necessities of the time, the prevalent moral and political theories, intuitions of public policy, avowed or unconscious, even the prejudices which judges share with their fellow-men, have had a good deal more to do than the syllogism in determining the rules by which men should be governed." *The Common Law* also stressed the importance of understanding law in a broad social context because "the law embodies the story of a nation's development through many centuries, and it cannot be dealt with as if it contained only the axioms and corollaries of a book of mathematics." The conception of the law as a geometric proof was pure fantasy, in Holmes's view.[32]

Any mention of *The Common Law* requires some qualification. Despite Holmes's bold and sweeping introductory remarks, reviews of the book indicate that his ideas were not wholly iconoclastic but rather reflective of a nascent movement. And the remainder of the book—which covered various topics such as torts, contracts, and criminal law—did not rigorously apply realist philosophy. Holmes, for instance, focused on the substance of legal doctrine, with little concern for external factors. *The Common Law*, then, was important primarily for the influence of its first paragraphs.[33]

Thayer appreciated the full significance of Holmes's contribution immediately, which is to say long before most other jurists, who came to consider *The Common Law* one of the classic texts of American law beginning in the 1920s.[34] As Holmes was converting his Lowell Lectures into *The Common Law* in early 1881, Thayer was quietly working to elevate Holmes to even greater heights. The professor sent a letter to governor John Long concerning a recent vacancy on the Massachusetts Supreme Judicial Court. "You will have an abundance of advice to the vacancy made by Judge Ames' resignation, but I will not abstain from adding a contribution," Thayer wrote optimistically.

"Would not O W Holmes Jr. be the man? His recent course of lectures at the Lowell Institute was very remarkable and indicated the highest sort of legal capacity."[35] Decades later, Holmes would observe that "deciding to give [the] Lowell Lectures on the Common Law, a matter which the weight of a hair decided, changed the whole course of my life."[36] Holmes could have easily added that those lectures were valuable in part because Thayer seized on them to advance Holmes's interests. After Governor Long chose another candidate to fill the seat on the court, Thayer turned his sights on a new vocation for Holmes: an endowed professorship at Harvard Law School.

In the latter part of 1881 Harvard University president Charles William Eliot and Holmes began to discuss the prospect of his appointment to the faculty. Eliot assured Holmes that an endowment for a professorship was forthcoming. Thayer would later recount that Holmes "deliberated for a considerable time and concluded to come and to come at once." But then Holmes learned that Eliot did not have the promised funds and was attempting to raise them from Holmes's fellow lawyers. Holmes withdrew his acceptance, explaining that he did not want his friends to bankroll an academic post for him. Given this turn of events, Thayer's colleagues at the law school did not see how an endowment could be raised and thus saw no merit in pursuing Holmes any further. But Thayer pressed on. He conferred with both Eliot and Louis Brandeis (whose role in this episode is discussed in the next chapter) about possible paths to a Holmes appointment. Thayer and Brandeis contemplated a number of potential benefactors, including Thayer's former student W. F. Weld, who agreed to endow the professorship with a slice of an inheritance he had just received from his grandfather. The fall of 1882 saw Thayer's labors come to fruition as Holmes became the Weld Professor of Jurisprudence at his alma mater.[37] Holmes's appointment, however, ended almost as soon as it had begun.

Thayer opened the *Boston Globe* on the morning of December 9, 1882, to uncover some unsettling news. "At a meeting of the Executive Council held yesterday," the paper reported, "Governor Long nominated Oliver Wendell Holmes, Jr. to the Supreme Bench."[38] Thayer was stunned that Holmes would abruptly leave Harvard Law after the considerable efforts undertaken to create the Weld Professorship for him. The *Globe*'s article sat so poorly with Thayer that he refused to believe it. The professor convinced himself of an alternative reality: surely Holmes had neither accepted nor declined the judgeship, but the governor, who simply presumed that Holmes would accept, prematurely announced the nomination. Thayer was so confident in the foregoing narrative that he offered the Harvard Law librarian a $500 bet (around $13,000 today) that Holmes must have "told the Governor that he would consider the subject and the Governor has gone forward upon that." Had the librarian taken that bet, he would have emerged the richer for it.[39]

In fairness to Holmes, he had informed Eliot a year earlier that he would assume a professorship with the understanding that he might well leave the law faculty for the bench if given the opportunity.[40] Holmes's offense, then, was not that he abandoned his academic post for a judgeship but that he did so with undue haste. He had failed to consult a single person at Harvard, including Eliot, before accepting Governor Long's nomination. The governor had expected Holmes to make an immediate decision, and according to Thayer's diary, Holmes "made no struggle for more time." Thayer took this as an insult to himself, to the law school, and to the student body. He felt particular sympathy for the law students, for whom "the year at the School had only begun." Many of Holmes's pupils "had been mainly induced to come [to Harvard Law] by his being here," and they deserved significantly more consideration than Holmes had afforded them. Thayer recognized that Long's expectation of a same-day response had put unjust pressure on Holmes, but he blamed Holmes for not requesting additional time. When Holmes formally announced his departure at a faculty meeting the following Tuesday, he was met with silence from all those present, save for President Eliot, who later admitted that he spoke only because "it did not seem kind" to "leave him talking all alone." In the confines of his diary, Thayer raged that Holmes, for all his legal acumen, was "wanting sadly in the noblest region of human character"—he was "selfish, vain, thoughtless of character."[41]

Despite the adulatory language in his correspondence with Holmes and his clear respect for the intellect of the newly appointed justice, Thayer's diary reveals that this sudden affront was not the first time Thayer had harbored negative feelings about Holmes. The professor wondered whether Holmes's acceptance of the governor's offer was indicative of a temporary lapse in judgment, asking, had "he lost his head perhaps?" But then, Thayer concluded, the earlier "experience with him in editing Kent, which I had been willing to forget, comes all back again and assures me that this conduct is characteristic."[42] Although a decade earlier Thayer had been outwardly magnanimous when Holmes arrogated to himself the sole editorship of Kent's *Commentaries*, it appears that Thayer had in fact felt wounded at the time. And the wound was now reopened by Holmes's hubris.

The relationship between Thayer and Holmes could easily be described as a pattern of exploitation. In two separate instances, Thayer gave Holmes a rare opportunity to ascend the legal ladder, and Holmes seized each opportunity— only to publicly slight Thayer. And yet the two never disentangled themselves. The motivation for Thayer's continued support of Holmes remains a matter for speculation. Perhaps Thayer so appreciated Holmes's legal mind that he was willing to ignore the younger man's character flaws. Maybe Thayer reasoned that Holmes, now on the bench, could be an effective vehicle for the implementation of their shared jurisprudence, and the professor hoped to exercise continued influence over Holmes. Still another possibility is that Thayer was not quite so utilitarian, and his instinct for mentorship inevitably outran his fleeting moments of resentment. Most likely, Thayer's motivations were a complex mix of the professional and the personal.

What is certain, however, is that the two men maintained an extensive correspondence long after Thayer could do much to enhance Holmes's meteoric career trajectory. Holmes continued to see Thayer as someone whose legal views were to be solicited and respected, not an erstwhile benefactor to be discarded. For instance, Holmes wrote to Thayer in October 1884 seeking advice about a pending case, *Winthrop Delano v. Trustees of Smith Charities*. This particular case turned on the scope of witness testimony. In his letter to Thayer, Holmes asked if there was precedent for determining whether a witness who was testifying that a specific event took place could speak on matters beyond the event in question. "Do you know any cases," Holmes inquired, "on the proposition that a party who has testified directly to a fact discernible by the senses is/is not entitled as of right to testify to collateral facts not otherwise material?"[43] Thayer wrote back quickly, and although his reply is no longer extant, he was apparently eager to provide guidance about evidence law and not so put off by previous events as to not respond.[44]

Holmes issued a ruling that individuals did not enjoy the right "to fortify their testimony by swearing to other facts merely for the purpose of making it more probable that what they said upon the principal point was true."[45] In a follow-up letter to Thayer's response, Holmes wondered whether his seeking Thayer's advice had violated some standard of judicial ethics and acknowledged that he did not "quite know what principle should be adopted by a judge as to difficulties which occur to him." Holmes ultimately decided that tapping Thayer's expertise was the sort of practice that "might properly enough fall within the discretion of the presiding Judge"—in other words,

Holmes himself.[46] That Holmes was willing to risk a possible breach of professional protocol in order to learn Thayer's thoughts is suggestive of the justice's enduring esteem for his old mentor.

As Holmes settled into life on the bench and Thayer carried on with his work on the faculty at Harvard Law, their correspondence grew increasingly erudite. The letters between the two jurists lengthened, as did their respective bodies of published works. Whether the topic was judicial deference to legislatures, procedural aspects of law, or the perils of legal formalism, Holmes and Thayer marched largely in lockstep. In 1886, during an address marking Harvard's 250th anniversary, Holmes acknowledged the excellent scholarship that the law faculty was producing and said he hoped we "may soon add Thayer on Evidence," indicating his desire for the venerated professor to write a comprehensive treatise on American evidence law.[47] Their mutual regard, however, did not preclude occasional disagreement.

One such instance of minor discord involved Holmes's majority opinion in *Commonwealth v. William B. Briant* (1886), concerning the liability of a bar owner for the actions of his bartender. The bartender in question had served alcohol to minors—illegal then as now—and the commonwealth brought a case against the owner for the bartender's illicit sale. The trial court judge instructed the jury to presume that the provision of alcohol in an owner's shop was authorized by the owner himself. Accordingly, the burden of proof fell on the bar owner to demonstrate his rectitude. Holmes took issue with this judicial intervention, claiming that the bench's instructions to the jury "went too far." He contended that, although the jury was allowed to make such an inference of its own volition, the court had overstepped by directing jurors to treat the owner's foreknowledge as presumptively true.[48] In so doing, Holmes emphasized the distinction between a presumption of law and a presumption of fact—at least as he conceived it.

A presumption of law in his schema is a factual extrapolation mandated by law (statutory or common) that a jury or judge must hold as true unless there is evidence undercutting that presumption. Functionally, a presumption of law allocates the burden of proof for a particular allegation of fact to one party over the other. For example, one presumption of law in Thayer's era obliged courts to assume that any person who had been missing for seven years was deceased. The burden of proof thus fell on a party wishing to show that the missing person was alive. If neither party furnished any evidence, the person was considered dead for the purposes of that trial.[49]

A presumption of fact, alternatively, is an extrapolation based on common sense that juries are allowed to make but are not required to do so under the law. In the *Briant* case, Holmes argued that a jury might reasonably surmise that the bar owner was responsible for the actions of his employee, but it was beyond the trial judge's purview to instruct the jury to presume the defendant's guilt in the absence of relevant evidence. "A jury might be warranted in inferring that such a sale was authorized," Holmes held, so "there may be a presumption of fact; but, generally, it must be left to the jury to say whether there is one."[50]

Thayer was displeased. Having "long wallowed in presumptions," he felt compelled to write to Holmes in January 1888 to criticize the justice for conflating the concept of "inference" with "presumption of fact." Thayer was well aware that these terms were often treated as synonyms in legal jargon, but he found this usage problematic and told Holmes, "I think you use them both wrong here."[51] Thayer preferred a different schema: (1) *inference* should refer to all factual extrapolations, be they required by law or not; (2) *presumption* should refer only to those extrapolations required by law; and (3) the term *presumption of fact* should be dispensed with altogether. In a follow-up letter to Holmes, Thayer acknowledged that he held "a grudge which you do not share at the phrase pres[umption] of fact." He lamented that the entire system of categorizing presumptions was convoluted and asked rhetorically why legal practitioners did not speak "of inferences when one means that, and of presumptions when one means that?"[52]

The next year Thayer attempted a robust analysis of the subject in the *Harvard Law Review.* In his article "Presumptions and the Law of Evidence," Thayer refuted the notion that inferences and presumptions are interchangeable; rather, the latter is a subset of the former. Insofar as jurors are always using their logical faculties, inferences are commonplace at trial. But only some inferences—presumptions—are required by law. "A rule of presumption does not merely say such and such a thing is a permissible and usual inference from other facts," Thayer held, "but it goes on to say that this significance shall always, in the absence of other circumstances, be imputed to them." Thayer's decision to publish this article was probably prompted at least in part by his epistolary exchange with Holmes about presumptions. That he generally had Holmes in mind as he wrote the article is evident in his footnotes, which were effusive in their plaudits of *The Common Law.* "So many persons are indebted to this excellent book," Thayer declared.[53] So even in a law review article elaborating on a point of difference with Holmes, Thayer's scholarship made plain that the two jurists shared far more in common.

Holmes's reaction to Thayer's piece on presumptions was typical of their dynamic—general accord with some quibbling. The justice began his letter to Thayer with high praise: "I have read it and think it first class—you are a damn smart fellow." Holmes then quickly transitioned to a critique of "the extent which you give to the sphere of *logic*." To illustrate his point, he offered a colorful example involving philandery. "When a jury finds the proved fact that a man spent the night locked up in a bedroom with another chap's wife," Holmes argued, "the inference that swiving [sexual activity] ensued . . . depended not on logic but on the experience of life." In other words, the jurors were "illustrating their knowledge as men of the world [rather] than their capacity as logicians." Holmes then allowed for the possibility that any distinction between himself and Thayer was a matter of semantics rather than substance, suggesting, "I don't imagine that we should differ except in expression." After all, nothing in Thayer's piece indicated that the professor disagreed with Holmes's proposition that inferences, if properly drawn, are rooted in real-world experience. The justice well recognized, "You say nothing distinctly to the contrary of my obvious remarks—but give me a feeling as if you might for the moment overlook them."[54]

Holmes was correct that they diverged in terminology, not perspective. Whereas Holmes used the word *logic* to mean reasoning divorced from experience, Thayer used it to mean reasoning based on experience. They both abhorred empty logical abstraction. The professor took pains in the future to clarify his position on the relationship between logic and experience. For instance, in the foregoing article Thayer had written, "The law furnishes no test of relevancy. For this, it tacitly refers to logic."[55] Perhaps he was cogitating on Holmes's letter when he later produced his *Preliminary Treatise*, which repeated the above language while notably adding a key phrase: "The law furnishes no test of relevancy. For this, it tacitly refers to logic and general experience."[56] Logic had validity only when grounded in lived experience. The two jurists were saying much the same thing, albeit in different words.

A similar exchange—with a mix of commendation and objection—arose the following year after the appearance of another article by Thayer, "'Law and Fact' in Jury Trials," in the pages of the *Harvard Law Review*. Here, Thayer sought to dispel the myth of a tidy division of labor between judge and juror in the courtroom. "We are told that matters of law are for the court, and matters of fact for the jury," he observed. But this dichotomy was too facile, by Thayer's lights. With his characteristic emphasis on historical study, he asserted, "There is not and never was any such thing as an allotting of all questions of fact to the jury." By way of example, Thayer referenced the interpretation of documents, which is a factual inquiry undertaken by the judge. Complicating the issue is the reality that fact and law are not always easily disentangled. Insanity, negligence, and ownership are all "mixed questions of law and fact," raising doubts about where the jury's role ends and the judge's begins. Thayer contended that such cases ought to be treated as "mere matters of fact," noting that jurors might find it useful for a judge to provide them with a legal definition of insanity, negligence, or ownership, but the ultimate determination ought to be left to the jury.[57] Thayer may have had a unique perspective on insanity in particular, having served as a trustee of the Worcester Lunatic Hospital in the 1870s.[58]

Thayer's article elicited praise from Holmes, who wrote to him shortly after the piece was published "mainly to say what pleasure its learning and ability gave me." Holmes also challenged Thayer, albeit gently. The justice shared that "the only criticism which occurs to me" was Thayer's notion that judges engaged in a "usurpation" of the jury's role "when the courts dont [*sic*] leave anything and everything capable of being named by a single word [*insanity, negligence,* or *ownership*] to the jury." In Holmes's view, the bench had a significant part to play in such cases, and he was more fearful of the jury encroaching on the judge's remit than the reverse. Holmes was unsure whether he and Thayer actually disagreed about where to draw the line between the domain of the judge and that of jury, openly wondering whether "we differ at all." He figured that any deviation between them might have been more a matter of "tone" than substance.[59]

A year later, Thayer divulged to Holmes that he felt a measure of insecurity about his role in Holmes's life. The professor feared that his influence over the justice was fading. This confession appeared in a letter Thayer wrote to Holmes in October 1891 to congratulate him on his newly published *Speeches*, a collection of Holmes's orations. Thayer lauded the volume as "noble and precious" and remarked that the speeches had "the quality of *gems*." He went on to convey, however, a concern about Holmes's blunt rejection of some critics in his addresses. Thayer wrote that the speeches "make, it seems to me, in a certain way, an interesting and frank revelation of *yourself*," meaning that they reflected Holmes's disinclination to "withhold an intimation of dissent" from viewpoints contrary to his own. Thayer was not criticizing Holmes's candor—"these things do not trouble me"—but Thayer feared that he himself might fall into that category of people whom the justice summarily dismissed. "Sometimes I am left behind," Thayer admitted, before adding somewhat vaguely that he felt "a little as if you had passed out of that region where . . . noble sentiments are nourished." It was a striking moment of vulnerability for the professor. Just why Thayer felt anxious about his relationship with Holmes at this particular moment is unclear. It seems that even Thayer struggled to articulate the reason, for he conceded, "Very likely this isn't intelligible and perhaps I can't make it so."[60]

If Thayer fretted about being abandoned in some sense, Holmes's dissenting opinion in *Commonwealth v. Josiah Perry* (1891) six weeks later may have palliated the professor's unease. That dissent championed judicial deference to legislatures, a cardinal tenet of Thayer's jurisprudence. In *Perry*, the Massachusetts Supreme Judicial Court struck down a state law that prohibited employers from reducing the wages of weavers for "imperfections that may arise during the process of weaving." The majority contended that such a law infringed on the employers' rights of "acquiring, possessing, and protecting property" under the Massachusetts Constitution. Holmes was unconvinced by this reasoning. What mattered, Holmes insisted, was not whether he thought the law a good idea as a matter of politics and economics. His obligation as a judge was to defer to the legislature unless there was no plausible claim to the statute's constitutionality. "Speaking as a political economist, I should agree in condemning the law," Holmes conceded. "Still I should not be willing or think myself authorized to overturn legislation on that ground, unless I thought that an honest difference of opinion was impossible, or pretty nearly so."[61] This was precisely the position that Thayer had advanced in his 1884 article in the *Nation* and would soon reprise in his famous "Origin and Scope" article.

Two days after the *Perry* dissent appeared, Thayer penned a letter to Holmes "to express a hearty agreement with your views in this weaver's case," which were "precise, learned, [and] worthy." The professor was full of "gratitude, as a student of constitutional law," for Holmes's principled stand. Thayer was deeply concerned about "the prevailing confusion between law and political economy," which led judges to wrongly project their own preferred economic theories onto a constitution. He worried that there is "constant and great danger of our methods of handling such questions becoming petty."[62]

In 1893, after Holmes produced another dissent, he made sure that Thayer was aware. The justice, referring to himself in the third person, asked his mentor to turn "your attention to the dissenting opinion of Holmes J. in Hanson v Globe Newspaper Co . . . which I am told he doesn't feel particularly modest about."[63] Holmes's ribbing of his own sizable ego suggests that he had developed at least a modicum of self-awareness as he aged into his fifties. The case involved H. P. Hanson, a resident of South Boston who sued a newspaper for libel after it mistakenly identified him as a "prisoner in the criminal dock." The paper referred to "H. P. Hanson, a real-estate and insurance broker of South Boston," but the actual prisoner was A. P. H. Hanson. By chance, these two Hansons shared not only the same surname and two initials but also the same vocation and neighborhood. The county court found in favor of the paper, and the Massachusetts Supreme Judicial Court upheld that judgment. Writing for the majority, justice Marcus Knowlton determined that the newspaper had written about someone other than the plaintiff; the mere fact that the plaintiff's name was accidentally used did not mean the article was actually about him. Therefore, it was not libelous.[64]

Holmes dissented. In realist fashion, he accused Knowlton of fixating on a logical nicety while ignoring real-world outcomes. It was plain to see, in Holmes's eyes, that the newspaper's erroneous identification of the plaintiff as a prisoner in the criminal dock would damage his reputation. "The inevitable consequence of the defendant's acts is that the public, or that part of it which knows the plaintiff, will suppose that the defendant did use its language about him," Holmes reasoned.[65] After Holmes alerted Thayer to his dissent, the professor replied three days later. "Thank you also for the reference to the Hanson case," he wrote. "I agree with you entirely." He shared Holmes's aversion to Justice Knowlton's reasoning, complaining, "It seems very difficult to follow Knowlton." Thayer further observed of the majority opinion, "There is an odd literalness in laying down the law . . . as if the law hadn't its *imperfections*."[66] Straitjacketed formalism was a common bane for Thayer and Holmes alike.

Two months after Thayer published his signal contribution to constitutional law, "Origin and Scope," Holmes wrote to its author praising the article's defense of judicial restraint. "I agree with it heartily," the justice offered. "It makes explicit the point of view from which implicitly I have approached the Constitutional questions upon which I have differed from some of the other Judges." Holmes argued that "a state legislature has the power of Parliament, i.e., absolute power," except when limited by the state's constitution.

Rather than presume a *lack* of legislative authority except where expressly provided, judges ought to presume a *grant* of legislative authority except where expressly prohibited. As Holmes put it, "The question always is where do you find the prohibition—not, where do you find the power," adding, "I think the contrary view dangerous and wrong."[67]

The following day Holmes sent Thayer another letter, this one seconding the concern articulated in "Origin and Scope" that an overly robust exercise of judicial review makes legislators less attentive, at the front end of the legislative process, to the constitutionality of their statutes. Holmes, like Thayer, feared that "by repetition it necessarily becomes easier for courts to declare acts unconstitutional." As a result, "legislatures more and more rely on the Court and enact [statutes] tentatively—subject to the Court's opinion." Holmes also described as "remarkable" any "decision declaring an act unconstitutional with two Judges dissenting."[68] The very issuance of a dissent meant that the act could plausibly be construed as constitutional; thus the legislation in question would pass the Thayer test.

Following "Origin and Scope," Thayer's next major endeavor was a two-volume casebook entitled *Cases on Constitutional Law* (1894). Holmes sent a congratulatory letter upon the publication of the first volume, observing that "it is done, as all your work is, as well as possible."[69] Following the second volume's appearance, Holmes wrote to Thayer again, thanking him for sending a copy and directing the professor to a recent article of his in the *Harvard Law Review*.[70]

That article, "Privilege, Malice, and Intent," set forth a central tenet of legal realism: the bench should reject syllogistic reasoning and instead balance competing interests on a case-by-case basis. Judicial decisions, Holmes claimed, were merely social policy formulations involving cost-benefit analyses, even if judges were loath to admit it. "Questions of policy are legislative questions, and judges are shy of reasoning from such grounds," he explained. As a result, opinions from the bench "often are presented as hollow deductions from empty general propositions." But in reality, "the worth of the result, or the gain from allowing the act to be done, has to be compared with the loss which it inflicts." This balancing act must hinge on the particularity of the case rather than the universality of some abstract principle. In Holmes's words, "the conclusion will vary, and will depend on different reasons according to the nature of the affair."[71] One historian has contended that Holmes's depiction of law here constituted a revolutionary conceptual leap, and "perhaps it is the moment we should identify as the beginning of modernism in American legal thought."[72]

Apparently, Thayer did not read the article, as Holmes wrote again several months later to remind him of its existence. The justice was self-flattering in his appraisal of the piece: "I regarded it as a somewhat important addition to theory." Holmes's letter was plainly a bid to solicit Thayer's validation. But Holmes did not want to seem like he was begging for it, so he insisted, unconvincingly, that "these remarks are not intended to elicit a laudatory reply."[73] If Thayer did pen a response to this missive, it is lost to history.

The following year, after Thayer published the initial abridged version of his *Preliminary Treatise*, Holmes penned a word of congratulations. Holmes could see that Thayer's work would hasten the much-needed reform of evidence law. "It is useful and almost necessary to the enlightened reconsideration of doctrine for which we are almost ready," the justice declared.[74]

Thayer attended a speech that Holmes delivered at Boston University some seven months later. In printed form, that address—"The Path of the Law"—would stand among the most important law review articles in American history. Holmes sought to advance many elements of legal realism, including an emphasis on the actual consequences of law. "A body of law," he announced, "is more rational and more civilized when every rule it contains is referred articulately and definitely to an end which it subserves." The speech also sought to dispel the myth of law as some ethereal essence, a natural entity immanent within the universe. Despite the lofty claims of the courts, the law is neither a "system of reason" nor a "deduction from principles of ethics or admitted axioms." It is a man-made concoction. In one of his most famous statements, Holmes declared, "The prophecies of what the courts will do in fact, and nothing more pretentious, are what I mean by the law." Law is what judges do—nothing more. Holmes well understood the psychological appeal of treating the law syllogistically, but with Olympian detachment he disabused his readers of such a fantasy: "The logical method and form flatter that longing for certainty and for repose which is in every human mind. But certainty generally is illusion, and repose is not the destiny of man."[75]

"The Path of the Law" also nodded to Thayer's influence. Holmes hoped to demonstrate the role that "history necessarily plays in the intelligent study of the law," noting that legal historians at Boston University and Harvard, including "Mr. Thayer there have made important contributions which will not be forgotten."[76] Unlike his enthusiastic embrace of Holmes's *The Common*

Law, Thayer was wary about Holmes's instinct to publish the lecture immediately. In a January 1897 letter, three days after Holmes's address at Boston University, Thayer implored Holmes to adjust his arguments before submitting it to the *Harvard Law Review*. Thayer prefaced his caution with flattery, which surely appealed to Holmes's considerable self-regard. "I heard your address the other day with delight," Thayer wrote. "You speak as a master and a leader." Then Thayer grew circumspect. He was concerned that readers might misconceive Holmes's argument about the use of legal history. "The Path of the Law" had predicted that legal scholarship could eventually move beyond historical study of the law toward a greater emphasis on present-day outcomes. Thayer feared that most judges—who, unlike Holmes, were poorly versed in history—would take Holmes's words as license to ignore history altogether. "*You* have a right to go ahead in the way you suggest. But consider what would happen if the mob of judges who know so little of the groundwork should do the same thing," Thayer fretted. "You know it all. But there are very few who do." Thayer did not want to see Holmes unwittingly "seem to play into the hands of the rash ignoramuses." The professor closed his letter by writing, "Pray consider this danger and believe me."[77]

Holmes responded the next day, promising that "when I print certainly I will consider what you say." He assured Thayer that he wanted to avoid using language that could be susceptible to misconstrual of his intended meaning: "If there is anything that would be taken to run counter to it I must change my words."[78] In the end, however, Holmes opted not to heed Thayer's advice. The justice explained in a subsequent letter, "I anxiously considered your kind suggestion" but ultimately determined that Thayer's concerns were overblown. After all, Thayer had listened in person to the live lecture, a form of communication more easily misinterpreted than a printed version of the address. "I could not think that a reader (as distinguished from a hearer) would misapprehend my views," Holmes reasoned. Moreover, he had "a feeling that a speech [should] be printed as she is spoke."[79] As Holmes later found himself issuing one dissent after another on the US Supreme Court, perhaps Thayer's warning about the shortcomings of other judges rang ever truer in Holmes's ears.

In November 1898 Holmes wrote to Thayer to congratulate him on the publication of the expanded *Preliminary Treatise*. The justice reminded Thayer of his already "very high appreciation of your work" even "before receiving your new book." And now that the new book had come, Holmes was "more than ever struck by it on reading and rereading." He then hedged his flattery by reviving his disagreement with Thayer on whether negligence—a topic taken up in the *Preliminary Treatise*—should be treated as a matter of law or fact. Holmes preferred the former, Thayer the latter. "I reserve my rights and take a different view," the justice stated. (He would take this dispute public the next year in a law review article, which argued that the *Preliminary Treatise*, though "admirable," was wrong about negligence.) Holmes concluded this particular letter by chiding Thayer for using an English publisher, reminding the professor that "an American owes himself to his country and should secure all the credit of his work to it."[80] In truth, Thayer's book had been issued by the Boston-based publisher Little, Brown for the American market and by the London-based Sweet & Maxwell for British readers. Apparently, Holmes had come into possession of the Sweet & Maxwell edition and did not realize that the primary publisher of the *Preliminary Treatise* was located just a short distance from his own courthouse.

Upon reading the tome yet again, Holmes wrote to Thayer a week later to share that he had perused it with "constant pleasure and appreciation and with very few criticisms." Holmes was especially grateful for Thayer's efforts to expose the way that judges wrongly subsumed substantive law into evidence law. "I long have noticed the disguise of substantive law under the form of rules of evidence," Holmes shared, "and am glad to see it brought out so fully."[81]

Even with his take on the merits of Thayer's *Preliminary Treatise* fulsomely expounded, Holmes composed yet another letter to the professor two days later. He again commended Thayer's text but took issue with two appendices in the treatise, both of which were reprints of articles that Thayer had not written.[82] Appendix A was a piece about presumptions appearing in an English legal periodical, and appendix C was a paper by an English barrister on legal interpretation. Holmes's criticism of the former was brief. He asserted that the essay, which attempted to define presumptions of law, presumptions of fact, and inferences in legal systems, "is troubled by overnicety of speech." Holmes advocated a more concise definition of presumptions of fact that centered on the validity of making presumptions based on everyday experience. "When I speak of a presumption of fact," he explained, "I mean a major premise or general proposition reached by experience that men generally under such circumstances do or are so & so."[83] Thayer had long ago expressed his concern to Holmes about the phrase *presumption of fact*, which he thought muddled the difference between presumptions of law that judges direct juries to apply and ordinary factual inferences that jurors make of their own volition. If Thayer had forgotten their disagreement over presumptions from the prior decade, he was now freshly reminded.

The majority of Holmes's letter was reserved for his grievances with appendix C, "On the Principles of Legal Interpretation," by F. Vaughan Hawkins. The Hawkins piece asserted that parsing a given word in a contract or other legal document was difficult because one must "ascertain the meaning or intention of the writer," and therefore, "the interpretation of a legal writing is a collecting of the intent—of what the writer meant, that is—from the marks or signs used."[84] Under Hawkins's conception, authors imbue legal documents with their own intentions and thereby establish themselves as the gatekeepers of meaning. Courts, if they adopt this understanding, must then admit evidence related to the writer's intent in order to correctly construe legal texts. Holmes strongly objected to this principle, devoting almost a full page to its rebuttal in his letter to Thayer. "We dont [*sic*] care what the individual user meant," Holmes argued, but rather "what the words used would mean in the mouth of a reasonable man."[85] This notion of the "reasonable man" as a workable legal guideline had been an important strand in Holmes's thought since he published *The Common Law*, where he contended that courts should employ a reasonableness standard in assessing the liability of defendants. If "the ideal average prudent man" could not have foreseen an injury, then the tribunal should not hold him liable, Holmes suggested in his treatise.[86] Reasonableness became critical to the legal realist agenda because its inherent malleability allowed courts to adapt law to the contingencies of individual cases and to the exigencies of a quickly changing society.

A few days later, Holmes again wrote to Thayer concerning legal interpretation. The justice made the case once more that the *general* meaning of language mattered, not the *particular* intent of a document's author. "The question is not the meaning of the party, but the meaning of the words according to the usage of speech," Holmes insisted. A practicable legal standard would ask, "What would the normal man competent to use English . . . mean by such a document?" Holmes indicated that he had "half a mind to send a note to the H. L. Rev. [*Harvard Law Review*]," where he could voice his frustrations publicly. He also announced that he had just reached the end of Thayer's casebook on constitutional law. As was typical, the justice reacted with praise and a touch of criticism. "I have this minute finished your cases on Const. Law—with profit but with weariness of the flesh over the spongy longwindedness," Holmes confessed.[87]

Although Thayer had seen fit to reprint Hawkins's essay in the *Preliminary Treatise*, he was hardly offended by Holmes's critique. "I write to beg that you *will* send the law review something on the matter of Hawkins," implored Thayer. He also took to heart Holmes's concerns about the length of his casebook. As Thayer conceded, "the subject is large, but perhaps you may have a suggestion" for "shortening it" should there be a revised edition in the future.[88] With Thayer's encouragement, Holmes published a rebuttal to Hawkins titled "The Theory of Legal Interpretation" the following month in the *Harvard Law Review*. The article responded directly to Hawkins's argument and advanced Holmes's own theory of interpretation, which centered on how a "normal speaker of English" would construe language. Holmes acknowledged Thayer's *Preliminary Treatise* in the article's opening paragraph, calling the volume "excellent."[89]

About a year and a half later, Holmes ascended to the chief justiceship of the Massachusetts Supreme Judicial Court. Thayer was, of course, highly pleased by the promotion. "You must allow me to express my sense of the general satisfaction at the recent appointment," he wrote to Holmes. "For one, I am heartily glad to see at the head of our court one who, knowing his law books, knows also how to give effect to the current of modern opinion, [and] who isn't afraid to use his discretion." The mention of "modern opinion" reflected Thayer's enthusiasm for seeing a like-minded realist, attuned to novel conditions, assume such a prominent seat on the bench. And Thayer was happy for Holmes as an individual, lauding the justice as "chock full of intelligence" and anticipating that his new role would furnish "opportunities of fortune, influence and work" beyond those Holmes had previously enjoyed. "If this [praise] be unsuitable for a chief justice, you must pardon it as coming from an old friend," Thayer concluded.[90]

A year later, in July 1900, Thayer was preparing the second edition of his evidence casebook and planned to incorporate passages from Holmes's "The Theory of Legal Interpretation." Thayer reached out to Holmes to share the text of an editorial footnote that he wanted to append to excerpts from Holmes's article. Thayer's footnote specifically endorsed Holmes's "normal speaker of English" standard and argued that even someone who was "inclined to differ" with some of Holmes's analysis should nevertheless "find in it the true limitation" of legal interpretation, which must stop short of "giving effect to a writer's intention."[91] Holmes replied that he would be "proud to appear" in the second edition of the casebook, all the more because of his esteem for the first.[92] This is the final surviving letter exchanged between the protégé and his mentor. Thayer died just shy of Holmes's nomination in 1902 to the US Supreme Court.[93]

Thayer's legacy endured in Holmes's career as a Supreme Court justice. Dubbed the "Great Dissenter" for his eloquent and prescient minority opinions, Holmes left a mark so profound on American law that only one or two other justices throughout history have rivaled his influence. What was arguably his most famous dissent was also the one that most vividly embraced Thayerian restraint.

In *Lochner v. United States* (1905), a five-to-four majority on the Supreme Court struck down a New York state law that, for health reasons, restricted the number of hours an employer could expect a baker to work during a given day and week. Justice Rufus Peckham did *not* frame the majority opinion as defending an individual's absolute liberty to contract his labor against the creeping power of the state. Peckham readily conceded that "a fair, reasonable and appropriate exercise of the police power of the State" in codifying health regulations would pass constitutional muster. However, in the particular case before him, Peckham determined that the factual record failed to legitimize the state law. "The limitation of the hours of labor as provided for in" the New York labor statute bore "no such direct relation to, and no such substantial effect upon, the health of the employee as to justify us in regarding the section as really a health law." Although the high court may have been unconvinced of the danger posed to bakers, it did not sanctify the free market as inviolable.[94]

Nevertheless, Holmes blasted the majority for arbitrarily reading laissez-faire into the US Constitution. In one of the more celebrated dissents in American legal history, he announced, "This case is decided upon an economic theory which a large part of the country does not entertain." Holmes suggested that the majority opinion erroneously interpreted the due process clause of the Fourteenth Amendment to mandate a laissez-faire approach to economic policy. The clause in question prevents states from denying anyone their "property" without "due process of law." According to Holmes, Peckham mistakenly found in that constitutional language an inviolate liberty of contract, wherein workers supposedly enjoy the right to hire out their labor under whatever conditions they please without government interference. But the Constitution, Holmes argued, was agnostic on economics. "The Fourteenth Amendment does not enact Mr. Herbert Spencer's Social Statics," he wrote, referring to the British scholar's 1851 book that argued laissez-faire is of a piece with natural law. For Holmes, a judge's personal economic views were immaterial: "I strongly believe that my agreement or disagreement [with laissez-faire] has nothing to do with the right of a majority to embody their opinions in law." Thayer's test of a statute's constitutionality was not whether a judge believed it to be constitutional but whether anyone rationally could, and Holmes—without citing Thayer—applied his mentor's theory of judicial restraint. "A reasonable man might think it a proper measure on the score of health," Holmes wrote of the New York statute, and therefore it ought to stand unmolested by the bench.[95]

This dissent became a rallying cry for progressives who were outraged by courts' willingness to invalidate regulatory legislation.[96] It was so influential that even though Holmes mischaracterized the majority opinion, historians have traditionally parroted his straw-man take on *Lochner*. They describe the decision as embodying the "night watchman" ideal of the state, which requires courts to brook no legislative interference in the free market. In this reading of *Lochner*, the majority opinion was formal legal thought par excellence: the Supreme Court (many historians allege) extolled liberty of contract, a doctrine that made sense only in a logical vacuum; real-world disparities in bargaining power between capital and labor meant that liberty of contract was effectively a hollow pretext for the exploitation of workers. Companies could force upon their employees grueling hours and meager wages. *Lochner*-era jurisprudence has long served as a synonym for contemporary legal formalism writ large.[97] (To be fair, most social welfare legislation in this era actually withstood judicial scrutiny, but cases in which courts struck down progressive laws, like *Lochner*, garnered outsized attention and became political lightning rods.[98])

Holmes's celebrated dissent in *Lochner* was a revival of his 1891 dissent in *Commonwealth v. Perry*, wherein the Massachusetts high court voided a law protecting weavers. In both instances, Holmes contended that the majority was conflating its preferred economic theory with constitutional law. Each time, he stressed the importance of judicial deference to lawmakers, insisting that his perspective on the merit of the legislation was irrelevant to the question of its constitutionality. The *Perry* dissent had prompted Thayer to send Holmes one of his most laudatory letters in which he expressed "a hearty agreement" with Holmes and praised the justice's analysis as "precise, learned, [and] worthy."[99] In other words, the justice's withering critique of the *Lochner* majority was a reincarnation of Thayer's favorite dissent from his protégé.[100] The main difference was that, as a US Supreme Court justice, Holmes now had a far more elevated platform from which to promote the jurisprudence that had bound the professor and justice together. It is not difficult to imagine the exuberant letter that Thayer, had he lived to see *Lochner*, would have mailed to Holmes.

Liberals were drawn to the *Lochner* dissent because its theory of judicial restraint was highly serviceable to them in a historical period when conservative courts sometimes invalidated progressive legislation. It would be a mistake to assume that Thayer's motivations were similarly partisan. After all, he began advocating judicial deference to legislatures as early as the 1850s—long before the grand battles of the Progressive Era that pitted reform-minded legislators against conservative judges. Thayer did *not* endorse judicial restraint as a convenient justification for his preferred policy agenda; rather, he was committed to restraint from the bench as a matter of principle. The presumption of constitutionality that he championed was not inherently left wing or right wing; it could apply as readily to conservative legislation as to progressive. It just so happened that, as an accident of history, Thayer's ideas resonated with liberals in the wake of his death.

Holmes nicely illustrates how Thayerian restraint was a jurisprudential principle and not merely a partisan tool. The justice was not enamored of progressive policies, which he thought wrongheaded. But he believed that, as a judge, his views on the virtue of a given statute were inapposite. If an ill-advised majority enacted bad policies, it was not his job to set them right. "Personally I bet that the crowd if it knew more wouldn't want what it does— but that is immaterial," Holmes wrote to an English jurist.[101] If anything made Holmes a Thayerite, it was his willingness to let the crowd have its way, even when he thought the results would be harmful.

If the *Lochner* dissent represents the most high-profile application of Thayerian deference in all of American legal history, then Holmes's noteworthy dissent in *Abrams v. United States* (1919) is easy to construe as a rejection of Thayerian principles. In *Abrams*, the Supreme Court heard an appeal from two Russian immigrants in New York who had been found guilty of violating the Espionage Act, a wartime law passed in 1917 and amended in 1918 that restricted free speech. America was at war with Germany—not Russia—but the defendants feared that the production in the United States of ammunition intended for use against Germany would eventually be turned against the Russian Revolution, a cause that the defendants supported. And so they distributed pamphlets exhorting American ammunition workers to strike. A jury deemed them guilty of disseminating materials "intended to incite, provoke and encourage resistance to the United States." On appeal before the Supreme Court, the defendants argued that the Espionage Act was repugnant to the First Amendment and ought to be nullified as unconstitutional. A seven-to-two majority sustained the statute and the guilty verdicts.[102]

Holmes's dissent—among the most acclaimed in American constitutional history—offered a robust defense of free speech. He set forth his belief that the First Amendment protects the marketplace of ideas so that truth has a chance to win out over falsehood. "When men have realized that time has upset many fighting faiths," Holmes wrote in one of his most quoted lines, "they may come to believe even more than they believe the very foundations of their own conduct that the ultimate good desired is better reached by free trade in ideas—that the best test of truth is the power of the thought to get itself accepted in the competition of the market." The justice did not believe that free speech would *necessarily* produce good results for society. Perhaps it would not. But in Holmes's view, that was a risk the First Amendment required the country to take. He mused about the marketplace of ideas: "It is an experiment, as all life is an experiment."[103]

In theory, Holmes's dissent was consistent with Thayer's concept of judicial restraint, insofar as he did not call for the Espionage Act to be annulled. But in a sense, Holmes was abandoning Thayerian deference to legislatures because he interpreted the statute so narrowly that he would have effectively rendered the law moot had he been speaking for the majority. Holmes's dissent in *Abrams* is all the more striking given that he had ruled against dissidents in *Schenck v. United States* (1919) a mere eight months prior. The *Schenck* case involved defendants who, in violation of the Espionage Age, had distributed pamphlets encouraging individuals to avoid the draft. Writing for a unanimous majority, Holmes did not employ a speech-protective interpretation of the Espionage Act (much less strike it down as unconstitutional). His opinion stated that the government can lawfully ban speech presenting a "clear and present danger that will bring about the substantive evils which Congress has a right to prevent."[104] When the Supreme Court decided *Abrams* later that year, the majority relied in part on Holmes's *Schenck* opinion, even as Holmes himself undertook an about-face.[105]

Holmes's evolution on free speech rights between *Schenck* and *Abrams* was due in large part to the efforts of friends and contemporaries who urged the justice to reconsider his position.[106] It is notable that *Abrams* was decided close to twenty years after Thayer's death. The relationship between Thayer and Holmes had been replaced in Holmes's world by new friends advancing new ideas under new circumstances. If Holmes's dissent in *Abrams* suggests a departure from his late mentor, it also hints at a common thread running through Holmes's long career—behind legal doctrine lies the profound, if overlooked, influence of interpersonal relationships.

4. Thayer's Students: Louis Brandeis, John Henry Wigmore, Roscoe Pound, and Learned Hand

For nearly three decades, aspiring lawyers who passed through the halls of Harvard Law School came under the tutelage of James Bradley Thayer. They learned from him not just the elemental features of American law but a philosophy that stayed with them long after Thayer's passing. The legal realism that he imparted to them in the classroom they, in turn, promoted on the bench and from the lectern. Of the many thought leaders in the legal world who studied at Thayer's feet, four stand out for their towering contributions to realism: Louis Brandeis, Learned Hand, John Henry Wigmore, and Roscoe Pound. Brandeis and Hand rank among the greatest judges in the history of the federal bench; Wigmore and Pound were the most prolific law school deans of their generation. All were faithful Thayerites who spent their careers engaging with the legal legacy that their shared mentor bequeathed to them.

LOUIS BRANDEIS

Louis Dembitz Brandeis was born in 1856 in Louisville, Kentucky. He was the youngest of four children in a Jewish family that had emigrated from Prague. Both sides of his family, though not quite wealthy, had belonged to the ranks of the sophisticated middle class in the Old World. And thanks to a measure of success that his father enjoyed in America, Brandeis and his siblings grew up with a degree of comfort and culture. Brandeis's intellectual prowess was evident from a young age; he won a gold medal for academic excellence in school. When he was fifteen his family returned to Europe for three years, and during this time abroad Brandeis took up studies in the German city of Dresden. The German methods of schooling struck him as draconian. After the family came back to America in the spring of 1875, the eighteen-year-old Brandeis made plans to attend Harvard Law School.[1]

He arrived in Cambridge in the midst of the Langdellian revolution in legal pedagogy. Brandeis thrilled to the case method of instruction, with its emphasis

Louis Brandeis during his tenure as a law student, circa 1876. (Harvard Law School Library, Historical and Special Collections)

on thinking over memorization and dialogue over recitation.[2] Although C. C. Langdell's approach suited Brandeis, it was James Bradley Thayer with whom the young law student cultivated a closer personal relationship. "He was my best friend among the instructors at the Law School," Brandeis recalled years later. Thayer was a "very fine man."[3] Outside the classroom, Brandeis joined the prestigious Pow Wow Club, which operated as a moot court and gave him a chance to hone his courtroom skills.[4]

In several respects, Brandeis's tenure as a Harvard student mirrored Thayer's own a generation earlier. Both tutored on the side to pay their way. Both graduated first in their respective classes in law school. And both were selected to be orators on graduation day (Thayer for Harvard College, Brandeis for Harvard Law). But unlike Thayer, Brandeis was denied the opportunity to give a commencement address owing to a technicality. Although the students and faculty had chosen Brandeis for the honor, he was a victim of his own precociousness—Brandeis was not yet twenty-one years old and therefore, according to a Harvard bylaw, was ineligible to receive his degree until his next birthday. University president Charles William Eliot determined that if Brandeis could not yet graduate, then he could not serve as the class orator. Harvard ultimately made a partial concession to Brandeis, however. On the morning of the commencement exercises, he learned that he would be permitted to accept his diploma alongside his classmates that day. The board and the faculty had made a special exception in honor of Brandeis's singular academic performance: he not only ranked first in his class but had earned the highest grades in the six-decade history of Harvard Law.[5]

While Thayer met Ralph Waldo Emerson by way of marriage, Brandeis did so by way of Thayer. In March 1878 Emerson was slated to give a lecture to a group of friends at Thayer's home one evening on the theme of education. Thayer sent a note inviting Brandeis, who had finished his degree the prior year but stayed at Harvard Law to undertake additional study. "If you would like to see him it would give us great pleasure to have you come," Thayer wrote, especially since "you and I ought to be interested in 'Education.'" Indeed, Brandeis would nurture a deep interest in the subject, particularly in legal education at Harvard, long after his graduation.[6]

Thayer's letter also sought to manage Brandeis's expectations for the lecture. Emerson was a legend, to be sure, but he was also well into his seventies and not quite the dynamic presence of yesteryear. "He is, you know, old now," Thayer acknowledged, "and perhaps one who had not seen him [in his prime] would not quite understand the great charm that he and all he says have for his friends."[7] Brandeis accepted the invitation, and Thayer's gesture of generosity stayed with his mentee for years to come. More than a decade later, Brandeis reminisced about the event in a letter to his fiancée. "One of the first good things he did for me was to ask me to his home to meet Emerson," Brandeis recalled.[8]

As Brandeis launched his legal career, he turned to Thayer as a trusted source of advice. Brandeis initially practiced law in St. Louis at the urging of his sister, who had moved there. But neither the work nor the city satisfied him. So when the chief justice of the Massachusetts Supreme Judicial Court offered Brandeis a role as his assistant in 1879, the opportunity to return to the Boston area was enticing.[9] Brandeis explained to a roommate from his law school days that he had consulted Thayer, among others, and all agreed that the job with the chief justice would prove "very valuable as a stepping stone." The plan now was for Brandeis to practice law in Boston while juggling his new responsibilities to the chief justice, which were part time and paid only $500 (around $13,500 today). The prospect of upending his life in St. Louis gave Brandeis no small measure of "hesitation & doubt," he confessed to his former roommate, "but happiness & contentment are rare birds worth chasing."[10]

Brandeis described his post–law school relationship with Thayer as "quite intimate," and many of their shared energies were directed at improving Harvard Law.[11] In late 1879 the university at large had acquired a sizable cash gift, and Thayer naturally hoped that a substantial portion would be allotted to the law school for the construction of a new building. At Thayer's suggestion, Brandeis published a newspaper piece in support of that agenda.[12] Soon Brandeis was aiding Thayer in the professor's preparation of a course on constitutional law.[13] Brandeis was also a critical ally in Thayer's bid to add Oliver Wendell Holmes Jr. to the law school faculty. As mentioned in chapter 3, the key issue in the latter endeavor was where to secure the funds for a professorship. Holmes was not opposed to the university raising an endowment for the position, but he would refuse to accept the job if the money came from his friends in the legal community. So on January 10, 1882, President Eliot addressed a meeting of the law school faculty to inquire about the prospects of fundraising under the conditions spelled out by Holmes.[14]

With the issue fresh on Thayer's mind, he met Brandeis for supper three days later and elicited his protégé's opinion. Brandeis recommended a number of "young fellows" who might contribute to an endowment. These "fellows" were recent alumni whom Brandeis had personally tutored, and the list corresponded with Thayer's own roster of potential donors. Newly energized by his meal with Brandeis, Thayer swung into action. "I went at the business in earnest," he recorded in his diary. He met with Brandeis a second time, and they decided to focus their attention on a former student, W. F. Weld, who had just inherited $3 million (about $80 million today) from his grandfather, a shipbuilder. Thayer was unsure where to locate Weld, so Brandeis undertook some reconnaissance.[15]

Brandeis tracked down Weld the next morning and informed him in person of the opportunity to endow an academic post. Despite having failed Thayer's class, Weld was highly amenable to the proposition owing to his warm feelings for his former professor. "He liked me better than anybody," Thayer later wrote. Although Weld was enthusiastic about an endowed professorship, he did express one misgiving to Brandeis: Weld had never graduated, and he wished to return to Harvard Law and complete his coursework, but he feared that others might assume his philanthropic gift was a bribe in exchange for the passing grades he would need to finish his degree. And so Weld asked that any donation remain anonymous for the time being. Brandeis arranged for Weld and Thayer to convene at three o'clock to discuss the matter further.[16]

At that afternoon meeting, Weld conveyed his concern about the appearance of impropriety. Thayer assured him that his identity as the benefactor could be kept under wraps until after Weld's graduation and that the law school would treat him as a student, not a donor, on principle. "You may rely on our dealing with you with absolute impartiality," the professor insisted. Weld explained that he needed thirty minutes to review his finances and would seek out Thayer in his office thereafter. When Weld resurfaced, he committed to funding an endowment of $90,000 (about $2.3 million today), which would provide Holmes an annual salary of $4,500 (around $120,000 today). The position was to be called the Weld Professorship in honor of the donor's grandfather, rendering educated guesses about the undisclosed source of the money none too difficult.[17]

Holmes took the job, only to summarily leave Harvard Law for the bench without a word of warning. Thayer privately fumed, and understandably so. It is unknown whether Brandeis—who had been just as crucial to procuring the endowment—was similarly piqued. If so, Brandeis showed no trace of it in a warm letter to Holmes written after the latter's judicial nomination was announced. "As one of the bar I rejoice. As part of the Law School I mourn. As your friend I congratulate you," Brandeis offered.[18] The efforts of Brandeis and Thayer were not entirely for naught, as Thayer himself assumed the Weld Professorship.[19]

Perhaps more importantly, Thayer learned a lesson from the experience: he and Brandeis working in tandem were capable of raising money for the law school they both loved. "Having got this so easily," Thayer wrote of the Weld Professorship, "I determined, in conference with Brandeis, to go ahead and get more—a fund of $50,000 [about $1.3 million today] for the library."[20] They fell far short of this lofty figure.[21] Still, it mattered to Thayer, acting very much in character, that Brandeis share in the credit for whatever success they did enjoy. As another professor at Harvard Law wrote to Brandeis, "Mr. Thayer tells me that we are under obligation to you for your active interest in our behalf. It is particularly gratifying to know that any benevolence to the school is stimulated by its recent graduates."[22]

By securing financial support to expand the research faculty and library holdings, Thayer and Brandeis were lively participants in the modernization of legal academia. Only a well-endowed library could provide professors with the requisite sources to produce original scholarship and furnish students with the necessary materials to meet the rigors of a revamped curriculum.

Thayer and Brandeis were willing to spend their social capital to help realize that vision.[23]

Shortly after securing the Weld endowment, Thayer made plans to take a sabbatical the following academic year. Unsurprisingly, he recommended that Brandeis teach his evidence course in his absence. President Eliot acted on Thayer's advice and invited the young lawyer to join the faculty for the coming year. When Brandeis forwarded Eliot's letter to his parents, they were delighted that their son would teach at the finest university in the land. It was "the greatest honor that can be given to a young man of your age," his father affirmed. "The profession of an academic teacher and possibly a writer is the most satisfying and desirable," he continued, though he feared "it may have been imprudent on my part to have expressed my opinion so unreservedly." Brandeis's father also harbored concerns that the job might tax the health of his son—who had struggled with lethargy and vision troubles—and urged him not to "exert yourself too much in accepting these new and difficult duties." His mother was beyond elated. "My dearest child, how happy you make me feel!" she gushed. "My heart is a prayer of thanksgiving, and at the same time it is filled with the deepest wish that heaven may protect you." She made her way to her brother's house to show off the letter from Eliot, and Brandeis's uncle promptly wrote his own missive to his precocious nephew extending all due accolades.[24] While an appointment at Harvard would have filled any family with pride, it is not difficult to imagine that an immigrant Jewish family would find it particularly meaningful to see one of their own reach such rarefied heights.[25]

Brandeis did well as an instructor—so well that he was afforded the opportunity to transition into an assistant professorship at Harvard Law. But Brandeis felt more inclined toward the courtroom than the classroom. "I may refuse the Cambridge offer," he wrote to his father about the faculty post. "What I should prefer is some position that would give me practice in trying cases. I feel I am weak in this experience and think that with practice I could do well at it." And so, like Holmes, Brandeis gave up an academic life for a professional one. But unlike Holmes, Brandeis's departure occasioned no scandal.[26]

Brandeis maintained close ties with the law school. As a model alumnus, he made sure that his law firm in Boston always hired a current Harvard Law student for part-time help in the office. Brandeis also seized on Harvard University's 250th anniversary in 1886 to establish, with six others, an alumni group called the Harvard Law School Association. These founding alumni were ardent supporters of Langdell's reforms, and the dean later credited the association with playing a critical role in bringing his forward-looking agenda to fruition. Although Brandeis was the secretary rather than the president, he was the association's de facto leader. He would continue to serve as an officer in the alumni association even after his ascension to the US Supreme Court.[27]

Brandeis also had a hand in originating the *Harvard Law Review*, which began publication in 1887 and became an important outlet for his scholarship as well as Thayer's. When three enterprising students approached Brandeis with the idea of establishing a law review, he gave them their first donation and arranged for other alumni to follow suit. Brandeis served on the board of the *Harvard Law Review* and, in Thayerian spirit, was an attentive mentor to its student editors. Law reviews were conspicuous symbols of the modernization of legal academia. They embodied the professoriate's newfound commitment to research, reflected a culture of specialization, and nationalized academic discourse. Brandeis, who made his various commitments to the law school mutually reinforcing, ensured that a copy of the *Harvard Law Review* was distributed to every member of the alumni association.[28]

His involvement with his alma mater extended to the curriculum as well, and on matters of pedagogy, he and Thayer were of a piece. In 1889 Harvard Law first considered offering a course on Massachusetts law and tapped a young alumnus, Frank Brewster (class of 1883), to teach it. Brandeis produced a course proposal for Brewster's use, but somehow it never came to his attention. Without the benefit of Brandeis's insight, Brewster wound up teaching a course on Massachusetts law for three years that not only failed to be "inspiring" but even bordered on "depressing," as Brandeis explained in a letter to President Eliot. Brewster had focused exclusively on statutory law, which entailed boring topics like conveyancing; meanwhile, he neglected the state's common law, which would have been "highly interesting" to students. Massachusetts's judicial decisions contained much to excite the student body, Brandeis told Eliot, for the "local customs, traditions and the peculiar habits of mind of its people, have resulted in a spirit [in its common law] which is its own." Brandeis envisioned a revised curriculum that would foreground the state's "distinct individuality" while excluding those "details from which the student's mind recoils." He went on to explain that Thayer had spoken to Brewster about the necessity of reforming the course and that he himself had "supplemented Prof. Thayer's remarks" in his own communications with Brewster. Plainly, Thayer and Brandeis had devised a coordinated plan to correct Brewster's wayward path. Brandeis reported that, happily, Brewster proved eager to heed their advice. As it turns out, Eliot had been stalling on the decision whether to reappoint Brewster to the faculty. Once Brandeis emphasized Brewster's willingness to adapt, Eliot opted to give the instructor another chance.[29]

Brandeis was also attuned to Thayer's scholarly output. After Thayer published "Presumptions and the Law of Evidence" in an 1889 issue of the *Harvard Law Review,* Brandeis quickly sent off a congratulatory note. Recall that Holmes praised the same article but also needled Thayer over his use of the term *logic.* Brandeis, too, had a quibble, but a more generous one, sharing, "I read the article with one deep regret—the regret that there was not more of it." Having found "equal pleasure + profit" from turning its pages, Brandeis pleaded with Thayer to "put into permanent force the much [*sic*] which fifteen years of careful study has brought together"—by this, Brandeis meant a full-blown treatise on evidence law. He worried that Thayer's wish to study every last detail of the subject would indefinitely delay the appearance of such a treatise. "You should not let us wait longer for the results you have achieved," Brandeis insisted. In his view, Thayer ought not be concerned about publishing a treatise that left the topic "unfinished"; the professor merely needed to "remember the opportunities of a second edition" that would allow him to expand and update his text as his research in the field advanced. Brandeis concluded his letter by reflecting on "the great inspiration" that Thayer had been "many years ago" during Brandeis's law school days, adding that "your teaching should have a wide field." In other words, a treatise would allow those who never set foot in a Harvard Law classroom to reap the benefits of a Thayer education.[30]

Brandeis's encouragement notwithstanding, he and the rest of the legal profession would have to wait another seven years for the first installment of Thayer's *Preliminary Treatise* to appear. Thayer published *Cases on Evidence* in the interim. Like the article on presumptions, the casebook impressed Brandeis, but he wished that Thayer had written more. The casebook featured excerpts from cases, without an abundance of commentary from Thayer himself. Brandeis told his old professor that while the casebook "brings me a wealth of learning and of ideas," still "I regret only that . . . your opinions are not more frequently expressed."[31]

Thayer reached the twilight of his life as Brandeis's star was shining ever brighter. Upon Thayer's death, it was Brandeis's wife, Alice, who sent a letter of condolence to Thayer's widow. Perhaps Brandeis was otherwise preoccupied—or maybe the grief was too acute for him to pen the letter himself.[32]

The years after Thayer's passing saw Brandeis gain increasing renown for his work as a lawyer and reformer. Felix Frankfurter, a fervent Thayer acolyte in his own right, noted that Brandeis's experience as a practicing lawyer crystallized a belief in the living constitution that Brandeis had originally derived from Thayer. As Frankfurter observed, "Rich experience at the bar confirmed the teachings which Mr. Brandeis had received from James Bradley Thayer, the great master of constitutional law, that the Constitution had ample resources within itself to meet the changing needs of successive generations."[33]

As a lawyer, Brandeis is most celebrated for his trailblazing litigation in the landmark case *Muller v. Oregon* (1908) before the US Supreme Court. At question was the constitutionality of an Oregon statute that limited the working hours for female laborers. On behalf of Oregon, Brandeis submitted to the high court what would become known as the "Brandeis brief." It was a tour de force in data-driven jurisprudence. He dedicated merely two pages to legal analysis and more than a hundred to sociological and medical research about the dangers that lengthy work hours posed to women. Brandeis won the case, and the groundbreaking nature of his brief became even more famous than the majority opinion upholding the law.[34]

Although *Muller* is best remembered for the novel manner in which Brandeis privileged data over doctrine, his litigation strategy also reflects a Thayerian belief in judicial restraint. During oral argument, Brandeis told the justices that bad laws are not necessarily unconstitutional. A statute under judicial scrutiny "may be found afterwards to be unsound—and yet the constitutionality of the act would not be affected thereby," he explained. The high court's inquiry should not extend to a determination of whether the Oregon statute is "wise or unwise" but "merely whether you can see that legislators had no ground on which they could, as reasonable men, deem this legislation appropriate."[35] This was classic Thayer: if there is any rational argument in favor of the law's constitutionality, the court must sustain it.

Eight years later, Woodrow Wilson named Brandeis to the US Supreme Court, the first Jew to receive that honor. He sat on the court for twenty-three years and earned his place in its pantheon of great judges. From the bench, he applied the same principle of restraint that he had urged the justices to adopt in *Muller*. In *Jay Burns Baking Co. v. Bryan* (1924), for instance, the Supreme Court voided a Nebraska law regulating the size of bread loaves on the grounds that the state was unreasonably interfering with private industry. Brandeis dissented. He contended that the majority's willingness to second-guess the Nebraska legislature constituted "an exercise of the powers of a super-legislature—not the performance of the constitutional function of judicial review."[36] The factual record did not overcome the presumption of constitutionality owed to the statute, by Brandeis's lights.

He was not inclined to credit Thayer in his footnotes; citations to Thayer are conspicuously absent from Brandeis's judicial decisions and legal scholarship.[37] That Brandeis was as close to Thayer as any of the protégés mentioned in this book makes these silences curious indeed. Still, the jurisprudence that Thayer taught was largely the same that Brandeis championed. It would be folly to think that Brandeis's views on judicial deference to legislatures did not emerge, at least in part, from the warm personal relationship he shared with his favorite professor. Melvin Urofsky's definitive biography of Brandeis speculates, and rightly so, that the justice's take on judicial restraint originated in Thayer's teachings.[38] If Thayer was seldom mentioned in the letter of Brandeis's work, the revered professor was very much alive in its spirit.

All that said, Brandeis's commitment to restraint was not unconditional. He was comfortable with an activist role for the judiciary in the protection of civil liberties. For example, Brandeis signed on to Holmes's dissent in *Abrams v. United States* (1919), which construed statutory language so narrowly as to run amiss of congressional intent in order to safeguard freedom of speech.[39] And Brandeis was willing to depart from Thayerian restraint even when Holmes was not. The two justices diverged, for instance, in the free speech case *Gilbert v. Minnesota* (1920). The majority, which included Holmes, upheld a Minnesota law that rendered it illegal to dissuade Minnesotans from aiding the US government in any war against the nation's enemies. Brandeis in dissent found that the "law is inconsistent with the conceptions of liberty" and favored striking it down to preserve the First Amendment's "right to speak freely concerning functions of the federal government."[40] Notably missing from Brandeis's dissent was his usual anxiety about the high court becoming a superlegislature.

A possible explanation for the differing votes from Holmes and Brandeis in *Gilbert* relates to their views on economic legislation. Both justices promoted judicial restraint when the Supreme Court reviewed statutes regulating industry (Holmes, for instance, signed on to Brandeis's dissent in the above-mentioned *Jay Burns Baking*). That they voted the same way in such cases might lead one to overestimate the congruence between their views. Holmes was dubious of progressive statutes but sustained them, despite his own misgivings, because he did not think it was his place, as a judge, to substitute his policy preferences for those of the people's representatives. Brandeis, in contrast, genuinely believed in social reform. Arguably, Brandeis saw in Thayerian deference a useful tool to ensure that progressive legislators could experiment without interference from the bench. Brandeis surely found it easy to let stand legislation that he considered meritorious. But when confronting a statute he disliked, as was the case in *Gilbert*, Brandeis wanted the court to abandon judicial restraint and instead pursue his desired policy outcome. Unsurprisingly, Holmes, having already stayed his hand when faced with economic legislation he thought misguided, could more easily do the same with the statute at issue in *Gilbert*. If Brandeis was more principled in his defense of liberties, Holmes was more principled in his deference to majorities.

JOHN HENRY WIGMORE

John Henry Wigmore was born in 1863 in San Francisco, California. He planned to attend the nearby University of California at Berkeley for his undergraduate degree, but as his sister recalled, "Mother was under the spell of the New England men and women of letters of the time, and nothing would do but that [John Henry] must go to Harvard." Unsettled at the thought of her firstborn so far from home, Mrs. Wigmore insisted that she, her husband, and John Henry's numerous younger siblings move to Massachusetts in 1879 to join her sixteen-year-old son in this new phase of life.[41]

At Harvard, Wigmore performed with distinction, and the experience bolstered his confidence in his intellect. The family returned to San Francisco after Wigmore earned his bachelor's degree, and there the recent graduate took a job in the family lumber business. His parents wanted him to work for the business in perpetuity, but after a year, to their displeasure, Wigmore struck out on his own. He resurfaced at Harvard in 1884 to attend law school. This time, he came to Cambridge alone. Another indication of the widening breach between Wigmore and his parents was their absence from his wedding.[42] They always kept his room, with a view of the Golden Gate, just as he had left it as a boy—perhaps a comforting reminder of an earlier day when the parents still had some control over their son.[43]

John Henry Wigmore at the time of his graduation from Harvard Law in 1887. (Northwestern University Archives Photographic Collection)

Wigmore thus came into Thayer's orbit just as the young man's estrangement from his family was beginning. In Thayer, Wigmore found a substitute father figure who inspired in his mentee a veneration bordering on hero worship. In Wigmore, Thayer found precisely the kind of precocious student who had always attracted his attention. Wigmore ranked first in a class of sixty-one students at the end of his first year of law school, and he served on the inaugural board of the *Harvard Law Review* in his third year.[44]

Thayer continually encouraged Wigmore as he set out on his post–law school career. When Wigmore was only twenty-five and soon to embark on an academic life in the late 1880s, Thayer wrote, "I am truly glad that you are making yourself favorably known."[45] In another letter dated 1889, Thayer asked Wigmore to "remember that I shall always be glad to hear from you and of you and always ready to say or do anything which may help you."[46] And a few years later, Thayer offered, "Let me know if I can help you in any exigency."[47] These words of support from such an eminent scholar meant a great deal to his young protégé.

Wigmore spent the early 1890s teaching Anglo-American law at Keio University in Japan before joining the faculty at Northwestern Law in 1893. There he would remain for the rest of his long career, much of it as the school's enterprising dean. In his early days as a professor, he consulted Thayer on a range of academic issues. Often, Wigmore sought clarification of a historical point or advice in revising a scholarly article.[48] He also looked to Thayer as an authority on the reform of legal education. Lamenting the "desperately Philistine" approach of most educators, Wigmore lauded Thayer in 1895 for the "exalted tone" and "high standards" of his celebrated speech "The Teaching of English Law at Universities" (discussed in chapter 2).[49] Moreover, Wigmore valued Thayer's recommendations for additions to the law faculty at Northwestern.[50]

Part of what bonded the two men together is that Wigmore, more than any other Thayerite, chose to make Thayer's specialty of evidence law his own.

Wigmore once said that he never considered a rule of evidence "without imag-ining what [Thayer] would think of it."[51] Wigmore's evidence classes at North-western relied heavily on Thayer's teaching materials. After Thayer published his evidence casebook, Wigmore assured the author, "My men [i.e., students] have enjoyed extremely the Cases on Evidence."[52] When Thayer produced the second edition in 1900, Wigmore conveyed to Thayer his appreciation of the updated text. "I was deeply impressed, on turning over its pages, with the im-mense amount of detailed care spent in the revision," Wigmore marveled. "It is indeed a new book, for every page seems to have been given some breath of new life." Praising the "copious citations" and "new minor conveniences," he concluded, "It will all be a decided advantage for students and teachers."[53] Not only did Wigmore use *Cases on Evidence* in the classroom but he would later reference it in his own treatise on evidence.[54]

Thayer, in turn, drew from Wigmore when developing curricular materials for his Harvard students. In 1899 Thayer commended Wigmore for his "ex-cellent article on *Confessions.*" Referring to his own pupils, Thayer informed Wigmore, "I shall turn my men loose on it. . . . This seems to me one of the best and neatest things you have done. I wish you would print it in a pamphlet and send a copy to every judge in the country."[55] Thayer was particularly taken with Wigmore's work as editor of a revised edition of Greenleaf's *A Treatise on the Law of Evidence* (hereafter, *Greenleaf*), the dominant reference work on evidence law since the 1840s. Wigmore's prefatory remarks in *Greenleaf* ex-plained to readers that he felt torn between his obligation to "leave the original text still available in its classical integrity" and his desire to "make the work as useful as possible to the profession and to the student of the present time." To fulfill the former objective, Wigmore included an appendix that reproduced sections he had deleted from the original text. To address the latter, he incor-porated three chapters entirely of his own authorship on physical evidence, circumstantial evidence, and exceptions to the hearsay rule.[56]

As an indication of the acclaim that met Wigmore's revision of *Greenleaf*, Thayer and his colleagues at Harvard Law awarded him the first Ames Prize, bestowed every four years for the best English-language contribution to le-gal scholarship.[57] Thayer assured Wigmore, "You have done all that can be to rehabilitate your learned author."[58] A few months later Thayer reported, "I am constantly referring my men to your new Greenleaf."[59] Thayer also referenced Wigmore's *Greenleaf* in the second edition of his *Cases on Evi-dence.*[60] Wigmore's reaction to the citation in the casebook was indicative of his adulation for Thayer: "I certainly did not for a moment dream of this compliment."[61]

The *Greenleaf* edition may have earned Wigmore high praise from Thayer, but the young scholar was frustrated with his own effort. Wigmore hungered to produce a wholly new treatise that would refashion evidence law to meet the demands of modern legal practice. "The Greenleaf, of course, contained many statements (by me) which must have made you shake your head," Wigmore wrote to Thayer, "but I can only assure you that I believe myself to have authority for it all, and will some day defend it where space will allow ample opportunity."[62] The following year—even as the thirty-eight-year-old Wigmore was assuming his new responsibilities as dean of Northwestern Law—he still longed to publish a treatise all his own. "As to Greenleaf," he told Thayer, "the condensation was such that I should not like to be judged by all I said there; some things had to be said roughly, and thus perhaps without necessary qualification; other things could be better defended if space allowed."[63] Wigmore would eventually get that opportunity.

Amid this intellectual exchange, one work in particular left an indelible mark on Wigmore: Thayer's *Preliminary Treatise*. In a letter addressed to Thayer shortly after its publication, Wigmore insisted, "Any other book on Evidence could be spared . . . but not this. I only wish that every judge who is to write an opinion on the law of evidence could be required to read this book." Thayer had paved the way for a wholesale overhaul of the rules of evidence, according to Wigmore. "The crying need of today is clear thinking; and there will be no clarifier more potent than your Preliminary Treatise," he exclaimed. "As an achievement merely in the writing of history, it would be unique and pioneer, but I do not know when a mark of history ever bore so immediately and practically upon concrete improvement in current practice."[64] Wigmore fully appreciated that Thayer's historical emphasis was more utilitarian than antiquarian.

The effusive praise that flowed between Wigmore and Thayer did not preclude disagreements on legal issues. Wigmore at first only sheepishly distanced himself from his former professor. After the *Preliminary Treatise* appeared, he confessed to Thayer, "on matters of classification and analysis, I am sometimes unfortunate enough to find myself taking a different attitude from yourself."[65] Two years later, referring to Thayer's evidence casebook, Wigmore belatedly offered "a suggestion [for the forthcoming second edition] which I wanted to make before this, but did not have the courage to advance." He went on to recommend a "larger selection of cases on the Examination and Impeachment of Witnesses" and added, somewhat obsequiously, "I hope you will not think me to be intruding with this suggestion."[66] Thayer, with characteristic humility, proved amenable to Wigmore's advice and implored, "Pray give me any other hints. I wish I had written to you before."[67] Soon after, Thayer again assured his protégé, "It would be a real favor if you would let me have good criticism."[68]

Eventually, Wigmore traded his deferential comments for direct critiques. Responding to Thayer's perspective on two legal doctrines, Wigmore bluntly wrote in a 1902 letter, "I doubt the significance you suggest."[69] According to the historical record, this was the last letter that Wigmore ever sent Thayer. The professor of legend died three weeks later. In a note to Thayer's widow, Wigmore described his connection to her late husband in religious terms, referring to Thayer as his "father-confessor" and to himself as one of his loyal "disciples." Wigmore continued, "It was a good word of his which helped me at almost every stage in the profession; and to him, more than to any one man, I was indebted for action which brought me advancement."[70] As Wigmore well knew, many others could make that same claim.

At the time of Thayer's passing, both he and Wigmore were at work on new evidence treatises. Now Thayer's would remain forever unfinished, and it fell to Wigmore alone to steward evidence law into modernity. Wigmore had an almost superhuman capacity for intellectual undertakings, but as he toiled on his treatise in the wake of Thayer's death, he surpassed even his own standards for sustained concentration. Robert Miller was a student at Northwestern Law during these years and remembered in vivid detail the intensity with which Wigmore focused his energies on his magnum opus. "Aided by numerous cigarettes," Miller recalled, "he applied himself to the work which was to give him imperishable fame." Although the smoking room in the old courthouse where Wigmore labored "was not the quietest place in the world," he remained "wholly undisturbed by the activity around him." Miller added, "With the absorption there attended an air of sureness and serenity, as of one who possessed the certainty that what he was doing would be in perfect fulfillment of his design."[71] The four volumes of his treatise appeared in late 1904 and early 1905; they spanned an arresting four thousand pages and included forty thousand judicial citations.

The *Harvard Law Review* gushed, "It is hardly too much to say that this is the most complete and exhaustive treatise on a single branch of our law that has ever been written."[72] In the course of promoting Wigmore's new publication, fellow Thayerite Louis Brandeis—whom Wigmore had solicited for advice as he worked on it[73]—nodded implicitly to Thayer's legacy: "Trained early by the masters of the Harvard Law School, and enriched by years of patient and devoted study, Professor Wigmore has produced a work which must prove of great value."[74]

While some of Thayer's acolytes acknowledged their debts to him in private correspondence and others did so in published footnotes, Wigmore paid homage to Thayer in both modes. The pages of Wigmore's treatise, often called *Wigmore on Evidence*, referenced Thayer's *Preliminary Treatise* dozens of times. Indeed, the entire organizing principle of *Wigmore on Evidence* was explicitly borrowed from Thayer's tome. The *Preliminary Treatise* delineated two "fundamental" tenets that governed evidence law and made it a "rational system." The first "forbids receiving anything irrelevant" into court; the second dictates that "unless excluded by some rule or principle of law, all that is logically probative is admissible."[75] Thayer's two-tiered metaprinciple appealed to Wigmore, who restated Thayer's dual precepts as follows: (1) "*None but facts having rational probative value are admissible,*" and (2) "*All facts having rational probative value are admissible, unless some specific rule forbids.*" Wigmore gave all due acknowledgment to Thayer. After quoting the relevant language from the *Preliminary Treatise* at length, Wigmore added, "This notable passage fitly expresses the marked spirit of our law of evidence for the last century and a half,—that is, since the beginning of our consciousness of it as a system."[76]

Wigmore on Evidence was a consummate expression of legal realism, and its particular brand of realism bore the unmistakable marks of the *Preliminary Treatise*.[77] Consider their parallel treatments of the parol evidence rule. Thayer reviewed a dissent relating to parol evidence authored by the English judge Lord Chief Justice John Holt (1642–1710). Holt had argued that the meaning of a will should derive only from its terms and not from evidence of the circumstances in which the will was formulated. In Thayer's estimation, Holt had lapsed into a false sense of absolutism that was unresponsive to the contingencies of the real world. "The Chief Justice," wrote Thayer, "here retires into that lawyer's Paradise where all words have a fixed, precisely ascertained meaning." Though "men have dreamed of attaining" an "absolute security" through "rigid rules," they ultimately cannot escape "the fatal necessity of looking outside the text in order to identify persons and things [which] tends steadily to destroy such illusions and to reveal the essential imperfection of language."[78] Thayer's rebuke of formalism and its empty promises resonated with Wigmore, who quoted this very passage in his own treatise's commentary on parol evidence. Wigmore also chided the opinion of yet another English judge who, like Holt, presumed that "certainty of interpretation can be had," and Wigmore drew the same conclusion as Thayer: "It is a dream of the impossible."[79] Both Wigmore and Thayer saw a critical need to rescue evidence law from logical abstraction and confront with candor the messy realities of lived experience.

Perhaps the most innovative use of Thayer in *Wigmore on Evidence* was how Wigmore applied Thayer's theory of judicial restraint to the rules of evidence. Wigmore discussed those circumstances under which a tribunal is asked to investigate, as a factual matter, the validity of a legislative proceeding that culminated in the passage of a statute (e.g., whether the lawmakers' votes were accurately recorded in the house's journal). In determining whether the legislature followed proper procedure in enacting a law, a court risks overstepping its bounds and unduly voiding the statute, Wigmore cautioned. Great deference is owed to legislators. Attributing to the bench "a righteous desire to check at any cost the misdoings of Legislatures," he inveighed against the judiciary's efforts to fashion itself "a second and higher Legislature." Wigmore insisted that a democracy thrives by electing worthy representatives rather than by "trusting a faithful Judiciary to check an evil Legislature." Just as Thayer had in his article "Origin and Scope," Wigmore conceded that legislatures sometimes err and contended that the remedy has to originate from the source of the problem. "The sensible solution is not to patch and mend casual errors by asking the Judiciary to violate legal principle and to do impossibilities with the Constitution," wrote Wigmore, "but to represent ourselves with competent, careful, and honest legislators, the work of whose hands on the statute-roll may come to reflect credit upon the name of popular government."[80] An unelected bench cannot save democracy from itself.

Judicial review was also pertinent to evidence law because some rules of evidence were prescribed by legislative statute rather than by common-law doctrine, and here, Wigmore went further than Thayer in developing a theory of judicial restraint. Whereas Thayer maintained that a piece of legislation with any credible claim to rationality passes constitutional muster, Wigmore held that the bench should uphold even *irrational* laws. "If the Legislature can make a rule of evidence at all," he set forth, "it cannot be controlled by a judicial standard of rationality, any more than its economic fallacies can be invalidated by the judicial conceptions of economic truth." Here Wigmore was alluding to the bench's tendency (or perceived tendency) to read laissez-faire into the Constitution and thereby strike down regulations on industry. He added, "Apart from the Constitution, the Legislature is not obliged to obey either the axioms of rational evidence or the axioms of economic science." In his general deference to legislatures and in his particular view that the Constitution favors no specific economic school, Wigmore articulated the very analysis that traced its origins to Thayer and would achieve lasting fame in Holmes's celebrated *Lochner* dissent.[81] Yet Wigmore did not cite "Origin and Scope" on the topic of judicial review, perhaps because his standard that irrational laws should survive judicial scrutiny went well beyond the test Thayer championed.

Following Thayer, Wigmore did not argue for judicial deference in all instances. Most rules of evidence were not dictated by legislatures and thus were subject to considerable judicial discretion. Yet courts exercised such discretion infrequently, to the joint dismay of Thayer and Wigmore. "In our own administration of the law of evidence," warned the *Preliminary Treatise*, "too many abuses are allowed, and the power of the courts is far too little exercised in controlling the eager lawyer in his endeavors to press to an extreme the application of the rules."[82] *Wigmore on Evidence* sounded the same note of caution: "The typical tendency of the modern American judiciary is to abdicate that power of control over the trial which tradition and the due course of justice demand that they shall have, and to become more and more mere umpires, who rule upon errors and make no attempt otherwise to check the misconduct of counsel."[83] Wigmore applied this principle to innumerable doctrines throughout his treatise. For instance, in endorsing the expanded use of judicial notice—whereby a judge admits an alleged fact without evidence—Wigmore offered this quotation from the *Preliminary Treatise*: "It is an instrument of great capacity in the hands of a competent judge; and is not nearly as much used, in the region of practice and evidence, as it should be."[84]

The *Preliminary Treatise* and *Wigmore on Evidence* were constituent parts of a common enterprise, bound together by shared realist values. And yet they each had a distinct purpose: the former was a work of history and theory that planted the seed; the latter was a work of immediate practical use that reaped the harvest. Given that Thayer and Wigmore advanced the same jurisprudence, Thayer's sequel to the *Preliminary Treatise*—had he lived long enough to produce it—probably would have looked strikingly similar to *Wigmore on Evidence.*[85] Yet they surely would not have been identical. Wigmore was more diligent than Thayer in applying realist philosophy to evidence law. For example, the constructed nature of legal categories, to which Thayer briefly nodded in the *Preliminary Treatise*, was a more prevalent theme in *Wigmore on Evidence.*[86] Similarly, Thayer only sometimes alluded to the societal context of legal development, whereas Wigmore made a greater effort to situate law amid broader social forces.[87] In other words, there were discrepancies between them, but these were matters of degree, not of kind.

It is difficult to overstate the sweeping impact of *Wigmore on Evidence* on courtroom practice. In 1923 the *Yale Law Journal* reflected on the effect of Wigmore's treatise in the nearly two decades since its publication: "It is so far superior to any other treatise on the subject, that comparison is impracticable. It is by all odds the best, if not the only real, authority on the law of Evidence."[88] Because *Wigmore on Evidence* was so dominant and so Thayerian, no other branch of American law more thoroughly embodied Thayer's teachings. And if an obtuse reader of Wigmore's treatise missed the obvious signs of Thayer's profound influence, a mere glance at the dedication page would have sufficed. The tome was written in memory of "the great master" himself—James Bradley Thayer.[89]

ROSCOE POUND

Roscoe Pound was born in Lincoln, Nebraska, in 1870. The precocious Pound enrolled at age fourteen at the University of Nebraska, where he studied classics before turning to natural science. Four years later, Pound set off for Harvard Law at the behest of his father, a highly respected lawyer and former judge. The lengthy train ride to the East Coast proved onerous; Pound described the trip as "the most detestable bit of traveling I ever heard of." But after settling in Cambridge, Pound enjoyed an immersive experience. He lived a short walk from the law school and ate his meals at the recently constructed Memorial Hall just north of Harvard Yard. Pound managed to find time between law classes to frequent the theater and watch athletic events. He even stepped into the boxing ring himself, which left its bruises. "My countenance presents a rather singular appearance," Pound offered euphemistically. But the blows to his head did not inflict lasting damage, if his later scholarly output is any indication.[90]

Roscoe Pound during his deanship of Nebraska Law School, circa 1904. (Omaha Bee, *"Nebraskans," 1854–1904* [Omaha, NE: Bee Publishing Company, 1904], 58)

Thayer taught Pound constitutional law, and the lessons Pound gleaned from his professor would stay with him for the remainder of his career. He valued the Harvard Law faculty in general for teaching law not as some ivory tower abstraction but as a grounded reality, and he ranked Thayer among those educators "who made law teaching a specialized branch of the legal profession without divorcing it from the law as practised."[91] (In that same spirit, Pound later titled an article "Law in Books and Law in Action," which became one of the most commonly cited publications on his lengthy curriculum vitae.)[92] Pound's opportunity to learn from Thayer was limited because he dropped out of Harvard after just one year. Completion of law school was not a prerequisite for taking the bar at that time, and Pound's ailing father needed him to return to Nebraska and help with his law practice.[93]

Pound soon scored his first victory in a jury trial; opposing counsel was the future populist firebrand William Jennings Bryan. As the 1890s progressed, Pound built a formidable reputation in the local legal community. The thirty-year-old Pound became a state judge in 1900 and shortly thereafter assumed the deanship of the University of Nebraska's College of Law. Pound often lunched during these years with the famed sociologist Edward A. Ross at a local haunt called Jimmie's. These meals first stimulated Pound's interest in sociological approaches to law, for which he would become renowned.[94]

Pound's experience keenly illustrates that Thayerites constituted a tight-knit group. John Henry Wigmore introduced Pound to Oliver Wendell Holmes Jr. over dinner in 1907. "It would not be possible," Pound wrote to Wigmore, "to express my indebtedness to you for the opportunity of meeting him which you gave me."[95] Wigmore lured Pound to the Northwestern Law faculty that same year. Both men advocated reforms that they had experienced as students at a modernizing Harvard Law in the 1880s and 1890s: higher admission standards, a three-year degree, and more full-time faculty members. The University of Chicago soon poached Pound, only to have Harvard do the same not long after.[96] In 1912 Louis Brandeis remarked to Wigmore that "Roscoe Pound will be a potent influence at Harvard" in reversing the "waning respect for the law, the Courts and the profession."[97] Pound's reputation was instrumental in persuading yet another Thayerite, Felix Frankfurter (discussed in chapter 5), to join the Harvard Law faculty.[98] When Pound became the dean of Harvard Law in 1916 (succeeding Thayer's son in that role), Learned Hand told him, "Many of us look to you as the natural leader of legal education in the country today."[99] Lengthy volumes could be written about the dense networks among Thayer's protégés, but suffice it to say that the relationships were deep, enduring, and informed by the jurisprudence they had inherited from a common source.

Pound was breathtakingly prolific in his scholarly research, and despite spending relatively little time with Thayer, he regularly acknowledged his debt to the late professor. Among the Thayerian insights that surfaced in Pound's writings was the merit of living constitutionalism. Thayer wrote in the *Harvard Law Review* in 1899 that a loose construction of the Constitution did not betray the framers; if anything, the framers' genius lay in creating a dynamic legal charter that would prove equal to challenges unimagined by the convention in Philadelphia in 1787. In Thayer's words, the Constitution is "forever silently bearing witness to the wisdom that went into its composition, by showing itself suited to the purposes of a great people under circumstances that no one of its makers could have foreseen." Thayer called for a recognition of the Constitution's "large scope" and warned against a straitjacketed construal of the document's text: "Petty judicial interpretations have always been, are now, and will always be, a very serious danger to the country."[100]

Pound's central grievance with the judiciary was its unwillingness to see in the Constitution the powers required by the national and state governments to confront the unprecedented exigencies of an industrializing society. Drawing on Thayer's 1899 article, Pound published his own piece in the *Harvard Law Review* in 1908 that chided the courts for their "narrow and illiberal construction of constitutional provisions, state and federal. 'Petty judicial interpretations,' says Professor Thayer, 'have always been, are now, and will always be, a very serious danger to the country.'" Thayer saw strict constitutional interpretation as a perennial concern, and Pound deemed it especially hazardous amid "the industrial conditions of today."[101]

Pound was also influenced by Thayer's study of how a given regime could run a functional administration of justice without the rule of law—in other words, a legal system that could remedy disputes but do so without fair and equal justice. A prime case study was America's treatment of its indigenous peoples, and Thayer was unusually sensitive to their plight. In the *Atlantic Monthly* he pushed for legal equality between Indians and non-Indians but found little will among politicians to give the former the same rights as the latter. "The whole Indian question gets little hold on public men," he lamented, "and is crowded aside by tariffs and silver and President-making and office-jobbing and pension-giving."[102] Pound kept this example in mind when he himself wrote about the perils of an "administration of justice without law" in a 1913 article in the *Columbia Law Review.* He advised readers, "For an example of failure of justice without law in modern times see Thayer, Legal Essays," and he cited the relevant page numbers where Thayer advocated civic equality for Indians.[103]

Pound was likewise attuned to Thayer's displeasure with trial procedure. Thayer bristled at a "mechanical," or formalistic, conception of trial procedure that fetishized a strict adherence to rules at the expense of a rational search for truth. His *Preliminary Treatise* documented the judiciary's unhealthy fixation on the "mechanical following of form" in the past. Judges had been too narrowly focused on the stringent application of procedure and neglected to appreciate that procedure should be merely a means—and thus subservient—to the ends of justice. Thayer observed this phenomenon at work in English legal history: "The judges of the Common Pleas sat, like the referee at a prize-fight, simply to administer the procedure, the rules of the game."[104] In a 1910 contribution to Northwestern's law review, Pound decried that the preoccupation with form over substance chronicled by Thayer was no relic of the past; it survived in the "over-technical character and exaggerated importance of procedure in the American legal system." Pound lifted language from Thayer in asserting that much of the trouble was a residue of "rules originating in the archaic administration of justice by the 'mechanical following of form.'" Thayer had been sanguine about the evolution of modern procedure, concluding that "the method of reason" had largely triumphed; Pound, in contrast, bemoaned, "Escape from the past is always slow and difficult."[105]

Pound routinely exhorted the legal profession to build upon Thayer's legacy. For instance, in a 1912 speech Pound explained that the law was ripe for the last of a three-stage process. In the first stage, the law had been a litany of rules that bore little cogent relation to one another. The second stage had required industrious minds to impose order upon the different branches of law, and Pound offered up Thayer as one of the great contributors to this endeavor in the field of evidence law. "The advance from Greenleaf on Evidence to the system outlined by Thayer and carried out in thorough-going detail by Wigmore . . . shows what has been the task of American law teaching for the past forty years and that the task has been well done," Pound announced. "It is time now to essay a new task." That new task—the third stage—called for the legal guild to expand on the work of Thayer and of other treatise writers by furnishing a coherent system of law writ large. To redress the law's ongoing fracture into different branches, this final phase must erase "the persistence of lines of cleavage, existing only from accidents of historical development and subserving no useful purpose."[106] It is fitting that Pound paid homage to Thayer in this particular speech because he delivered it in his capacity as president of the Association of American Law Schools, an office whose inaugural holder had been Thayer himself.

Pound also challenged the legal academy to produce a treatise on criminal law in the mode of the great treatise writers, a pantheon that included Thayer. In a 1935 article titled "Toward a Better Criminal Law," Pound noted that every other branch of law had been "affected for the better by some creative text book written by a great teacher of law and embodying the results of his teaching and of his study in preparation for teaching." He named "Greenleaf and Thayer and Wigmore" as models for some enterprising scholar to follow.[107]

Pound did not merely encourage others to emulate Thayer; he positioned his own work in the Thayerian tradition. In a 1914 article in the *Harvard Law Review* Pound criticized the "legal idea of justice" for lagging behind the "sociological idea of justice." He felt that this discrepancy was particularly pronounced in the marketplace, where legal justice upheld the doctrine of liberty of contract—that is, workers enjoyed the liberty to contract out their labor on any terms—while sociological justice recognized that this doctrine was a farce in a modern age in which individual laborers had little bargaining power. "We have to ask," Pound wrote, "why did the legal idea come to be what it is and why does it so persistently remain such?" Only a proper understanding of the past can rectify the present, he insisted. To that end, Pound's historical inquiry involved recourse to the *Preliminary Treatise.* He quoted at length from Thayer's discussion of formalistic modes of trial procedure, where Thayer described how a "convenient form or formula" of deciding cases often exhibited "little or no relation" to the "probable truth of fact" and thus had all the arbitrary results of "a child's rigmarole in a game."[108] For Pound and Thayer alike, formalism led to negative outcomes, be it liberty of contract or capricious trial procedure. Pound also shared this particular portion of the *Preliminary Treatise* with students in a law course. That this course was jurisprudence, and not evidence, is telling; Pound recognized that Thayer had taken a highly technical branch of law and recast it as a robust exercise in legal philosophy.[109]

In using Thayer's historical work as a foundation for legal reform, Pound was heeding a call that Thayer himself had sounded years earlier. Thayer praised the law school in an 1886 address for its progress in "methods of historical research." Those methods, Thayer affirmed, constituted an incremental step upon which future generations would build: "We know, with an absolute conviction, that we are helping to lay a better foundation for those who will follow us." The speech was not merely a meditation on the utility of historical study; it also offered a history lesson on how law became an academic discipline at Harvard. Thayer noted that this curricular development had been unlikely, given that Harvard's Puritan founders had no special regard for the subject. "It is not altogether strange that our law at that time should seem to a plain Puritan to be a dark and knavish business," Thayer explained, "for it was still heavily encumbered with the formalism of the Middle Ages."[110]

Although Pound had not yet arrived at Harvard at the time of Thayer's address, he managed to secure a copy of it at some point because he quoted it in a 1914 article in the *Michigan Law Review* that explored the historical reasons for the modern distrust of lawyers. In a section on early colonial Massachusetts, Pound remarked that "the pious Puritan" was "naturally disposed to regard law as 'a dark and knavish business' and to regard lawyers as mischievous parasites upon society." Pound in the end was content to accept a certain level of derision toward the bar as inevitable. He reasoned that lawyers would always assume an outsized role in government, and their political power was destined to incite jealousy.[111]

Pound also followed Thayer's lead in producing pedagogical materials for students. Beginning in 1899 Pound taught a course at the University of Nebraska on the "history and system of our law," and he eventually aggregated primary sources from that course into a book titled *Readings on the History and System of the Common Law*. This volume was designed to work in tandem with his lectures and provide fodder for class discussion. It thus followed in the tradition of Thayer's *Cases on Constitutional Law*. Indeed, Pound had Thayer's *Cases* in mind as he prepared *History and System*—the latter book relied upon the former for translations of foreign-language documents.[112]

Pound's book directed student readers to Thayer's scholarship on the importance of judicial restraint. Under the heading "the supremacy of the law," Pound referred students to Thayer's classic article "Origin and Scope." Pound also cited Thayer's essay about advisory opinions.[113] Recall that Thayer—a consummate proponent of minimalism from the bench—insisted that advisory opinions from the judiciary are not binding on coordinate branches of government.[114] Given that Pound was far more enamored of progressive statutes from legislatures than of conservative decisions from judges, Thayer's premium on judicial deference dovetailed perfectly with Pound's agenda.[115]

Although they were both legal realists, they had distinct orientations toward their shared jurisprudence. Thayer explicated a legal philosophy for the ages; Pound applied legal philosophy in service of an agenda that was specific to his historical moment. Thayer advocated judicial deference to legislatures to preserve the foundational principle of democratic rule; Pound saw judicial deference as a means to preserve progressive legislation. Thayer admonished the legal world to consider the real-world consequences of doctrine as a general matter of sound reasoning; Pound stressed the exploitative consequences of formalistic adjudication for laborers in an industrial age. Thayer generically argued that law should accommodate social change; Pound called on courts to adapt law to the particular exigencies of the Progressive Era. Thayer sought to expose the irrationalities of outdated rules within the legal system; Pound aimed to instrumentalize the law in his quest for sweeping societal reform.

Beyond these differences in tenor, Pound promoted elements of legal realism that Thayer did not. Pound, for instance, thought of law as an exercise in the pragmatic balancing of competing social interests. He also embraced the use of social scientific data in adjudication. These two tenets were interrelated for Pound. In a complex society, social scientific investigation—or what he sometimes simply termed "science"—was required to gather facts about the various social interests to be balanced. "This task of valuing new interests," Pound maintained, "balancing them against old ones and reshaping legal doctrines accordingly is primarily a scientific work, calling for more science and more research than has been demanded in the past."[116] Still another realist precept that appears in Pound's writing but not in Thayer's is the notion that law must be oriented around the needs of the collective rather than the rights of the individual. Pound dismissed the "isolated individual" as "an abstraction" that "has never had a concrete existence," adding, "we look instead for liberty through society."[117] In recovering the extent of Pound's realism, we see the limits of Thayer's own.

Notably, Pound failed to cultivate as close a personal relationship with Thayer as did some other students. Both Brandeis and Wigmore completed their law degrees and then stayed in the Boston area for at least some time following graduation; Pound did neither and thus lacked the same chance to benefit from Thayer's sustained mentorship over a period of years. Still, Thayer's teachings remained top of mind for Pound as he ascended to the loftiest perch in legal academia. Pound appreciated that Thayer had given the legal profession not hard-and-fast answers but rather a set of tools. As Pound reflected, "Professor Thayer caused us to think for ourselves."[118]

LEARNED HAND

Learned Hand is widely considered the greatest judge in American history to have never sat on the US Supreme Court. He was born in Albany, New York, in 1872 under the name Billings Learned Hand, but he feared Billings was insufficiently masculine and dropped its usage as a teenager. Hand lionized his father, Samuel, whose towering intellect was peerless, at least in his family's eyes. Samuel could also be aloof and intimidating. He died when Learned was only fourteen, robbing the son of the eventual opportunity to confront his father's fallibility from an adult perspective. Instead, Hand lived under the shadow of an idealized memory of his father, which proved to be a source of both insecurity and motivation.[119]

As an undergraduate at Harvard, Hand was initially drawn to philosophy and even considered earning a doctorate in the subject. But when the time

Learned Hand at the time of his graduation from Harvard College in 1893. (Harvard University Archives)

came to pursue an advanced degree, Hand defaulted to the family tradition: law. His grandfather, father, and uncles had all been judges, lawyers, or both (his older cousin Augustus would later sit alongside Hand as an appellate judge on the Second Circuit). In the fall of 1893 Hand began his first semester at Harvard Law.[120]

He initially lived in the dormitories in Hastings Hall but then relocated to a boardinghouse at 52 Brattle Street, a seven-minute walk from campus. There he happily fell in with a group of classmates who shared his intellectual curiosity. Hand throve as a student, joining Harvard Law's two most prestigious extracurricular activities: the law review, where he served as an editor, and the Pow Wow Club, which had claimed Brandeis as a member. Hand eventually decided, however, to abandon both endeavors and focus his intellect on his coursework. And no courses left a deeper mark on Hand than those taught by Thayer.[121]

In Thayer, Hand found a mentor with an intellect that rivaled his father's yet who provided a paternalistic warmth that had been absent from Hand's childhood.[122] Jerome Frank (a Thayerite in his own right) sat on the Second Circuit with Hand and observed that Thayer had profoundly molded Hand in law school. "What we learn from some of our teachers may shape our basic attitudes for the rest of our lives. From such influences, future judges are not immune," Frank posited. "So it was with Thayer and Learned Hand."[123] Hand himself would later tally Thayer among "the great names that had originally grouped themselves about Langdell at the Harvard Law School."[124] And of these great names, Thayer was "on the whole the best of the lot," "the most original," and the "teacher who counted most with me."[125] Hand, like Wigmore, used religious language to describe Thayer, referring to him as "the prophet of a new approach" to law.[126]

Hand's initial course with Thayer was evidence law for second-year students. Decades later, Hand fondly remembered that he "had the advantage of sitting under that great master in the laws of evidence, J. B. Thayer."[127] The first lecture of the semester began with a theme that had long preoccupied Thayer: the misguided inclusion of substantive law in the rules of evidence. As the opening lines of Hand's student notebook from that course read: "Much of the law of Evidence is really no more than rules of reasoning. Much of it is substantive law and must be excluded."[128] It was a lesson that stayed with Hand. In a speech years afterward, he said of Thayer's course, "One rule after another, as it came up, he laid aside and showed us, without any peradventure or possibility of question, had nothing to do with evidence whatever, but was a rule of substantive law."[129] During Hand's time at Harvard Law, Thayer was in the midst of working on his *Preliminary Treatise*, which was deeply concerned with disentangling substantive law from evidence law.

Thayer's evidence course reflected the central tenets of legal realism. He revealed that judges do more than adjudicate—they inevitably make policy in the manner of legislators. Hand recorded in his student notebook that courts engage in "judicial legislation."[130] Thayer also emphasized that although legal principles do exist, they are not directives so much as guidelines full of caveats. At times, it must have seemed to Hand and his fellow students that such caveats were numerous enough to render a given principle nearly meaningless. Late in the fall semester, for instance, Thayer spent merely half a class period discussing the hearsay rule before dedicating several class periods to its litany of exceptions.[131]

Thayer conveyed to students that legal principles are something of a necessary fiction. In Hand's words, Thayer "did indeed recognize that law must pretend to generality, if it is to have an authority greater than the personal word of the judge, but [Thayer was] content to accept the variants with the theorem, and to let consistency take care of itself as best it could."[132] Even mere pretenses to generality were sometimes impossible, and in those instances Thayer was candid with his students about the law's lack of coherence. During one class period, for example, he covered "fact" versus "opinion"—witnesses can typically testify to the former but not to the latter. The distinction, however, is often messy, and as Hand penned in his notebook, "there is no uniformity of decisions" from the courts.[133] Another notable feature of Thayer's evidence course was its heavy emphasis on history as a tool to make sense of present-day doctrine. "We must always remember . . . that the historical method is the only clear one," Hand dutifully inscribed in his notebook.[134] Almost half a century later, when an evidence scholar asked for Hand's take on select passages from Thayer's *Preliminary Treatise*, Hand replied, "My recollection of Thayer is not from the Preliminary Treatise, which I never read, but from what he taught me nearly fifty years ago."[135]

If Thayer's evidence course demonstrated to Hand the merits of realism, then Thayer's constitutional law course the following year showed Hand the perils of formalism. Realists saw legal formalism as a delusional exercise in airtight logical precision that was hopelessly divorced from reality, and Thayer taught that the field of constitutional law was in thrall to this formalist fantasy. "What one did learn, step by step," Hand later explained, "was that most of constitutional law had been constructed out of circular propositions." Thayer stressed to his students that the law was frequently too indeterminate for even flexible guidelines, much less the kind of universal axioms that were central to formalism. "One did not get—at least I did not—many working propositions out of it," Hand observed of the constitutional law course. Amid such uncertainty, Thayer was necessarily "tentative and moderate, as though dealing in an unpredictable medium on which no one could count," recalled Hand.[136]

Having disabused students of whatever comforting illusions they might have entertained about an all-wise judiciary, Thayer promoted his theory of judicial restraint. "The result," Hand reflected, "was to imbue us with a scepticism about the wisdom of setting up courts as the final arbiters of social conflicts, which many of us, at any rate, always retained." Given the fallibility of the bench, there was little defense for the conceit of "a judicature [that was] invulnerable to popular assaults," Hand wrote in a paraphrase of Thayer's teaching. "Origin and Scope" had been published just as Hand commenced law school, and its thesis plainly formed a critical component of Thayer's pedagogy. In Hand's telling, Thayer was "subversive" for advancing an antiformalist mode of jurisprudence that "came to be feared and deeply deprecated by those who set their hopes for the existing order upon [a] repository of eternal principles." Thayer was not quite as subversive as Hand would have it—some other jurists were also rebuking formalism in the 1890s—but Hand nevertheless aggrandized

Thayer as a fearless trailblazer. For Hand, Thayer's course on constitutional law was "the fitting crown of the whole three years" at Harvard Law, and he would carry its insights with him for the rest of his life.[137]

After graduating sixth in his class in 1896, Hand returned to Albany and took a position in his uncle's law practice.[138] Hand undoubtedly had Thayer in mind as he began his work as an attorney. The former student once lauded the professor for possessing "a kind of Rhadamanthine detachment that has always remained to me a paragon of what a lawyer's attitude to law should be," a reference to a judge in Greek mythology who was hailed for his unimpeachable integrity.[139] Thayer made a habit of maintaining a lively correspondence with his best students after they left Harvard Law, and Hand was included in this inner circle. The year after Hand received his degree, Thayer sent him a copy of an article he had just published in the *Yale Law Journal* on a topic Hand no doubt remembered from his evidence course: presumptions. Thayer argued that the legal profession commonly conflated concepts that were, in fact, separate. He was concerned that the "presumption of innocence" and the standard of "proof beyond a reasonable doubt" were confused for one another. A presumption of any kind merely imposes the burden of proof onto the party operating against the presumption, so that in the absence of evidence, the presumption stands. Precisely how much evidence is required to overcome the presumption varies, depending on the presumption in question. For instance, the "presumption of innocence" places the burden of proof on the prosecutor; the threshold of "proof beyond a reasonable doubt" is a discrete rule that specifies the degree of that burden. In Thayer's words, "A mere presumption involves no rule as to the weight of evidence necessary to meet it." As was his wont, Thayer's analysis drew from a rich repository of historical materials to clear up a present-day misunderstanding.[140]

Having been schooled in presumptions by Thayer himself, Hand unsurprisingly agreed with his professor's findings about "the distinction between presumption proper and the rule determining how much proof is necessary." However, Hand feared that the great mass of lawyers who had not been privileged to learn such nuances in Thayer's classroom would be lost. "The purposes of teaching this is no doubt useful," Hand granted, "but it would greatly confuse an ordinary lawyer in practice, I believe, who unites the real presumption with the rule which requires a certain quantum of evidence in each case to establish the opposite conclusion to that of the presumption." He also offered Thayer an update on his career in Albany. The uncle who had hired him had just passed away, and Hand would soon be joining the practice of a lawyer of "reportorial fame." This language was a reference to his new employer's prior role as the court reporter for the New York State Court of Appeals, a prestigious position that Hand's own father had once occupied. "I believe I shall have as good an opportunity as I could have anywhere in this city," Hand concluded.[141]

Two months later, Thayer reached out to Hand for help. The professor was in the midst of revising his evidence casebook into a second edition. It was a text that Hand knew intimately—Thayer had assigned it as part of his evidence course, and Hand's copy was filled with copious notes in the margins.[142] "I am going to beg you to do me a little favor," wrote Thayer. He was "perplexed by the inexact reporting" of a particular case in the New York courts, and Hand was an obvious resource, given that he practiced in the Empire State. Thayer asked, "Will you do me the kindness to look at the record and let me know." The professor also inquired after the young lawyer's new job: "Tell me a word about yourself and how business opens." Thayer's letter went on to remark that it was commencement day at Harvard, and with the thermometer reaching seventy degrees even before breakfast, he looked forward to the "prospect of a good, hot, satisfactory occasion" for that year's graduates.[143] Hand, of course, was happy to accommodate Thayer's request and sent him the information sought about the New York case. "It is a great favor that you have done me," Thayer replied, "and I thank you heartily for your full and careful statement." He assured Hand that the forthcoming edition of the casebook would have "the appellants now fairly described, thanks to you."[144]

Hand found daily legal practice unstimulating, and he sought intellectual fulfillment by undertaking research for an article on a troublesome issue within evidence law: expert testimony.[145] Being a Thayer disciple meant beginning any inquiry into a legal topic with a study of its history. And no one was better situated than Thayer himself to advise Hand on the history of evidence law. When Hand solicited advice from his old professor about where to find germane cases from centuries past, Thayer did better than merely suggest sources. He generously offered to send Hand a "biggish book" of particular relevance—by express mail, no less. Thayer added, "I am heartily glad that you are at work on this." And the professor had an ask of his own: if Hand was planning to reference the *Preliminary Treatise* in his article (which of course Hand was), Thayer wanted Hand's citations to direct readers to the new expanded edition due out later that year.[146]

Hand's article "Historical and Practical Considerations Regarding Expert

Testimony" first appeared in November 1900 in the *Albany Medical Annals* and was reprinted six months later in the *Harvard Law Review*.[147] Expert testimony was a thorny topic. As society grew more complex, the division of labor accelerated, and the development of professional expertise across a wide array of fields became a critical element of modernity. Yet even as the premium on specialized knowledge increased—in society at large and in the courts—expert testimony generated a number of problems in the legal system. If the promise of expertise was a single authoritative opinion, it was a promise all too often left unfulfilled at trial. Experts routinely contradicted one another in court and thereby appeared to be exploiting their credibility so as to benefit a given party in exchange for lucrative fees. Disagreements among experts may have been a normal part of professional life in many fields, but airing those differences in the context of a legal dispute made for poor optics.[148]

In consummately Thayerian fashion, Hand's article spilled most of its ink on the history of expert testimony before turning to a diagnosis of the current problem. He noted that the very purpose of expert opinion, rooted in professional experience, was to guide jurors on matters too complex for ordinary citizens to understand. But if the experts themselves were not in accord, "what hope have the jury, or any other layman, of a rational decision between two such conflicting statements?" Hand proposed a creative solution: an independent body of experts, neither called by nor accountable to either party, who could advise jurors on the pertinent field of knowledge.[149]

Eager to recognize Thayer's assistance, Hand included the following footnote on the first page of his article: "So far as concerns the attempt to trace the outline of the origin of expert evidence, I must acknowledge my great indebtedness for materials to Professor James B. Thayer, who has so much made the whole subject of evidence his own that no one can come into it without feeling, to a certain degree, a trespasser." Hand also took pains to explain that he was not trying to trade on Thayer's stature to enhance the credibility of his article. "Professor Thayer is in no sense the sponsor of any of the conclusions in this article, historical or otherwise," he clarified. "I do not even know that any one of them would meet with his approval, however grateful to me might be such a result."[150] Hand's caveats aside, Thayer surely took great pride in seeing one of his most promising protégés make an important contribution to the field of evidence—just how important, Hand could little imagine. Over the course of his long career, he published dozens of law review articles, but none would be cited more often, in either scholarship or judicial decisions, than the foregoing piece on expert testimony that he produced as a young lawyer still in his twenties.

It is worth noting that in the Thayer-Hand correspondence, requests for advice went both ways. One time Thayer asked for Hand's help with a reference to a particular case and then thanked him in a postcard featuring the image of Thomas Jefferson. Perhaps Thayer deliberately chose a historical icon who was no great enthusiast of judicial review.[151] When the new edition of the *Preliminary Treatise* was about to appear, Thayer told Hand, "I should welcome any criticisms that occur to you."[152] In so doing, Thayer repeated a pattern that can be found in his letters to Wigmore. Thayer may have been the country's preeminent specialist in the history of evidence law, but he had the humility to not merely accept but actually elicit critiques from his former students.

When Hand received word that Thayer had suddenly died, he was "really much grieved." The void at Harvard Law was unfillable, for "no one of the rest of the Law School was quite such a scholar as he," Hand remarked. It was Thayer who "more sympathetically reflected the character of our law" than did "any of the others" on the faculty. And the loss for Hand, of course, went beyond the professional. "I had a real personal regard, perhaps almost an affection for him," Hand shared with a Bostonian. Thayer "represented the very best you people in Eastern New England can produce."[153]

Thayer was gone, but his jurisprudence lived on in Hand. Six years after Thayer's death, Hand published an article in the *Harvard Law Review* that considered the constitutionality of statutes capping work at eight hours per day. As mentioned, some courts had nullified such legislative acts as violations of the liberty-of-contract doctrine derived from the due process clause of the Fourteenth Amendment. Like many other realists, Hand viewed liberty of contract as a ruse by which the bench smuggled its laissez-faire policy preferences into law. Hand, in Thayerian spirit, fulminated against judges who invoked liberty of contract to invalidate statutory limits on working hours. He held that the bench must extend considerable deference to such legislative reforms. "Only in those cases in which it is obvious beyond peradventure that the statute was the result, either of passion or of ignorance or folly, can the court say that it was not due process of law," Hand declared.[154] He did not cite Thayer in the article, but his intellectual debt was obvious. As Jerome Frank commented, "Learned Hand, in an article on the constitutionality of state eight-hours-of-labor statutes, boldly followed Thayer."[155]

Hand ascended to the national judiciary the following year, 1909, at the age of thirty-seven. While on the bench as a federal district judge, he continued to tout a Thayerian jurisprudence. In another *Harvard Law Review* article, in 1916, Hand accused judges of obscuring their "class prejudice" behind a fictitious veneer of self-abnegating formalism: "No ritualistic piety can save them from the necessity of an active partisanship amid the contests of their time."[156] It would be far better for his fellow judges to admit that they exercise discretion, Hand suggested, so that they might avoid using it exclusively for the benefit of the privileged stratum they themselves occupied. Yet again, Thayer did not appear in the footnotes, but the lineage was clear to Frank, who observed, "Here Judge Hand, aged 44, once more disclosed himself as an eager advocate of the lesson he had learned from Thayer. He never forgot that lesson."[157]

Hand was a vocal critic of the US Supreme Court when the justices struck down various forms of social welfare legislation. In *Coppage v. Kansas* (1915), for instance, the high court voided a state law that protected an employee's right to join a labor union.[158] Hand argued publicly that the Kansas statute fell within the commodious bounds of rationality. "Between all reasonable differences of opinion the legislature has the right to choose," he affirmed in the pages of the *New Republic*.[159] Although the article made no explicit allusions to Hand's mentor, the sentiment was classic Thayer. Hand later proposed that in cases implicating liberty of contract, a six-to-three majority should be required on the Supreme Court to annul legislation.[160]

Hand's commitment to Thayerian restraint was less steadfast in the realm of free speech. In 1917, before the Supreme Court heard the *Schenck* and *Abrams* cases (discussed in chapter 3), Hand became the first judge in America to interpret the Espionage Act. Pursuant to that act, the US Postal Service banned the distribution of a radical publication called the *Masses*, and its publisher looked to the courts for redress. Hand overturned the ban in *Masses Publishing Co. v. Patten*, bravely bucking public opinion amid the hysteria of wartime. His judicial opinion celebrated that "the tolerance of all methods of political agitation . . . is a safeguard of free government." He did not go so far as to invalidate the Espionage Act, so in that sense, Hand's opinion was technically compatible with Thayerian restraint; Hand himself insisted that his decision proceeded from "the greatest deference" to Congress. But he was unquestionably motivated by a fervent faith in the value of dissent, and he construed the wording of the statute so narrowly as to effectively overturn the will of Congress. It would be difficult to credibly claim that Hand's speech-protective interpretation of the Espionage Act was consistent with judicial deference to a Congress that, swept up in war fervor, manifestly sought to silence contrarians.[161]

The following year, by coincidence, Hand happened upon Oliver Wendell Holmes on a train heading from New York to New England. Both judges were journeying north to their summer homes. Hand seized the opportunity to impress upon the celebrated Supreme Court justice the imperative to protect dissident voices. Following that train ride, Hand began corresponding with Holmes, urging him to embrace a more liberal position. Given the younger judge's veneration of the elder, it is a testament to the strength of Hand's convictions that he beseeched Holmes so vehemently. They continued to exchange letters through 1919, as the justice issued a majority opinion in *Schenck* that showed little regard for free speech before pivoting in *Abrams* to a more speech-friendly construction of the Espionage Act.[162] Holmes's famous dissent in *Abrams* effectively mirrored Hand's ruling in *Masses*, in that neither judge deemed the statute unconstitutional; instead, they both construed its wording strictly enough to defend freedom of speech. To what extent Holmes was influenced, consciously or otherwise, by Hand remains unknown, but there is a striking similarity between Hand's convictions and the approach Holmes eventually adopted.

Although Hand as a young district court judge may have promoted free speech in the face of congressional censorship, Hand as an older appellate court judge erred on the side of judicial deference even when free speech was implicated. In *United States v. Dennis* (1950), Hand upheld the convictions of Communist Party officials who had been found guilty of violating the Smith Act, which criminalized speech that advocated the violent overthrow of the government.[163] Some commentators contend that Hand, having succumbed to Cold War anxieties, abandoned his earlier libertarian streak in *Masses*. Others claim that Hand felt bound by Supreme Court precedents that were more speech-restrictive than he would have personally preferred. But if we take Hand at his word, his ruling in *Dennis* was about deference to Congress rather than to the Supreme Court. "We had no alternative," Hand said of the Second Circuit's ruling. "Many is the time that I have declared valid a law I should have never voted to pass." What mattered to Hand was not his view of the Smith Act's merit but his recognition, as a judge, of the legislature's right to enact it. *Dennis*, then, was a straightforward application of Thayer's theory of judicial restraint.[164]

If *Masses* and *Dennis* taken together indicate a measure of inconsistency on Hand's part, then the celebrated judge confused matters further in a famous lecture series in 1958. The eighty-six-year-old Hand was still a practicing judge, with forty-nine years of experience on the bench. In the words of the *New York Times*, Hand was "the most revered of living American judges."[165] The lectures were hosted by his alma mater, Harvard Law, and the series was called the Holmes Lectures, so named for Hand's fellow Thayerite.

Hand dedicated his lectures to the vexing topic of judicial review. He maintained that the principle of judicial deference to legislatures was just as germane to statutes regulating fundamental liberties as those concerning economic welfare. "I do not think the interests mentioned in the First Amendment are entitled in point of constitutional interpretation to a measure of protection different from other interests," Hand argued. He then abruptly reversed himself, warning that in "periods of passion or panic," legislative majorities might exact "serious damage" on freedom of speech, so there is "a substantial and important advantage of wide judicial review."[166] Hand's self-contradiction here is hard to paper over.[167]

This halfhearted exception for free speech aside, Hand's lectures otherwise mounted a forceful defense of judicial restraint. He cautioned that judges were Trojan-horsing their political biases into their decisions under the spurious mantle of objectivity. In Hand's words, his fellow judges "disguise what they are doing and impute to it a derivation far more impressive than their personal preference." His deference to legislatures was especially notable because it ran counter to the trajectory of the Warren Court, which had embraced an activist agenda with respect to personal liberties. Hand well understood that proponents of robust judicial review were holding fast to a belief that "courts may light the way to a saner world." But he was highly skeptical. "For a judge to serve as a communal mentor appears to me a very dubious addition to his duties," Hand warned. In a democracy, the hastening of a saner world must come from the ballot, not the bench. "For myself it would be irksome to be ruled by a bevy of Platonic Guardians," he memorably added.[168]

Thayer had said it all before. Indeed, Hand privately acknowledged that his lecture series was something of an homage to the late professor. When Hand sent a copy of the lectures to a friend, he described them as attending to "an old grievance I have nurtured for over sixty years, derived from one of the great masters I had the good luck to be under at the Law School." That Hand delivered the lectures in the very building where he had taken Thayer's constitutional law course must have made the nostalgia all the more poignant. The following year, Hand wondered in a letter whether Thayer—were he still alive—would acknowledge as readily as Hand did the consistency between their approaches. "I have often asked myself how far [Thayer] would recognize as legitimate descendants my own views about constitutional law," Hand mused. "There is no doubt that—bastards or not—they are his get."[169] Nearly a lifetime after meeting Thayer, Hand's memory of his mentor burned as brightly as ever.

Each of the protégés profiled in this chapter engaged in his own distinct way with Thayer and his teachings. Brandeis and Hand cultivated close relationships with Thayer that endured past graduation, and although they were disinclined to cite Thayer, his residual effect on their jurisprudence is undeniable. Pound offers a mirror image of these two judges; he never enjoyed the opportunity to forge a close bond with Thayer, but he was not shy in his scholarship about positioning the professor's work as a lodestar to guide the legal profession. Wigmore combined all these elements, claiming an intimate personal connection with Thayer marked by prolific correspondence while also regularly crediting Thayer in his publications. It might be tempting to conclude from this sample that those on the bench were less apt than their counterparts in the academy to publicly acknowledge their debts to Thayer. But as the next chapter reveals, the most loyal of all Thayer devotees donned judicial robes.

5. Thayer's Heir: Felix Frankfurter

The legacy of James Bradley Thayer did not hinge alone on those followers who personally knew him. Such was his impact that, even after his death, jurists who never had the opportunity to study under Thayer hewed to his teachings. The posthumous admirers most in thrall to Thayer's memory were, unsurprisingly, mentees of Thayer's most famous acolytes—especially of Oliver Wendell Holmes Jr., Louis Brandeis, and Learned Hand. Despite being one step removed from Thayer, some second-generation Thayerites were much more diligent in citing Thayer than those who had actually learned at the feet of the storied professor. This chapter features the most iconic of these figures: Felix Frankfurter.

Felix Frankfurter was born in 1882 and grew up with three brothers and two sisters in Vienna, Austria.[1] When Felix was on the cusp of his teenage years, his father, Leopold, took a solo trip to the United States and "fell in love with the country, and particularly with the spirit of freedom that was in the air," Felix later recounted.[2] Leopold decided to send for the rest of his family, and within a year they had relocated to the humming metropolis of New York City.[3] "From the moment we landed on Manhattan," Felix recalled, "I knew, with the sure instinct of a child, that this was my native spiritual home."[4]

His faith by birth was Judaism. In fact, Felix Frankfurter was descended from a long line of rabbis dating back centuries.[5] Yet neither his rabbinic lineage nor his upbringing in an observant Jewish home was sufficient to bond him to his family's religion as he came of age. When Frankfurter was an undergraduate at City College, he attended a Yom Kippur service and was suddenly struck by its insignificance to him. "I looked around as pious Jews were beating their breasts with intensity of feeling and anguishing sincerity"—here referring to the practice of tapping one's chest in repentance—"and I remember with the greatest vividness thinking that it was unfair of me, a kind of desecration for me to be in the room with these people . . . adhering to a creed that meant something to my parents but ceased to have meaning for me." Frankfurter promptly walked out and never again resurfaced at a Jewish service. For the remainder of his life, he still thought of himself as a Jew—and

understandably so, as Jewish identity entails more than just liturgical prac-
tices—but he was never again a Jew in a devotional sense.[6] Frankfurter instead
came to embrace a new religion: American democracy.

He was a dedicated adherent of what he called the "true democratic faith"
and routinely described the American legal system in decidedly religious terms.[7]
"Society has breathed into law the breath of life and made it a living, serving
soul," Frankfurter once wrote in language mirroring the book of Genesis's description of God animating Adam with breath.[8] The US Constitution, he suggested, was "Delphic," an allusion to the high priestess of the Temple of Apollo.[9]
Frankfurter extolled legislatures as the heart of representative democracy and
lauded them for exercising "prophetic judgment."[10] Harvard Law, where he enrolled at the age of twenty in 1903,[11] was, in effect, his house of worship; he acknowledged having "a quasi-religious feeling about the Harvard Law School."[12]

The circumstances leading to his matriculation at Harvard must have
seemed an exercise in divine predestination to the young Frankfurter. He initially intended to enroll at Columbia Law, but just as he was on his way to
the campus to register, he encountered a friend who convinced him that the
weather was too fine not to spend the day outside. Enrollment could wait;
Coney Island could not. Although Frankfurter had intended to postpone reg-
istration for only one day, he then came down with the flu and never made it
uptown to Columbia. His doctor ordered him to leave New York City for the
sake of his health, so Frankfurter absconded to Cambridge.[13]

If democracy was his faith, the Constitution his scripture, and Harvard Law
his temple, then Frankfurter's prophet was James Bradley Thayer.[14] Thayer's
iconic essay "Origin and Scope" was, for Frankfurter, "the compelling motive
behind my Constitutional views . . . the Alpha and Omega." Here he invoked
the two Greek letters that together refer to God in the book of Revelation.[15] To
be sure, there were other prophets in Frankfurter's civic faith, but even these
prophets were themselves disciples of Professor Thayer. As Frankfurter neared
the end of his life, he told the historian Arthur Schlesinger, "Both Holmes and
Brandeis influenced me in my constitutional outlook, but both of them derived theirs from the same source which I derived mine, namely, James Bradley Thayer."[16] Elsewhere, Frankfurter included Learned Hand in this pantheon
of Thayerites, writing that his own experience on the Supreme Court "deci-
sively confirms the philosophy in which Mr. Justice Holmes, Judge Learned
Hand, Mr. Justice Brandeis and I were bred, to wit: James B. Thayer's outlook
on the reviewing power of this Court."[17]

Felix Frankfurter in the early years of his career, circa 1910. (Harvard Law School Library, Historical and Special Collections)

Given Frankfurter's profound reverence for Thayer, it is striking that the two never met. The Harvard professor of legend had passed away just the year prior to Frankfurter's arrival in Cambridge. Frankfurter spent the remainder of his years lamenting that he had narrowly missed the opportunity to learn from Thayer directly. "That James Bradley Thayer was no more when my class entered the School has been a lifelong bereavement for at least one member of that class," he reflected nearly four decades after his graduation.[18] Even in his golden years, Frankfurter was still recalling how often others had remarked "that I came too late to the School to encounter the mind I would have found most congenial to mine, that of James Bradley Thayer; and I am sure [this] was right, judging by everything I have heard of Thayer and everything of his I have seen in print."[19] Thayer may have been gone, but the professor's memory still permeated the law school while Frankfurter was earning his degree. In a speech that Frankfurter delivered late in life at Harvard Law, he exalted "the traditions of James Bradley Thayer, echoes of whom were still resounding in this very building in my student days."[20] It appears that Frankfurter's failure to encounter Thayer in the flesh only strengthened his affection for the deceased scholar. Unencumbered by the foibles that come with interpersonal familiarity, Frankfurter effortlessly turned Thayer into an idol.

When Frankfurter had occasion to produce pieces commemorating for-mer professors or colleagues upon their deaths, he often paid his respects by comparing their legacies to Thayer's. He wrote of Edmund Morgan, "History will surely account him with Thayer and Wigmore as a trinity in the law of evidence."[21] And about professor Eugene Wambaugh, Frankfurter declared, "In range and depth and precision of scholarship he was not unequal to his illustrious associates on the faculty of the Harvard Law School—Ames and Gray and Thayer, to speak only of the dead."[22]

After graduating first in his class from Harvard Law in 1906, Frankfurter worked in private legal practice for a few short months. He then opted to take a substantial pay cut by accepting a job in a federal prosecutor's office in New York.[23] In 1914 he was invited to return to Harvard as a faculty member.[24] The prospect daunted him, as Frankfurter struggled to conceive of himself in the same position as the likes of Thayer and other leading faculty: "My first concern was that I wasn't qualified. When I thought of Gray, Ames, Thayer, I couldn't think of myself in those terms."[25] But return he did, serving on the Harvard Law faculty for twenty-five years. During his long tenure in aca-demia, Frankfurter championed causes such as Zionism and raising the min-imum wage. He also helped found the American Civil Liberties Union and served as an adviser to Franklin Delano Roosevelt. In 1939 FDR named him to the US Supreme Court. Throughout Frankfurter's lifetime of work as a scholar, activist, and justice, the constellation of his legal realism was oriented around a single star: Thayer.

One of the many realist tenets that Frankfurter inherited from Thayer was a belief in living constitutionalism. Both men held that the Constitution is an adaptable document that courts ought to interpret in light of changing conditions. Frankfurter approvingly wrote in the *New York Times Magazine* of "the influential teaching of Professor James Bradley Thayer that the Con-stitution has within itself ample resources for meeting the changing needs of successive generations."[26] A Thayerian embrace of the living constitution easily accorded with Frankfurter's worldview, which was characterized by an earnest optimism about modernity. He teemed with enthusiasm for human-ity's progress. In a 1915 law review article, Frankfurter rejoiced over what he considered the "almost magical industrial growth" experienced since the Civil War. He celebrated the "vast nervous system of telephones and telegraphs [that] has electrified our scattered country into one self-conscious unit," as well as the "radiating railroads . . . which have pulled into a co-ordinate and articulate body the detached and sprawling members of our great domain."[27] Frankfurter welcomed this modern era that—he was sure—heralded a new premium on collective action for the general welfare. As Frankfurter asked rhetorically, "Does it not mean that we are in the very midst of a definite shift of emphasis from individualistic ends to co-operative ends?"[28] If Holmes was the most cynical of Thayerites, Frankfurter was the most idealistic.[29]

Among all the principles that Frankfurter gleaned from Thayer, by far the most important was judicial deference to legislatures. As both a law school professor and Supreme Court justice, Frankfurter was known for his dogged— even dogmatic—commitment to the theory of judicial restraint formulated by Thayer in "Origin and Scope." Frankfurter went so far as to pronounce Thayer's article "the most important single essay" on American constitutional law. It was "the great guide for judges and therefore, the great guide for understanding by non-judges of what the place of the judiciary is in relation to constitutional questions."[30] Throughout his long career penning law review articles and judicial decisions, Frankfurter defended time and again the Thayerian position that a court should not strike down a statute if anyone could rationally find it constitutional. He spoke reverentially of "Thayer's statesmanlike conception of the limits within which the Supreme Court should move" and pledged to "be loyal to his admonition regarding the restricted freedom of members of that Court to pursue their private views."[31] This narrow conception of judicial review was "not merely a gesture of courtesy" from the judiciary to the legislature, in Frankfurter's perspective. Rather, it was "the formulation of a basic truth in the distribution of governmental powers. . . . To this consideration our great master of constitutional law, James Bradley Thayer, attached the utmost weight."[32] Of Thayer's many acolytes who picked up the mantle of judicial restraint, Frankfurter was arguably the most emphatic—as well as the most diligent in crediting Thayer.[33]

Frankfurter fully subscribed not just to Thayer's theory of judicial deference but also to Thayer's underlying rationale. Both jurists posited that, in a democracy, the people are sovereign; they express their will through elected representatives, and unelected judges ought to nullify statutes enacted by those representatives only in extreme cases. In his biography of John Marshall, Thayer extolled the legislative branch of government as the "majestic representative of the people." It followed for Thayer that "to set aside the act of such a body, representing in its own field, which is the very highest of all, the ultimate sovereign, should be a solemn, unusual, and painful act. Something is wrong when it can ever be other than that."[34] Frankfurter quoted this passage in the *Harvard Law Review* in 1923, paying heed to these "abiding words of warning by James Bradley Thayer" about the "grave dangers" inherent in "the power of our judiciary to disregard unconstitutional legislation."[35] If the bench was too willing to substitute its opinion for that of elected officials, then judges risked undermining the paramount principle of democratic rule.

Frankfurter seconded Thayer's concern that a robust exercise of judicial review would mistakenly convince the public and their representatives that such encroachment on the legislative sphere was proper. Thayer repeatedly stressed that judicial activism cultivates among the citizenry and elected lawmakers an unhealthy dependence on the courts. Legislators cease to be concerned about the constitutionality of their statutes, Thayer fretted, if they know that the bench will be quick to intervene. The people, through their chosen representatives, need to correct legislative mistakes. In a 1915 law review article, Frankfurter endorsed Thayer's thesis that it was not the judiciary's duty to protect society from legislative malfeasance. For that, there was no replacement for an engaged citizenry. Frankfurter declared that "the admonition is profoundly important" and "was sounded long ago before the controversial days by a great teacher of constitutional law with the vision of a statesman, James Bradley Thayer, to the end that responsibility for mischievous or inadequate legislation may be sharply brought home where it belongs—to the legislature and to the people themselves."[36] Frankfurter was effectively plagiarizing Thayer's "Origin and Scope" article, which called for judicial restraint "so that responsibility may be brought sharply home where it belongs."[37]

Frankfurter used his perch as a Supreme Court justice to champion this viewpoint. "A democracy need not rely on the courts to save it from its own unwisdom," he wrote in a 1949 decision, for "if it is alert—and, without alertness by the people, there can be no enduring democracy—unwise or unfair legislation can readily be removed from the statute books. It is by such vigilance over its representatives that democracy proves itself."[38] Arguably no other justice on the high court did more than Frankfurter to echo Thayer's conviction that it was up to democracy to rescue itself.

Thayer and Frankfurter alike feared that the unduly expansive purview of courts had led lawmakers to think in terms of whether a statute could pass judicial muster instead of the legislation's virtue. As Thayer observed in 1893, "No doubt our doctrine of constitutional law [i.e., judicial review] has had a tendency to drive out questions of justice and right, and to fill the mind of legislators with thoughts of mere legality, of what the constitution allows."[39] For Thayer, the remit of the Supreme Court was straightforward and limited: either the legislation in question could rationally be said to fit within the provisions of the Constitution or it could not. Any matter beyond this strict inquiry—be it morality or merit—was the exclusive prerogative of the voters and their representatives. Frankfurter reiterated Thayer's sentiment in the pages of the *Harvard Law Review* in 1955, suggesting that lawmakers and the people at large tended to spuriously conflate the constitutionality of a given act with its worthiness. "The emphasis on constitutionality and its fascination for the American public," he lamented, "seriously confound problems of constitutionality with the merits of a policy."[40] If the public and legislators alike better understood the constrained role of courts, they would take more seriously the imperative of passing laws that are not merely constitutional in form but also commendable in function, Frankfurter contended.

A critical element of Thayer's theory of judicial restraint was his opposition to advisory opinions, a stance that left an imprint on Frankfurter. As discussed in chapter 2, Thayer first took up the topic in the 1880s, inveighing against advisory opinions and praising the US Constitution for granting the judiciary solely an after-the-fact influence. Courts could invalidate a law only subsequent to its passage, and even then, only if the act in question occasioned litigation. Thayer reprised this line of reasoning in his Marshall biography. There, he admonished the courts to "consider how narrow is the function which the constitutions have conferred on them—the office of deciding litigated cases," not of providing advisory opinions prior to a law's enactment. Aside from the small handful of states where advisory opinions are allowed by their constitutions, legislators have "no authority to call upon a court for advice; they must decide for themselves, and the courts may never be able to say a word" unless and until a legal dispute arises. Thayer argued that the principal onus for ensuring the constitutionality of the laws must rest on the branch of government tasked with passing them. "By adhering rigidly to its own duty, the court will help, as nothing else can, to fix the spot where responsibility lies," he maintained, "and to bring down on that precise locality the thunderbolt of popular condemnation."[41] The thunderbolt is one of the world's most ancient symbols for the wrath of God; it appears that Thayer, too, could frame democratic processes in quasi-religious terms.

In a 1924 law review article on advisory opinions, Frankfurter quoted the foregoing passage from Thayer. At the time, Frankfurter was concerned about "the proposal, variously made, that opinions of the Supreme Court in advance of legislation would be 'constructive.'" Like Thayer, Frankfurter thought that advisory opinions would weaken a sense of obligation among elected representatives to preserve constitutionality in their lawmaking. Legislators would simply punt to the courts. In ominous language, Frankfurter warned, "Advisory opinions are not merely advisory opinions. They are ghosts that slay."[42] Judicial review *after* the fact and advisory opinions *before* the fact were flip sides of the same pernicious coin.

Frankfurter also followed Thayer's lead in citing a historical precedent from the Washington administration to make the case against advisory opinions. In Thayer's 1885 essay on the subject, he approvingly noted that the Supreme Court justices had abstained from weighing in when George Washington sought their legal opinion about a matter not under litigation. Their refusal was a divergence from English legal practice. Thayer reasoned that if the justices had acquiesced to Washington, then "the Court might, not improbably, have slipped into the adoption of a precedent that would have engrafted the English usage upon our system."[43] Frankfurter quoted this excerpt from Thayer in a 1938 law review article discussing the same episode from Washington's presidency and added in his own words, "Despite the most tempting appeals of patriotism, the Supreme Court at the very outset of its career declined the rôle of adviser even on legal aspects of policy, and defined its function strictly as that of a court of law."[44] Thayer and Frankfurter both admired how the early Supreme Court had circumscribed its own power.

If Frankfurter used religious language with respect to legislatures—once describing legislative deliberation as an "exercise in prophecy"[45]—he explicitly repudiated the idea that the judiciary deserves the kind of reverence afforded to faith. In Frankfurter's words, "Five Justices of the Supreme Court *are* molders of policy, rather than impersonal vehicles of revealed truth."[46] The justices on the high court were no gods, Frankfurter insisted, just "nine mere mortals."[47]

Thayer's notion of judicial deference went hand in hand with two other tenets of legal realism: privileging practicality and rejecting universal maxims. Here again, Frankfurter took Thayer as his guide. In a discussion of interstate commerce in *Cases on Constitutional Law*, Thayer argued that a regulation's applicability to a given region is a matter of pragmatism and therefore lies properly in the province of congressmen rather than judges. His discussion of laws concerning the importation and sale of opium suggested that a "desirable rule for California, where there are many Chinamen, and for Vermont, where there are few, may conceivably be different." The commerce clause of the Constitution lacks "any requirement of uniformity," so it is a matter of "practical judgment" how regulations ought to vary across jurisdictions. Thus, "the question . . . appears to be a legislative one; it is for Congress and not for the courts" to decide (except, of course, in those rare cases in which the legislation is unquestionably unconstitutional).[48]

Frankfurter parroted Thayer's emphasis that laws must be attuned to case-by-case practicalities and as such are the special preserve of legislatures. In a 1925 article in the *Yale Law Journal*, Frankfurter discussed the regulation of electrical power in those terms. "The circumstances of the individual situation control," he stressed. "Being a judgment on practical affairs its exercise is primarily and persuasively for Congress, not for the courts." Frankfurter was quick to acknowledge his view's venerable lineage: "The profound reasons for deference to the Congressional judgment have been put in classic language by James Bradley Thayer." He then reproduced at length the above quotation from Thayer's *Cases on Constitutional Law*.[49]

So cautious were Thayer and Frankfurter about judicial discretion that even the greatest of American judges, John Marshall, was not above their reproach. To be sure, they both esteemed the famed chief justice, particularly for his landmark ruling in *McCulloch v. Maryland* (1819), which fortified the supremacy of the federal government over the states. Thayer's biography of Marshall described *McCulloch* as "probably his greatest opinion," adding, "there is nothing so fine as the opinion in McCulloch."[50] Frankfurter, too, thought *McCulloch* was Marshall's signal contribution to American law. "I should like to follow James Bradley Thayer," Frankfurter said in a 1955 speech, "in believing that the conception of the nation which Marshall derived from the Constitution and set forth in *M'Culloch v. Maryland* is his greatest single judicial performance."[51] But they each recognized that Marshall, despite his brilliance, was fallible. As Thayer averred in the biography, "Even so great a man as Marshall erred sometimes."[52] Frankfurter repeated that observation in his speech, admonishing the audience, "It is important not to make untouchable dogmas of the fallible reasoning of even our greatest judge."[53] In Frankfurter's pantheon of legal legends, Thayer alone merited his unquestioning loyalty. It is unsurprising—given Frankfurter's anxiety about judicial activism—that only someone like Thayer who had never sat on the bench could elicit his unmitigated adoration.

In a number of landmark cases before the Supreme Court, Frankfurter helped immortalize Thayer's theory of judicial restraint. *Minersville School District v. Gobitis* (1940), for example, afforded Frankfurter a prime opportunity to showcase Thayerian deference. Two young Jehovah's Witnesses in Pennsylvania faced expulsion from public school for refusing to comply with a requirement that students salute the American flag during the Pledge of Allegiance. The students considered the salute a form of idolatry that violated their religious beliefs, and they filed suit on free exercise grounds. After the school board lost at trial and again in the Third Circuit, it appealed to the Supreme Court.[54]

The pledge requirement was promulgated by a legislative body: the local board of education. So while the case did not implicate a high-profile institution like Congress or the state assembly, the question of judicial deference to a legislature was nonetheless at play. Frankfurter was so eager to pen the decision for *Gobitis* that he supposedly begged the chief justice for the privilege of writing it, which he was granted.[55] As Frankfurter worked on the majority opinion, he sent a letter to a fellow justice describing his forthcoming decision as a platform for exalting the centrality of judicial restraint to representative democracy. The opinion was to be "a vehicle for preaching the true democratic faith of not relying on the Court for the impossible task of assuring a vigorous, mature, self-protecting and tolerant democracy." In so doing, Frankfurter would be "bringing the responsibility . . . directly home where it belongs—to the people and their representatives."[56] Once again, the echo of "Origin and Scope" was so pronounced that it edged on plagiarism.[57]

Frankfurter did just as his letter promised, and although his opinion did not reference Thayer explicitly, his reasoning reflected his devotion to Thayer's teachings. The *Gobitis* decision set forth that the very idea of representative democracy requires courts to intervene only when a violation of the Constitution is beyond rational debate. "Except where the transgression of constitutional liberty is too plain for argument," Frankfurter insisted, "personal freedom is best maintained—so long as the remedial channels of the democratic process remain open and unobstructed—when it is ingrained in a people's habits, and not enforced against popular policy by the coercion of adjudicated law."[58] In *Gobitis*, he could find no such unequivocal transgression of the Constitution and, consistent with Thayer's guidelines for judicial review, felt duty-bound to uphold the school board's mandate that all students salute the flag. He believed that just as judicial activism would enervate democracy, judicial deference would energize it. Frankfurter proclaimed in Thayerian terms, "To fight out the wise use of legislative authority in the forum of public opinion and before legislative assemblies, rather than to transfer such a contest to the judicial arena, serves to vindicate the self-confidence of a free people."[59] Here, Frankfurter diverged from other Thayer acolytes who had sat on the high court. Holmes and Brandeis were more willing to stray from Thayerian restraint when fundamental liberties were violated; Frankfurter, by contrast, was more consistent in applying Thayer's presumption of constitutionality. But amid the troubling aftermath of *Gobitis*, Frankfurter's consistency would strike many as dogmatism.

Following *Gobitis*, an outburst of hate crimes against Jehovah's Witnesses occurred in Pennsylvania and elsewhere. It seemed to many liberal observers that the Supreme Court was partly to blame. Newspapers throughout the country excoriated the court for enabling the violence and failing to stand up for civil liberties. A number of the justices came to regret the *Gobitis* decision, and some signaled publicly that they would be open to reversing the precedent if a similar case arose.[60] Frankfurter bore the brunt of the backlash after *Gobitis*. "I was literally flooded with letters," Frankfurter told a fellow justice, "by people who said that I, as a Jew, ought particularly to protect minorities."[61] Yet his faith in Thayerian deference remained unbroken.

West Virginia v. Barnette (1943) featured a reprise of *Gobitis* as yet again Jehovah's Witnesses declined to salute the flag in a public school for religious reasons, this time in violation of a statewide board of education policy. In a six-to-three decision, the Supreme Court overruled *Gobitis* and sided with the students. Frankfurter, however, remained true to his credo, issuing an impassioned dissent. He once more applied Thayer's test to the question of constitutionality: if there is any rational basis by which the law might pass constitutional muster, it must stand. This case "presents a question upon which men might reasonably differ," Frankfurter determined; he thereby found it "beyond my constitutional power to assert my view of the wisdom of this law against the view of the State of West Virginia." He acknowledged there might well be merit in West Virginia's making religious accommodations for Jehovah's Witnesses. "But the real question is, who is to make such accommodations, the courts or the legislature?" Frankfurter asked. "This is no dry, technical matter. It cuts deep into one's conception of the democratic process."

To him the answer was clear: any accommodations for minority faith groups must come from lawmakers, not judges. Otherwise, the bench risks becoming a "super-legislature," and a dangerous one at that, since federal judges are not subject to elections. Frankfurter made plain that his commitment to judicial restraint did not vary based on which constitutional provision was in play. Even when a fundamental right like religious liberty was implicated, the judge's role remained the same. "In no instance is this Court the primary protector of the particular liberty that is invoked," he declared.[62]

Although Frankfurter had not cited Thayer in *Gobitis*, he left no doubt in *Barnette* where his intellectual debts lay. His dissent in the latter case referred to "an utterance as wise as any that I know in analyzing what is really involved when the theory of this Court's function is put to the test of practice. The analysis is that of James Bradley Thayer." Frankfurter then lifted a nearly seven-page passage from Thayer's *John Marshall* about the limits of judicial review.[63] There, Thayer warned that an overly robust exercise of judicial review would have harmful effects on representative democracy. In Thayer's words, invalidating a statute is "always attended with a serious evil, namely, that the correction of legislative mistakes comes from the outside, and the people thus lose the political experience, and the moral education and stimulus that come from fighting the question out in the ordinary way, and correcting their own errors." Frankfurter used the lengthy Thayer quotation as a coda, giving the late professor the final word about the hazards of judicial interference.[64]

Even with respect to capital punishment, which Frankfurter considered profoundly immoral, he demonstrated a steadfast fidelity to Thayerian deference. He cast the tie-breaking vote in a notorious 1947 case that condemned inmate Willie Francis to death. The matter reached the Supreme Court after the state of Louisiana botched Francis's electrocution; the justices were asked to determine whether allowing Louisiana to electrocute him again would violate the double jeopardy clause and cruel and unusual punishments clause in the Bill of Rights. Frankfurter—who had once offered his summer cottage as a headquarters for anti-execution activists—signed on to a five-member majority that permitted Louisiana to send the inmate to the electric chair a second time. Later Frankfurter would acknowledge, "It offended my personal sense of decency to do this. Something inside of me was very unhappy, but I did not see that it violated due process of law." Still, he worked behind the scenes in his capacity as a private citizen in the hopes of orchestrating a gubernatorial commutation of the sentence. His attempts were fruitless, however,

and the execution proceeded as planned. Frankfurter defended the disjunc-
ture between his personal and judicial views in a letter to a friend more than
a decade after the Francis case, writing, "Few of the arrangements of our society are more repellent, more of an expression of barbarism, than is capital
punishment." But on the bench, he refused to "apply my 'sense of right and
justice and honor' in rejecting capital punishment, and vote to set aside the
conviction merely because the sentence was death."[65] Had Frankfurter joined
the four dissenters on the high court, Willie Francis would have lived, but
Frankfurter's devotion to Thayer's legacy overrode his own moral compass.

There was, however, one area of jurisprudence in which Frankfurter violated that commitment: church-state relations. In a series of iconic cases involving the rights of religious groups, he voted counter to the groups' interests,
even when doing so required forsaking the Thayer test to which he otherwise
piously adhered.[66] The first of these cases, *Everson v. Board of Education* (1947),
concerned a New Jersey statute that allowed school districts to use tax dollars
to reimburse parents for the cost of busing their children to private schools,
including religious ones. A five-to-four majority found that the New Jersey
statute did not run afoul of the establishment clause. In the court's reasoning,
the fire department would not refuse to train its hose on a school engulfed
in flames just because the school was Catholic rather than public. Similarly,
the establishment clause did not require the state to withhold busing—another public welfare service—from children who happened to attend religious
schools. To do so would make the state the "adversary" of religion in a way
that the establishment clause hardly required.[67]

Despite Frankfurter's lifelong insistence on judicial restraint, he voted with
the minority to void the law. He did not author a dissent, so it is impossible
to state with certainty his rationale. One could certainly claim that the law *did*
violate the establishment clause, and indeed, two of the four justices in the
minority wrote dissents to that effect. But to apply Thayerian deference is to
inquire whether there is *any* rational argument in defense of the statute. And
given that a majority of the justices found the New Jersey law valid, it easily
passed the Thayer test. Yet Frankfurter, who had so often stressed the importance of legislators rectifying their own errors, here preferred the bench to
substitute its judgment for that of the people's representatives.

If Frankfurter's silence in *Everson* left some question as to his motivations,
he offered greater insight the following year in *McCollum v. Board of Education*
(1948), when he again favored judicial activism to ensure that church and state

remained separate. In this case, the Champaign Board of Education in Illinois instituted a program that allowed privately funded religious classes with voluntary attendance to be offered on public school grounds during school hours. Frankfurter joined an eight-member majority that ruled the policy was repugnant to the establishment clause, and he penned a separate opinion explaining his vote. In Frankfurter's view, the public school system is a critical means for cultivating social harmony across a diverse population. He feared that the unifying effects of schooling would be at risk if a school became host to sectarian religious divides. The country's educational system is "designed to serve as perhaps the most powerful agency for promoting cohesion among a heterogeneous democratic people," and as such, it "must keep scrupulously free from entanglement in the strife of sects." Frankfurter called the public school "at once the symbol of our democracy and the most pervasive means for promoting our common destiny."[68] He was remarkably untroubled by his typical concern that if unelected judges corrected bad policy, it would sap a democratic people's sense of their own civic responsibility.

Under the Thayer test, the Champaign policy ought to stand if even one justice considers it constitutional. And in fact one justice did. Stanley Reed in dissent contended that the court was expanding the meaning of the establishment clause beyond its original intent. The founding generation, Reed maintained, had merely sought to ban a state-supported national church, and the judiciary was now using the establishment clause to justify more sweeping prohibitions on religious activity. Thayer's test required merely that Reed's stance fall within the wide boundaries of rationality—and surely it did—for Frankfurter to vote with him. Yet Frankfurter was uninterested in joining Reed's exercise in restraint.[69]

Frankfurter's neglect of Thayerian deference resurfaced in yet another landmark establishment clause case, *Zorach v. Clauson* (1952). Pursuant to state law, the city of New York implemented a policy that public school students, with parental permission, could leave school during regular school hours to either attend religious classes or worship off campus. The remaining students stayed in school. A six-to-three majority upheld the program, finding that it was consistent with the First Amendment and underscoring the fact that the participating religious organizations neither received public funds nor used public facilities. Frankfurter penned a concise dissent that offered little in the way of legal theory. He argued instead that the factual record was too incomplete for the majority to justify its ruling. Maybe he emphasized the facts over the law to avoid making a case for judicial activism, one that would trample his usual commitment to judicial restraint.[70]

Frankfurter had long before substituted the religious faith of his youth, Judaism, with the secular faith of his adulthood, American democracy. He was strikingly self-aware on that score. Frankfurter told his fellow justices, "As one who has no ties with any formal religion, perhaps the feelings that underlie religious forms for me run into intensification of my feelings about American citizenship."[71] His abiding fidelity to the "true democratic faith" undergirded his oft-stated conviction that an unelected bench ought not interfere with legislative processes, save in extreme cases. And yet he was willing to undermine that very faith in representative democracy to shield the republic from the influence of religion. Coming of age at a time when antisemitism was commonplace in the United States, perhaps Frankfurter felt, even subconsciously, that he could not be both fully Jewish and fully American, so he rejected the former for the latter. And he then begrudged others who attempted to do what he could not: harmonize a religious identity with a civic one. So deep was his concern about walling off religion from public life that it was the only issue for which he abandoned his otherwise unshakable adherence to Thayer's legacy.

Thayer's posthumous influence was far-reaching. The famed Benjamin Cardozo cited the *Preliminary Treatise* with greater frequency than did all his fellow justices combined during his stint on the US Supreme Court in the 1930s.[72] Alexander Bickel, who clerked for Frankfurter in the 1950s before becoming a renowned Yale Law professor, lauded "Origin and Scope" as a "singularly important piece of American legal scholarship."[73] Theodore Roosevelt was influenced by Thayer's writings after his presidency and speculated in his 1913 autobiography that, had he taken Thayer's courses, they might have altered the trajectory of his life. After finishing his undergraduate studies at Harvard, TR enrolled at Columbia Law, where he came to view the legal system as a tool that advantaged elite interests and opted not to complete his degree. He later expressed regret that he had not stayed at Harvard for law school, where Thayer could have demonstrated to Roosevelt that high-minded idealism is not incompatible with the legal profession. "If I had been sufficiently fortunate to come under Professor Thayer, of Harvard Law," TR mused, "it may well be that I would have realized that the lawyer can do a [sic] great work for justice."[74] Informed by his reading of "Origin and Scope," Roosevelt went even further than Thayer in denouncing judicial activism. He advanced a radical proposal in his ill-fated reelection bid in 1912: the popular recall of state court decisions, which would allow the people of a state, by majority vote, to reverse judicial rulings.[75]

It is impossible to neatly circumscribe a study of Thayer's influence after his death. Thanks to the sway of those protégés who knew the late professor personally, it extended widely. These acolytes passed Thayer's ideas on to a new generation of law students and court clerks who themselves went on to become leaders in the field. Thayer's thought endures today even as the origin of that thought has faded from memory. This chapter marks merely one attempt to consider how Thayer's ideas shaped American jurisprudence into the mid-twentieth century. An investigation of Thayer's reverberations through the remainder of the last century and the first decades of our own would be a worthy endeavor—and, if we are to fully understand the modern legal system, an essential one.

Conclusion

James Bradley Thayer's journey epitomized the possibilities and challenges of a modernizing world. His move from the bucolic meadows of the New England countryside to the burgeoning metropolis of greater Boston reflected a broader national trend toward urbanization. A dalliance with a journalistic career gave Thayer firsthand exposure to the railways that were revolutionizing transportation. And his ascension to the Harvard Law faculty just as the school began to pioneer innovations in legal training placed him at the vanguard of educational reform.

The very forces of modernity that made Thayer's path through life possible also rendered the legal system increasingly out of date. Having stood at the forefront of so many trends, Thayer proved well positioned to help fashion a novel jurisprudence attuned to the needs of a changing America. His legal realism—advanced in the classroom, in personal correspondence, and in his various writings—shaped the future giants of the bench and the academy. No other professor of his era could claim greater influence over so many legal luminaries in the United States. Had Thayer boasted a sharp mind and little else, he might not have exercised so much clout. But he was also a kind soul, with a deep commitment to mentorship, whose network of interpersonal relationships amplified his vision for American law.

Several of Thayer's disciples were not content with an honest appraisal of his venerable legacy. After his death, they felt compelled to overstate Thayer's exceptionalism. Learned Hand claimed that Thayer's contemporaries considered him "subversive" for rebuking formalism. In Hand's telling, Thayer had been a prescient skeptic who "came to be feared and deeply deprecated by those who set their hopes for the existing order upon [a] repository of eternal principles."[1] The renowned federal appellate judge Jerome Frank—who never knew Thayer but revered him nonetheless—painted a similar portrait. "When I was a law student, in the first and second decades of the 20th century, it was still heretical to agree openly with James Bradley Thayer," Frank insisted.[2] Undoubtedly, Thayer *was* ahead of his time in many ways, but he was not quite the image of iconoclasm that Hand and Frank liked to conjure; other commentators in the late nineteenth century also promoted elements of legal realism. Moreover, Thayer held an endowed chair at Harvard Law, the kind of establishment position that would have been unavailable to a true apostate.

The exaggeration about Thayer's singularity was compounded by another error: Thayerites embellished the continuity between his realism and their own. To be sure, there *was* considerable jurisprudential overlap, but his adherents were prone to hyperbole. In a 1916 article in the *Harvard Law Review*, Felix Frankfurter inaccurately attributed the origins of sociological jurisprudence to Thayer. Frankfurter lauded how the bench—formerly susceptible to seeing industrial regulations through the prism of logical abstraction—had come to respect the role of the social sciences in addressing such matters. "The courts," he recalled, previously "decided these issues on *a priori* theories, on abstract assumptions, because scientific data were not available or at least had not been made available for the use of courts." But now, Frankfurter observed, the judiciary placed newfound weight on social scientific findings. He described the "turning point" as *Muller v. Oregon* (1908), the famous Supreme Court case litigated by Brandeis that featured his trailblazing "Brandeis brief." As Frankfurter explained, "The Muller case is 'epoch making,' not because of its decision, but because of the authoritative recognition by the Supreme Court [of] the way in which Mr. Brandeis presented the case."[3]

While *Muller* was seminal in Supreme Court history, it was not without antecedents in the broader legal world, according to Frankfurter. "Lone voices of wisdom had been heard for almost two decades," he noted, citing three sources to support this claim. Two were from Thayer's pen: his "Origin and Scope" article and a letter from Thayer to a French legal scholar about the advisable limits of judicial power (the third source was Holmes's 1891 *Perry* dissent—discussed in chapter 3—which elicited praise from Thayer and prefigured the acclaimed *Lochner* dissent). In Frankfurter's view, *Muller* "marks the culmination" of the "technique" spearheaded by Thayer and Holmes.[4] *Muller* did entail judicial deference to a legislature, so in a broad sense, it embodied the kind of restraint that Thayer advocated. Still, Frankfurter was stretching here. In neither Thayer source cited by Frankfurter did the late professor offer any argument in favor of social scientific data. That Frankfurter was nevertheless eager to ascribe the genesis of the Brandeis brief to Thayer suggests more, then, about Frankfurter's adulation for Thayer than it does about the content of Thayer's writings.

Jerome Frank was especially guilty of erroneously resting his ideas on Thayer's body of work in a bid to position himself as a Thayerite. Most notably,

Frank argued that his own psychoanalytic jurisprudence was an extension of Thayerian thought. In 1930 Frank published his highly controversial book *Law and the Modern Mind*, which was informed by his experience as a patient in psychotherapy.[5] The book notoriously contended that society looks to the legal system as a father figure who absolves people from choosing between right and wrong by providing a false sense of moral certainty. Only by overcoming this childish impulse can we arrive at an adult conception of law and accept the law's shortcomings. Democratic self-rule represents the culminating phase in society's maturation, analogous to personal self-actualization. With this, *Law and the Modern Mind* established Frank's reputation as the most provocative of the legal realists.

Years after the book's publication, Frank claimed that Thayer had anticipated his Freudian take on the law. "Thayer was saying, in effect, that our democratic constitutions contemplate an adult, mature society, in which no one will play father to the citizens, treating them like children." According to Frank, he read Thayer only after writing *Law and the Modern Mind* and was struck by the apparent congruence between Thayer's jurisprudence and his own. "Before I had read Thayer," Frank recounted, "I published a book in which I envisioned a mature society where emotional father-dependence would vanish after childhood, in which each grown-up man would become, so to speak, his own father and thus eliminate the need for fatherly authority among adults. This comes close to Thayer's thesis."[6] Frank's superimposing of his psychoanalytic orientation onto Thayer was wildly overblown. It is ironic that Frank, who so stridently denounced the juvenile desire for a father figure, seemed to seek one out in Thayer.

Some of Thayer's most notable admirers thus advanced two distortions about him: that during his lifetime Thayer was unique in his realism (or largely so, when accounting for Holmes), and that his foresight extended to everything from sociological jurisprudence to Freudian legal theory. These dual myths were mutually reinforcing. The first positioned Thayer an isolated visionary who bravely assailed the shibboleth of legal formalism. The second myth solidified Thayer's bona fides as an oracle whose prescience was posthumously vindicated when his loyal disciples drew from his teachings to overthrow the benighted formalists who had once ostracized him.

Consciously or otherwise, Thayer's acolytes were invoking one of the oldest and most resonant motifs in history. The Bible depicts prophets whose revelations earn them reprobation in wicked lands beholden to false idols. Yet their spurned prophecies come to pass and their tormenters are vanquished. This archetype has surfaced countless times in mythology, folklore, and literature. Its romantic appeal is almost irresistible. Befitting the biblical trope of the scorned seer, Thayer's followers described him in overtly religious language. For Hand, Thayer was not merely a mentor but a "prophet." For Frank, Thayer was not merely forward-thinking but "heretical." For Frankfurter, Thayer's theory of judicial restraint was not merely an important contribution but the "Alpha and Omega." By infusing Thayer's memory with a sacred quality, his devotees bolstered their own stature, for in so doing they fashioned themselves descendants of a hallowed lineage, heirs to a righteous tradition of fearless truth-telling, apostles of a lonely soothsayer whose ultimate redemption rested in their own faithful hands.

Notes

ABBREVIATIONS

JBT   James Bradley Thayer Papers, Harvard Law School Library, Historical and Special Collections, Cambridge, MA

JHW   John Henry Wigmore Papers, 1868–2006, Series 17/20, Northwestern University Archives, Evanston, IL

LH   Learned Hand Papers, Harvard Law School Library, Historical and Special Collections, Cambridge, MA

OWHA   Oliver Wendell Holmes Jr. Addenda, Harvard Law School Library, Historical and Special Collections, Cambridge, MA

OWHH   Mark DeWolfe Howe research materials relating to the life of Oliver Wendell Holmes Jr., Harvard Law School Library, Historical and Special Collections, Cambridge, MA

OWHP   John G. Palfrey collection of Oliver Wendell Holmes Jr. Papers, Harvard Law School Library, Historical and Special Collections, Cambridge, MA

INTRODUCTION

1. "Funeral of Prof. Thayer," *Springfield (MA) Daily Republican*, February 18, 1902, 5.

2. For realism and the rejection of universal principles, see Neil Duxbury, *Patterns of American Jurisprudence* (Oxford: Clarendon Press, 1995), 145; Robert W. Gordon, "Legal Thought and Legal Practice in the Age of American Enterprise, 1870–1920," in *Professions and Professional Ideologies in America*, ed. Gerald L. Geison (Chapel Hill: University of North Carolina Press, 1983), 95.

3. For law as a historical social construct, see William M. Wiecek, *The Lost World of Classical Legal Thought: Law and Ideology in America, 1886–1937* (New York: Oxford University Press, 1998), 188–189, 193; Morton J. Horwitz, *The Transformation of American Law, 1870–1960: The Crisis of Legal Orthodoxy* (Oxford: Oxford University Press, 1992), 6, 104, 128.

4. For realism's view of law and society, see Brian Z. Tamanaha, "Understanding Legal Realism," *Texas Law Review* 87 (March 2009): 756.

5. For realism and consequentialism, see Wiecek, *Lost World*, 199; Horwitz, *Transformation of American Law*, 200; James E. Herget, *American Jurisprudence, 1870–1970: A History* (Houston, TX: Rice University Press, 1990), 156; Tamanaha, "Understanding Legal Realism," 737.

6. For realism and the primacy of experience over logic, see Duxbury, *Patterns of American Jurisprudence*, 96.

7. For realism and practicality, see Herget, *American Jurisprudence*, 156.

8. For realism and living constitutionalism, see Michael Kammen, "'A Vehicle of Life': The Founders' Intentions and American Perceptions of Their Living Constitution," *Proceedings of the American Philosophical Society* 131 (September 1987): 328.

9. For the realist critique of the formalist model of judging, see Wiecek, *Lost World*, 198.

10. For commentary on realism and judging, see Horwitz, *Transformation of American Law*, 142; Duxbury, *Patterns of American Jurisprudence*, 47–48; Gordon, "Legal Thought and Legal Practice," 94; Tamanaha, "Understanding Legal Realism," 749, 752.

11. John Henry Wigmore to Mrs. Thayer, February 16, 1902, box 25, folder 9, JBT.

12. Learned Hand, "Chief Justice Stone's Conception of the Judicial Function," *Columbia Law Review* 43 (September 1946): 697.

13. Quoted in Melvin I. Urofsky, *Felix Frankfurter: Judicial Restraint and Individual Liberties* (Boston: Twayne, 1991), 31.

14. Mark Tushnet, *Taking the Constitution Away from the Courts* (Princeton, NJ: Princeton University Press, 2001), 57. Thayer's article has been cited in law reviews with greater frequency than the most commonly cited articles written by a number of his leading contemporaries, including Roscoe Pound, Thomas M. Cooley, and John Chipman Gray.

15. James B. Thayer, "The Origin and Scope of the American Doctrine of Constitutional Law," *Harvard Law Review* 7 (October 1893): 144.

16. For Thayer's ascension into the Brahmin ranks, see Andrew Porwancher and Austin Coffey, "Becoming Brahmin: A Country Boy's Journey to Harvard Yard," *American Nineteenth Century History* 23, 2 (2022). For a discussion of how Thayer's Brahmin identity informed his thought, see G. Edward White, "Revisiting James Bradley Thayer," *Northwestern University Law Review* 88 (1993): 63–73.

17. Brian Z. Tamanaha, *Beyond the Formalist-Realist Divide: The Role of Politics in Judging* (Princeton, NJ: Princeton University Press, 2009), 14, 20, 83–87.

18. "Editorial Notes and Comments. A Paper by Professor Thayer. Constitutional Law," *American Law Register and Review* 42 (January 1894): 73; *Nation* 57, 1484 (1884), box 16, folder 7, JBT.

19. For realism and balancing tests, see Wiecek, *Lost World*, 202; Horwitz, *Transformation of American Law*, 18, 131; Gordon, "Legal Thought and Legal Practice," 94; Herget, *American Jurisprudence*, 7.

20. For realism and social science, see Duxbury, *Patterns of American Jurisprudence*, 82, 92; Herget, *American Jurisprudence*, 3; Tamanaha, "Understanding Legal Realism," 737; John Henry Schlegel, *American Legal Realism and Empirical Social Science* (Chapel Hill: University of North Carolina Press, 1995).

21. For realism and the collective, see Horwitz, *Transformation of American Law*, 72, 110.

22. Wiecek, *Lost World*, 198; Horwitz, *Transformation of American Law*, 169, 208–209; Duxbury, *Patterns of American Jurisprudence*, 64–65; Tamanaha, "Understanding Legal Realism," 737–738; N. E. H. Hull, *Roscoe Pound and Karl Llewellyn: Searching for an American Jurisprudence* (Chicago: University of Chicago Press, 1997), 174–175.

23. David M. Rabban rightly identifies Thayer as a core contributor to the "historical legal science" school of jurisprudence in his book *Law's History: American Legal Thought and the Transatlantic Turn to History* (Cambridge: Cambridge University Press, 2012). Rabban's analysis reveals important elements of Thayer's thought that bear no relationship to legal realism, such as his emphasis on the Germanic roots of English legal traditions. Even so, much of Thayer's historical legal science—and indeed of contemporary historical legal science writ large—as described by Rabban overlapped with realism as described by the secondary literature generally. Both schools acknowledged the ambiguities, contradictions, and irrationalities plaguing the law; both stressed legal development in a social and historical context; both saw law as dynamic rather than static; both were reform minded; both expressly rejected legal formalism; both treated legal classification as a contingent exercise subject to future change; both favored an adaptive approach to constitutional interpretation; and both prized practical utility. For Rabban's discussion of these themes among historical jurisprudents in general and in Thayer's writings in particular, see *Law's History*, 4–6, 14, 270, 273, 283.

24. See Tamanaha, *Beyond the Formalist-Realist Divide*, 1–5; Rabban, *Law's History*, 2–6.

25. For the inaugural use of the term *legal realism*, see Jerome Frank, *Law and the Modern Mind* (1930; reprint, New York: Coward-McCann, 1949), 18–20.

26. The term *originalism* was coined in Paul Brest, "The Misconceived Quest for the Original Understanding," *Boston University Law Review* 60 (March 1980): 204; *living constitution* in Howard Lee McBain, *The Living Constitution* (New York: Macmillan, 1927); and *judicial activism* in Arthur Schlesinger Jr., "The Supreme Court: 1947," *Fortune*, January 1947, 202, 208. For the popularizing of the term *judicial review* in the twentieth century, see Matthew J. Franck, "James Bradley Thayer and the Presumption of Constitutionality: A Strange Posthumous Career," *American Political Thought* 8 (Summer 2019): 396.

27. See, for instance, the articles in "One Hundred Years of Judicial Review: The Thayer Centennial Symposium," *Northwestern University Law Review* 88 (1993); Steven G. Calabresi, "Originalism and James Bradley Thayer," *Northwestern University Law Review* 113 (2019): 1419–1454; Howard Sherain, "Thayer, Judicial Self-Restraint, and Watergate," *Albany Law Review* 38 (1973): 52–65; Eleanor Swift, "One Hundred Years of Evidence Law Reform: Thayer's Triumph," *California Law Review* 88 (December 2000): 2437–2476; David A. Sklansky, "Proposition 187 and the Ghost of James Bradley Thayer," *Chicano-Latino Law Review* 17 (1995): 24–45; Franck, "James Bradley Thayer," 393–417; Zachary Baron Shemtob, "Following Thayer: The Many Faces of Judicial Restraint," *Boston University Public Interest Law Journal* 21 (Fall 2011): 61–84; Vicki C. Jackson, "Thayer, Holmes, Brandeis: Conceptions of Judicial Review, Factfinding, and Proportionality," *Harvard Law Review* 130 (2017): 2348–2396; Wallace Mendelson, "The Influence of James B. Thayer upon the Work of Holmes, Brandeis, and Frankfurter," *Vanderbilt Law Review* 31 (January 1978): 71–87; David S. Schwartz, "An Excess of Discretion? 'Thayer's Triumph' and the Uncodified Exclusion of Speculative Evidence," *California Law Review* 105 (April 2017): 591–598.

28. J. B. Ames, John Chipman Gray, Jeremiah Smith, and Samuel Williston, "James Bradley Thayer," *Harvard Law Review* 15 (April 1902): 605.

29. Charles Sherman Haight, "James Bradley Thayer," *Columbia Law Review* 2 (1902): 240.

30. Michael Steven Green, "Legal Realism as Theory of Law," *William and Mary Law Review* 46 (April 2005): 1917.

1. THAYER'S ORIGINS

1. Harvard College, Class of 1852, 445, sequence (hereafter seq.) 582, Class Book, 1852–1908, HUD 252.714, Harvard University Archives.

2. See, for instance, *Essex Gazette* (Haverhill, MA), May 17, 1834, 3.

3. *Essex Gazette*, February 15, 1834, 3.

4. James Parker Hall, "James Bradley Thayer," in *Great American Lawyers*, ed. William D. Lewis (Philadelphia: John C. Winston, 1909), 8:347.

5. Susan I. Lesley, *Memoir of the Life of Mrs. Anne Jean Lyman* (Cambridge, MA: privately printed, 1876), 523–527.

6. Grace Williamson Edes, *Annals of the Harvard Class of 1852* (Cambridge, MA: privately printed, 1922), 179.

7. Lesley, *Memoir*, 503, 525; James Bradley Thayer, *Letters of Chauncey Wright: With Some Account of His Life* (Cambridge, MA: John Wilson, 1878), 19; Susan I. Lesley, *Recollections of My Mother* (1886; reprint, Boston: Houghton, Mifflin, 1899), 457. Thayer's brother William also reaped the benefits of Mrs. Lyman's generosity.

8. Samuel Atkins Eliot, *A History of Cambridge, Massachusetts (1630–1913)* (Cambridge, MA: Cambridge Tribune, 1913), 117, 119.

9. Eliot, *History of Cambridge*, 117, 119, 121, 125.

10. *Cambridge Chronicle*, October 5, 1848, 2.

11. Eliot, *History of Cambridge*, 119.

12. US Census Bureau, *2010 Census of Population and Housing: Population and Housing Unit Counts*, CPH-2-1, US Summary (Washington, DC: US Government Printing Office, 2012), 20.

13. Lawrence W. Kennedy, *Planning the City upon a Hill: Boston since 1630* (Amherst: University of Massachusetts Press, 1992), 43–45, 53, 56, 58, 67. On Thayer's entry into the Brahmin elite, see Andrew Porwancher and Austin Coffey, "Becoming Brahmin: A Country Boy's Journey to Harvard Yard," *American Nineteenth Century History* 23, 2 (2022).

14. Hall, "James Bradley Thayer," 8:348. On the relationship between Hall and Thayer, see Floyd R. Mechem, "James Parker Hall," *Illinois Law Review* 23 (May 1928): 3.

15. James Bradley Thayer, "Bound Notes 1854–56," box 1, folder 1, JBT. Thayer lifted the quotation from Matthew Arnold, *A French Eton: or, Middle Class Education and the State* (London: Macmillan, 1864), 27.

16. Hall, "James Bradley Thayer," 8:348; Edes, *Annals*, 179.

17. Class of 1852, 448, seq. 585.

18. Class of 1852, 15–16, seq. 24–25.

19. Class of 1852, 26, seq. 35.

20. Class of 1852, 30, seq. 39.

21. Lesley, *Memoir*, 526.

22. Class of 1852, 448, seq. 585.

23. See Richard White, *Railroaded: The Transcontinentals and the Making of Modern America* (New York: W. W. Norton, 2011).

24. James Bradley Thayer, "Railroads at the West," *New York Evening Post*, September 1853, box 24, folder 1, JBT.

25. Jay Hook, "A Brief Life of James Bradley Thayer," *Northwestern University Law Review* 88 (1993): 2.

26. James Bradley Thayer, "Fisher Ames," in *Homes of American Statesmen: With Anecdotal, Personal, and Descriptive Sketches* (New York: G. P. Putnam, 1854), 282.

27. Thayer, "Fisher Ames," 285.

28. Hall, "James Bradley Thayer," 8:349.

29. Thayer, "Fisher Ames," 282.

30. Class of 1852, 448, seq. 585.

31. Lesley, *Memoir*, 508.

32. Lesley, 527.

33. Lesley, 511.

34. *A Catalogue of the Law School of the University at Cambridge for the Academical Year, 1856–1857, First Term* (Cambridge, MA: John Bartlett, 1856), 11, seq. 423, Harvard Law School Library, Historical and Special Collections.

35. Daniel R. Coquillette and Bruce A. Kimball, *On the Battlefield of Merit: Harvard Law School, the First Century* (Cambridge, MA: Harvard University Press, 2015), 168.

36. Quoted in Bruce Kimball, *The Inception of Modern Professional Education: C. C. Langdell, 1826–1906* (Chapel Hill: University of North Carolina Press, 2009), 34.

37. Coquillette and Kimball, *On the Battlefield of Merit*, 168–169, 175.

38. Hook, "Brief Life," 2.

39. *Catalogue of the Law School*, 14.

40. *Catalogue of the Law School*, 14.

41. J. B. Thayer, "The Right of Eminent Domain," *Monthly Law Reporter* 19 (September 1856): 249.

42. Edes, *Annals*, 180.

43. Hall, "James Bradley Thayer," 8:350; Hook, "Brief Life," 3.

44. Class of 1852, 448, seq. 585.

45. See Porwancher and Coffey, "Becoming Brahmin"; Louis Menand, *The Metaphysical Club: A Story of Ideas in America* (New York: Farrar, Straus & Giroux, 2001), 6.

46. Edward H. Madden, "The Cambridge Septem," *Harvard Alumni Bulletin* 57 (1955): 310–311. There is disagreement as to the correct spelling: David M. Rabban, *Law's History: American Legal Thought and the Transatlantic Turn to History* (Cambridge: Cambridge University Press, 2012), and Hook, "Brief Life," refer to the "Septum" Club;

Madden as well as Menand, *Metaphysical Club*, and Kimball, *Inception*, refer to the "Septem" Club.

47. Quoted in Madden, "Cambridge Septem," 310.

48. See Madden, 311–315.

49. Charles Pelham Greenough, "Memoir of James Bradley Thayer," *Proceedings of the Massachusetts Historical Society* 52 (February 1919): 135.

50. Class of 1852, 448, seq. 585.

51. Hall, "James Bradley Thayer," 8:351.

52. Hall, 8:350; Bernard Ginsburg, "Masters in Chancery in Massachusetts," *Law Society Journal* 6 (August 1934): 296.

53. Hall, "James Bradley Thayer," 8:350.

54. Hook, "Brief Life," 3; "Commonwealth of Massachusetts," *Boston Daily Advertiser*, June 19, 1866, 3.

55. Hook, "Brief Life," 4; Hall, "James Bradley Thayer," 8:381. See also Porwancher and Coffey, "Becoming Brahmin."

56. James Bradley Thayer to Ralph Waldo Emerson, June 15, 1861, box 15, folder 7, JBT.

57. Thayer's letter is somewhat curious because the lieutenant in question, Ezra Ripley, had greater proximity to Emerson than to Thayer in the family tree. It is unclear why Thayer would need to champion the cause of someone to whom Emerson himself was more closely related.

58. For checks for deposit, see James Bradley Thayer to Ralph Waldo Emerson, September 27, 1866, box 15, folder 7, JBT. For financial advice and stock purchases, see Thayer to Emerson, May 25, September 19, and December 13, 1865, box 15, folder 7, JBT. For poetry, see Thayer to Emerson, February 28, 1869, box 15, folder 7, JBT; Emerson to Thayer, March 3, 1869, Letters to James Bradley Thayer from Various Correspondents (MS Am 1613), Houghton Library, Harvard University. On the copyright issue, see Thayer to Emerson, August 31 and October 8, 1869, box 15, folder 7, JBT.

59. Ralph Waldo Emerson to James Bradley Thayer, September 26, 1865, Letters to James Bradley Thayer from Various Correspondents, Houghton Library, Harvard University.

60. Ralph Waldo Emerson to James Bradley Thayer, November 22, 1868, Letters to James Bradley Thayer from Various Correspondents, Houghton Library, Harvard University.

61. Ralph Waldo Emerson, *The Essay on Self-Reliance* (1841; reprint, East Aurora, NY: Roycrofters, 1908), 43–44.

62. Hook, "Brief Life," 3–4.

63. See Thomas Haskell, *The Emergence of Professional Social Science* (Urbana: University of Illinois Press, 1977).

64. Hook, "Brief Life," 5.

65. Although details on the comparative salaries are elusive, Hook describes the Royall Chair as "more lucrative" than the Boylston Chair ("Brief Life," 5), and Hall notes the "pecuniary sacrifice" the Royall Chair involved compared to Thayer's private practice ("James Bradley Thayer," 8:352).

66. Hook, "Brief Life," 5; Hall, "James Bradley Thayer," 8:352.

67. Menand, *Metaphysical Club*, 230–232.

68. Menand, 231, 256–257.

69. Menand, 232.

70. Kimball, *Inception*, 203, 192–194.

71. Kimball, 4.

72. Kimball, 195–197.

73. Kimball, 4.

74. Kimball, 21, 27, 28, 199.

75. Coquillette and Kimball, *On the Battlefield of Merit*, 345, 354–355.

76. Mark DeWolfe Howe quotes from Thayer's diary in his "Preliminary Note" to James Bradley Thayer, "The First Law School Lecture of James Bradley Thayer," *Journal of Legal Education* 2 (Autumn 1949): 2–3.

77. Thayer, "First Law School Lecture," 5.

78. For examples of historians' conflation of classification and induction with formalism, see Neil Duxbury, *Patterns of American Jurisprudence* (Oxford: Clarendon, 1995), 15; Morton J. Horwitz, *The Transformation of American Law, 1870–1960: The Crisis of Legal Orthodoxy* (Oxford: Oxford University Press, 1992), 17–18; James E. Herget, *American Jurisprudence, 1870–1970: A History* (Houston, TX: Rice University Press, 1990), 101.

79. Thayer's jurisprudence neatly fits into the "balanced realism" described by Brian Tamanaha in *Beyond the Formalist-Realist Divide: The Role of Politics in Judging* (Princeton, NJ: Princeton University Press, 2009), 6. Tamanaha explains, "To say that law should be organized rationally . . . and to engage in this process are not to say that legal rules are immutable or autonomous, or that only logic matters in the development and application of the law" (52).

80. Thayer, "First Law School Lecture," 6.

81. Thayer, 9.

82. Thayer, 9.

83. Thayer, 14.

84. Thayer, 6.

85. Thayer, "Right of Eminent Domain," 242.

86. James Bradley Thayer, *A Western Journey with Mr. Emerson* (Boston: Little, Brown, 1884), 36–37.

87. Thayer, "First Law School Lecture," 15.

88. G. Edward White likewise concludes that Thayer's "embrace of secularization was partial" in "Revisiting James Bradley Thayer," *Northwestern University Law Review* 88 (1993): 71–72. For the secularization of academic knowledge, see Julie A. Reuben, *The Making of the Modern University: Intellectual Transformation and the Marginalization of Morality* (Chicago: University of Chicago Press, 1996).

89. Thayer, "First Law School Lecture," 5.

90. Thayer, 15.

91. Thayer, 6.

92. Thayer, 10.

93. Thayer, 13.

94. Thayer, 3.

95. Thayer, 17.

96. Thayer, 7.

97. Kimball, *Inception*, 207, 237.

98. Kimball, 207–208.

99. Kimball, 214–216.

100. J. B. Ames, John Chipman Gray, Jeremiah Smith, and Samuel Williston, "James Bradley Thayer," *Harvard Law Review* 15 (April 1902): 606.

101. Kimball, *Inception*, 195–196.

102. Quoted in Kimball, 216.

103. *The Centennial History of the Harvard Law School, 1817–1917* (Harvard Alumni Association, 1918), 280.

104. Ames et al., "James Bradley Thayer," 609.

105. Ames et al., 607.

106. Ames et al., 606.

107. Ames et al., 600.

108. Kimball, *Inception*, 239–240.

109. Note that the first half of Langdell's casebook appeared in 1870, followed by the full casebook in 1871. See C. C. Langdell, *A Selection of Cases on the Law of Contracts* (Boston: Little, Brown, 1871). His casebook is generally referred to by its abbreviated title *Cases on Contracts*.

110. Coquillette and Kimball, *On the Battlefield of Merit*, 313–315.

111. Kimball, *Inception*, 242. Thayer quoted in Coquillette and Kimball, *On the Battlefield of Merit*, 472.

2. THAYER'S SCHOLARSHIP

1. J. B. Ames, John Chipman Gray, Jeremiah Smith, and Samuel Williston, "James Bradley Thayer," *Harvard Law Review* 15 (April 1902): 604–605.

2. Aviva Orenstein, "Sex, Threats, and Absent Victims: The Lessons of *Regina v. Bedingfield* for Modern Confrontation and Domestic Violence Cases," *Fordham Law Review* 79 (October 2010): 116–117.

3. "Declarations as Part of the Res Gesta," *Columbia Law Review* 3 (May 1903): 351–353.

4. James B. Thayer, "Bedingfield's Case—Declarations as a Part of the Res Gesta. [Part] I," *American Law Review* 14 (December 1880): 818–820.

5. James B. Thayer, "Bedingfield's Case—Declarations as a Part of the Res Gesta. [Part] II," *American Law Review* 15 (January 1881): 10.

6. James B. Thayer, "Bedingfield's Case—Declarations as a Part of the Res Gesta. [Part] III," *American Law Review* 15 (February 1881): 107.

7. Thayer, "Bedingfield's Case . . . III," 77.

8. James Bradley Thayer, "Constitutionality of Legislation: The Precise Question for a Court," *Nation* 980 (April 10, 1884): 314–315.

9. Thayer, 314.

10. Thayer, 314.

11. Thayer, 315.

12. Robert G. Street, "How Far Questions of Public Policy May Enter into Judicial Decisions," *Annual Report of the American Bar Association* 6 (1883): 182–186.

13. Wm. M. Meigs, "The Relation of the Judiciary to the Constitution," *American Law Review* 19 (March–April 1885): 192, 198, 201, 192.

14. For a contemporary whose views on judicial review were more closely aligned with Thayer's than with Street's or Meigs's, see Charles B. Elliott, "The Legislatures and the Courts: The Power to Declare Statutes Unconstitutional," *Political Science Quarterly* 5 (June 1890): 257.

15. James Bradley Thayer, "Advisory Opinions," in *Legal Essays* (Boston: Boston Book Company, 1908), 42.

16. Thayer, 42.

17. Thayer, 46, 56, 59. On the reversal of the Maine precedent, see 56n1.

18. Bruce Kimball, *The Inception of Modern Professional Education: C. C. Langdell, 1826–1906* (Chapel Hill: University of North Carolina Press, 2009), 256.

19. Charles Sherman Haight, "James Bradley Thayer," *Columbia Law Review* 2 (April 1902): 239.

20. James B. Thayer, "Legal Tender," *Harvard Law Review* 1 (May 1887): 73.

21. Thayer, 79–80.

22. Thayer, 80.

23. James Bradley Thayer, *Select Cases on Evidence at the Common Law: With Notes* (Cambridge, MA: Charles W. Sever, 1892).

24. Jay Hook, "A Brief Life of James Bradley Thayer," *Northwestern University Law Review* 88 (1993): 5.

25. Thayer, *Select Cases*, iii.

26. J. M. N., "Select Cases on Evidence at the Common Law. Review," *Harvard Law Review* 6 (October 1892): 159–160.

27. "Select Cases on Evidence at the Common Law. Review," *American Law Review* 26 (September–October 1892): 804, 803.

28. James Bradley Thayer, *A Selection of Cases on Evidence at the Common Law: With Notes*, 2nd ed. (Cambridge, MA: Charles W. Sever, 1900).

29. William P. LaPiana, *Logic and Experience: The Origin of Modern American Legal Education* (New York: Oxford University Press, 1994), 125.

30. James B. Thayer, "The Origin and Scope of the American Doctrine of Constitutional Law," *Harvard Law Review* 7 (October 1893): 144.

31. Thayer, 151.

32. Thayer, 144.

33. Thayer, 149.

34. Thayer, 136, 153.

35. Thayer, 152.

36. Thayer, 138.

37. Thayer, 155–156.

38. Thayer, 144.

39. Thayer, 155.

40. Thayer, 138–145. For a discussion of the historical content of "Origin and Scope," see David Rabban, *Law's History: American Legal Thought and the Transatlantic Turn to History* (Cambridge: Cambridge University Press, 2012), 311–317.

41. Thayer, "Origin and Scope," 145–146.

42. Little, Brown to James Bradley Thayer, November 17, 1893, box 16, folder 8, JBT.

43. Correspondence concerning Thayer's article on constitutional law, box 16, folder 7, JBT: William B. Hornblower to Thayer, November 6, 1893; John F. Dillon to Thayer, November 21, 1893; H. von Holst to Thayer, November 11, 1893; Thomas M. Cooley to Thayer, November 23, 1893.

44. "Constitutional Law," *Law Book News* 1 (February 1894): 59.

45. Review of "The Origin and Scope of the American Doctrine of Constitutional Law," by James Bradley Thayer, *Yale Law Journal* 3 (February 1894): 108.

46. Wm. M. Meigs, "Expository Statutes Are Not Unconstitutional!" *American Law Register and Review* 44 (January 1896): 25.

47. "Editorial Notes and Comments. A Paper by Professor Thayer. Constitutional Law," *American Law Register and Review* 42 (January 1894): 75.

48. David M. Rabban, *Free Speech in Its Forgotten Years, 1870–1920* (New York: Cambridge University Press, 1997), demonstrates that although mainstream liberals sought to protect unpopular speech only with the advent of World War I and its attendant restrictions, free speech had been a salient issue for radical libertarians in the prewar decades. In other words, at least some of Thayer's contemporaries were engaged with free speech jurisprudence during his lifetime, even as he was not.

49. *Nation* 57, 1484 (1884), box 16, folder 7, JBT.

50. Thayer, "Origin and Scope," 154–155.

51. *Nation* 57, 1484 (1884).

52. Irving Browne, "American Letter," *Law Journal* 29 (January 20, 1894): 35.

53. E. Alix, "Section Df. La Langue Anglaise," *Bulletin Mensuel De La Société de Législation Comparée* 6 et 7 (Juin–Juillet 1894): 435–436; W. Harrison Moore, *The Constitution of the Commonwealth of Australia* (Glasgow: University Press, 1902), 1:84n1.

54. James Bradley Thayer, *Cases on Constitutional Law: With Notes*, 2 vols. (Cambridge, MA: Charles W. Sever, 1894–1895).

55. Hook, "Brief Life," 5.

56. John W. Burgess, "Cases on Constitutional Law. Review," *Political Science Quarterly* 10 (September 1895): 547.

57. W. D. L., "Cases on Constitutional Law. Review," *American Law Register and Review* 43 (June 1895): 417.

58. Simeon E. Baldwin, "Cases on Constitutional Law. Review," *American Historical Review* 1 (October 1895): 167.

59. James Bradley Thayer, "The Teaching of English Law at Universities," *Harvard Law Review* 9, 3 (October 1895): 169, 172. For a discussion of the historical content of Thayer's speech, see Rabban, *Law's History*, 10–15.

60. Thayer, "Teaching of English Law," 174.

61. Thayer, 175, 179, 183, 184.

62. James Parker Hall, "James Bradley Thayer," in *Great American Lawyers*, ed. William D. Lewis (Philadelphia: John C. Winston, 1909), 8:372.

63. William Howard Taft to James Bradley Thayer, May 4, 1896, box 18, folder 18, JBT.

64. William Howard Taft to James Bradley Thayer, May 15, 1896, box 18, folder 18, JBT.

65. Kimball, *Inception*, 281–287.

66. Daniel R. Coquillette and Bruce A. Kimball, *On the Battlefield of Merit: Harvard Law School, the First Century* (Cambridge, MA: Harvard University Press, 2015), 499–509, 521.

67. Hall, "James Bradley Thayer," 8:353.

68. Simon Greenleaf, *A Treatise on the Law of Evidence* (Boston: Little, Brown, 1842).

69. The two dominant English treatises were Samuel March Phillipps, *A Treatise on the Law of Evidence*, 2nd ed. (London: A. Strahan, 1815), and Thomas Starke, *A Practical Treatise on the Law of Evidence, and Digest of Proofs, in Civil and Criminal Proceedings*, ed. Theron Metcalf (Philadelphia: Wells & Lilly, 1826). Only one evidence treatise by an American author appeared before 1842: Zephaniah Swift, *A Digest of the Law of Evidence, in Civil and Criminal Cases. And a Treatise on Bills of Exchange, and Promissory Notes* (Hartford, CT: Oliver D. Cooke, 1810). Swift's work did little to replace that of Phillipps and Starke, which continued to monopolize the American market.

70. Simon Greenleaf, *A Treatise on the Law of Evidence*, 16th ed., rev. John Henry Wigmore (Boston: Little, Brown, 1899), 1:v–vi. Neither of the two American treatises on evidence from the latter half of the nineteenth century posed a serious challenge to Greenleaf's dominance: John Appleton, *The Rules of Evidence: Stated and Discussed* (Philadelphia: T. & J. W. Johnson, 1860); Alexander M. Burrill, *A Treatise on the Nature, Principles, and Rules of Circumstantial Evidence: Especially that of the Presumptive Kind in Criminal Cases* (New York: Baker, Voorhis, 1868). William Twining writes that the former proved successful "in enabling the accused to give evidence in criminal cases," while the latter "does not seem to have made much impact." William Twining, *Rethinking Evidence: Exploratory Essays*, 2nd ed. (Cambridge: Cambridge University Press, 2006), 55.

71. Greenleaf, *Treatise on the Law of Evidence*, 16th ed., 1:828. For industrialization and tort law, see G. Edward White, *Tort Law in America: An Intellectual History* (Oxford: Oxford University Press, 2003), 16. For the judiciary's acceptance of intent as germane to tort law, see John Henry Wigmore, *A Treatise on the System of Evidence in Trials at Common Law*, 4 vols. (Boston: Little, Brown, 1904–1905), 4:3374–3375, 4:3389–3390, 4:3390n2.

72. Greenleaf, *Treatise on the Law of Evidence*, 16th ed., 1:881; Wigmore, *Treatise on the System of Evidence*, 1:703–705.

73. Greenleaf, *Treatise on the Law of Evidence*, 16th ed., 1:850–851.

74. Wm. Reynolds, "National Codification of the Law of Evidence: Its Advantages and Practicability," *American Law Review* 16 (January 1882): 4.

75. James Bradley Thayer, *A Preliminary Treatise on Evidence at the Common Law* (Boston: Little, Brown, 1898), 511.

76. Tal Golan, *Laws of Men and Laws of Nature: The History of Scientific Expert Testimony in England and America* (Cambridge, MA: Harvard University Press, 2004), 143.

77. Thayer, *Preliminary Treatise*, 511.

78. James Bradley Thayer, *A Preliminary Treatise on Evidence at the Common Law. Part II. Other Preliminary Topics* (Boston: Little, Brown, 1898); Thayer, *Preliminary Treatise*.

79. Thayer, *Preliminary Treatise*, 531.

80. Thayer, 267; Oliver Wendell Holmes Jr., *The Common Law* (Boston: Little, Brown, 1881), 1; Thayer, *Preliminary Treatise*, 3–4, 273, 514. Note that the parol evidence rule actually falls under contract law, but it was often discussed in treatises on evidence.

81. Thayer, *Preliminary Treatise*, 518, 319.

82. For a discussion of the historical content of Thayer's *Preliminary Treatise*, see Rabban, *Law's History*, 269–289.

83. Thayer, *Preliminary Treatise*, 251–252, 204, 297.

84. Thayer, 536, 273–274, 529.

85. Thayer, 48, 181–182.

86. Thayer, 226.

87. Thayer, 274, 271, 343.

88. Thayer, 447, 382, 274.

89. Thayer, 531.

90. Thayer, 529–530. Thayer's handwritten notes produced while preparing the follow-up to the *Preliminary Treatise* are in box 11, folders 2–4, JBT. That Thayer saw his treatise as an exercise in prescription, not merely description, aligns with Christopher Tomlins's argument that the treatise as a genre was "not just . . . the means to instantiate a particular legal culture or legal ideology and a record of its alteration over time (although plainly it is that) but also . . . a means to achieve certain strategic ends." Christopher Tomlins, "Commentary: Effects of Scale; Toward a History of the Literature of Law," in *Law Books in Action: Essays on the Anglo-American Legal Treatise*, ed. Angela Fernandez and Markus D. Dubber (Oxford: Hart Publishing, 2012), 241.

91. Charles L. Wells, review of *A Preliminary Treatise on Evidence at the Common Law. Part 1. Development of Trial by Jury*, by James Bradley Thayer, *American Historical Review* 2 (January 1897): 341.

92. C. A. Graves, review of *A Preliminary Treatise on Evidence at the Common Law*, by James Bradley Thayer, *Virginia Law Register* 4 (March 1899): 794, 796.

93. Review of *A Preliminary Treatise on Evidence at the Common Law*, by James Bradley Thayer, *Western Reserve Law Journal* 5 (March 1899): 51.

94. Munroe Smith, review of *A Preliminary Treatise on Evidence at the Common Law*, by James Bradley Thayer, *Political Science Quarterly* 11 (December 1896): 734.

95. R. G., review of *A Preliminary Treatise on Evidence at the Common Law*, by James Bradley Thayer, *Harvard Law Review* 10 (December 1896): 318.

96. Review of *A Preliminary Treatise on Evidence at the Common Law*, by James Bradley Thayer, *Yale Law Journal* 8 (1899): 217.

97. Frederick Pollock and Frederic William Maitland, *The History of English Law before the Time of Edward I* (Cambridge: University Press, 1895), 2:602n1.

98. F. W. Maitland, review of *A Preliminary Treatise on Evidence at the Common Law*, by James Bradley Thayer, *English Historical Review* 12 (January 1897): 148.

99. Frederick Pollock, review of *A Preliminary Treatise on Evidence at the Common Law*, by James Bradley Thayer, *Law Quarterly Review* 15 (January 1899): 86. Notwithstanding fulsome praise on both sides of the Atlantic, Thayer engaged in a sparring match in the pages of the *Harvard Law Review* over his *Preliminary Treatise*. His critic was Jabez Fox, a practicing lawyer who would soon become a judge in Massachusetts. Fox wrote a short piece that took issue with some of Thayer's semantic niceties; see Jabez Fox, "Law and Logic," *Harvard Law Review* 14 (May 1900): 39–43. Thayer published a response that largely shrugged off his detractor: "I confess that I do not know what he means. . . . It seems to be a senseless opinion." He dismissed the critique as a "man of straw" and implied that Fox had failed to read the *Preliminary Treatise* with much care. See J. B. Thayer, "Law and Logic," *Harvard Law Review* 14 (June 1900): 141–142.

100. J. G. P., review of *A Preliminary Treatise on Evidence at the Common Law*, by James Bradley Thayer, *Harvard Law Review* 12 (January 1899): 439.

101. Melville M. Bigelow, review of *A Preliminary Treatise on Evidence at the Common Law*, by James Bradley Thayer, *American Law Review* 30 (September–October 1896): 799.

102. J. G. P., review, 439.

103. Graves, review, 796.

104. Brian Z. Tamanaha, *Beyond the Formalist-Realist Divide: The Role of Politics in Judging* (Princeton, NJ: Princeton University Press, 2009), 84, 86–87.

105. James C. Carter, "The Ideal and Actual in the Law," *American Law Review* 24 (September–October 1890): 773.

106. James C. Carter, "Provinces of the Written and Unwritten Law," *American Law Review* 24 (January–February 1890): 15.

107. James C. Carter, *Law: Its Origin, Growth, and Function* (New York: G. P. Putnam's Sons, 1907), 73.

108. Tamanaha, *Beyond the Formalist-Realist Divide*, 20, 83.

109. John F. Dillon, *Law and Jurisprudence of England and America: Being a Series of Lectures Delivered before Yale University* (Boston: Little, Brown, 1894), 267–268.

110. Albert V. Dicey, *Lectures on the Relation between Law and Public Opinion in England during the Nineteenth Century* (New York: Macmillan, 1905), 361.

111. In *Beyond the Formalist-Realist Divide*, Tamanaha makes two interrelated arguments about legal thought in the decades surrounding the turn of the twentieth century. In opposition to the traditional narrative—which posits a formalist age from the 1870s to the 1920s—Tamanaha argues that legal realism was mainstream in the very years when formalism supposedly held sway. Not only was realism common, he insists, but formalism was marginal.

Even those reviewers who are skeptical of Tamanaha's claims are not surprised that he uncovered evidence of realism predating the 1920s. See Brian Leiter, "Legal Formalism and Legal Realism: What Is the Issue?" *Legal Theory* 16 (June 2010): 115; Alfred L. Brophy, "Did Formalism Never Exist?" review of *Beyond the Formalist-Realist Divide: The Role of Politics in Judging*, by Brian Z. Tamanaha, *Texas Law Review* 92 (December 2013): 391. The question thus becomes not whether realists existed in Thayer's era but whether they or the formalists were dominant. Leiter poses the question in these terms: "are the antiformalist quotations [Tamanaha] adduces representative of views in the putatively 'formalist' age?" Brophy's review offers an answer to that question. Although Tamanaha finds proponents of realism during the allegedly formalist age, Brophy doubts that they reflected mainstream opinion: "Obscure thinkers are often given [by Tamanaha] outsized importance as representatives of their age" (396). By way of rebuttal, Tamanaha suggests that no amount of evidence about the dominance of realism would satisfy his critics: "What would be enough to falsify the conventional view of the formalist age? If every showing—no matter how plentiful—is dismissed as a counterexample, the story is impervious to refutation; immune from the evidence." Brian Z. Tamanaha, "The Mounting Evidence against the 'Formalist Age,'" *Texas Law Review* 92 (May 2014): 1676.

One point weighing in Tamanaha's favor is that he finds realist views among figures whom historians consider formalists. As he puts it: "The very jurists that historians have identified as *leading legal formalists*, themselves, offered realistic accounts of law and judging" ("Mounting Evidence," 1678). Tamanaha's findings dovetail with those of Bruce Kimball, who concludes that C. C. Langdell was unfairly derided as a formalist when in fact he espoused Holmesian views. See Bruce A. Kimball, "Langdell on Contracts and Legal Reasoning: Correcting the Holmesian Caricature," *Law and History Review* 25 (Summer 2007): 346–347. Similarly, historians have described John Henry Wigmore as a formalist even though he was a consummate realist; see Andrew Porwancher, *John Henry Wigmore and the Rules of Evidence: The Hidden Origins of Modern Law* (Columbia: University of Missouri Press, 2016). Further research could provide additional clarity by disaggregating the various realist tenets and investigating when each one became mainstream.

112. Dillon, *Law and Jurisprudence of England and America*, 208.

113. W. G. Hammond, "American Law Schools Past and Future," *Southern Law Review* 7 (August 1881): 413.

114. William G. Hammond, ed., *Legal and Political Hermeneutics, or Principles of Interpretation and Construction in Law and Politics, with Remarks on Precedents and Authorities*, by Francis Lieber (St. Louis: F. H. Thomas, 1880), 328.

115. Hall, "James Bradley Thayer," 8:372.

116. Steve Sheppard, ed., *The History of Legal Education in the United States* (Pasadena, CA: Salem Press, 1999), 2:1170.

117. Samuel Haber, *The Quest for Authority and Honor in the American Professions, 1750–1900* (Chicago: University of Chicago Press, 1991), 212.

118. Burton J. Bledstein writes, "As many professions as feasible would locate the center of their authority within university schools." Burton J. Bledstein, *The Culture of*

Professionalism: The Middle Class and the Development of Higher Education in America (New York: W. W. Norton, 1976), 325.

119. Brian J. Moline, "Early American Legal Education," *Washburn Law Journal* 42 (Summer 2004): 801.

120. James Bradley Thayer, "Our New Possessions," *Harvard Law Review* 12 (February 1899): 468.

121. Samuel Atkins Eliot, *A History of Cambridge, Massachusetts (1630–1913)* (Cambridge, MA: Cambridge Tribune, 1913), 117, 119, 121, 123, 125–126.

122. James Bradley Thayer, *John Marshall* (Boston: Houghton Mifflin, 1901), prefatory note.

123. *Marbury v. Madison*, 5 U.S. 137, 177 (1803).

124. Thayer, *John Marshall*, 96, 97, 84. Thayer included a footnote in "Origin and Scope" (130n1) belittling *Marbury* as "overpraised."

125. Thayer, *John Marshall*, 98–100. Thayer made a passing reference to the political questions doctrine in "Origin and Scope" (134–135) but did not tease out its implications as fully as he did in his Marshall biography.

126. Thayer, *John Marshall*, 103–104.

127. Thayer, 106, 107, 109.

128. Thayer, 105; *Ex Parte Robert B. Randolph* (1833).

129. Review of *John Marshall*, by James Bradley Thayer, *Harvard Law Review* 15 (June 1901): 162.

130. Joseph H. Beale, "Langdell, Gray, Thayer and Ames—Their Contribution to the Study and Teaching of Law," *New York University Law Quarterly Review* 8 (March 1931): 392.

131. Ames et al., "James Bradley Thayer," 606–607.

132. Hall, "James Bradley Thayer," 8:384.

133. Ames et al., "James Bradley Thayer," 602.

134. Hall, "James Bradley Thayer," 8:383.

135. Hall, 8:377.

136. Ames et al., "James Bradley Thayer," 606.

137. *The Centennial History of the Harvard Law School, 1817–1917* (Harvard Alumni Association, 1918), 283.

3. THAYER'S PROTÉGÉ

1. "The Law Loses a Humanist," *Boston Evening Transcript*, March 6, 1935, box 2, folder 15, seq. 5, OWHA.

2. *Quinquennial Catalogue of the Officers and Graduates of Harvard University* (Cambridge, MA: Harvard University Press, 1890), 23.

3. "Law Loses a Humanist."

4. Holmes also shared with Thayer an appreciation for Ralph Waldo Emerson. See Adam H. Hines, "Ralph Waldo Emerson and Oliver Wendell Holmes, Jr.: The Subtle

Rapture of Postponed Power," *Journal of Supreme Court History* 44 (March 2019): 39–52.

5. Mark DeWolfe Howe, *Justice Oliver Wendell Holmes*, vol. 1, *The Shaping Years, 1841–1870* (Boston: Harvard University Press, 1957), 258–259.

6. Oliver Wendell Holmes Jr., *Speeches* (Boston: Little, Brown, 1891), 70.

7. James Kent, *Commentaries on American Law*, 4 vols. (New York: O. Halsted, 1826).

8. Review of *Commentaries on American Law*, by James Kent, edited by Oliver Wendell Holmes Jr., *North American Review* 118 (April 1874): 386.

9. Review of *Commentaries on American Law*, 386.

10. James Bradley Thayer to James Kent, December 1869, box 1, folder 23, seq. 1–2, OWHA.

11. Sheldon Novick, *Honorable Justice: The Life of Oliver Wendell Holmes* (Boston: Little, Brown, 1990), 119.

12. Review of *Commentaries on American Law*, by James Kent, edited by O. W. Holmes Jr., *Central Law Journal* 1 (February 1874): 85.

13. "Career of Justice Holmes; Life of Long Public Service Beginning in Days of Civil War," *Springfield (MA) Daily Republican*, March 7, 1935, 8, box 2, folder 17, seq. 111, OWHA.

14. Oliver Wendell Holmes Jr. to James Bradley Thayer, July 15, 1872, box 1, folder 23, seq. 18, OWHA.

15. James Kent to James Bradley Thayer, December 16, 1873, box 1, folder 23, seq. 22–23, OWHA.

16. Quoted in G. Edward White, *Justice Oliver Wendell Holmes: Law and the Inner Self* (New York: Oxford University Press, 1993), 126.

17. James Kent, *Commentaries on American Law*, 12th ed., ed. Oliver Wendell Holmes Jr. (Boston: Little, Brown, 1873), 1:vii–viii.

18. Review of *Commentaries on American Law*, by James Kent, edited by Oliver Wendell Holmes Jr., *Albany Law Journal* 9 (March 7, 1874): 160.

19. Review of *Commentaries on American Law*, *Central Law Journal* 1 (February 1874): 85.

20. "Law Loses a Humanist."

21. O. W. Holmes Jr., "Possession," *American Law Review* 12 (July 1878): 688–720; O. W. Holmes Jr., "Common Carriers and the Common Law," *American Law Review* 13 (July 1879): 609–631.

22. James Bradley Thayer to Oliver Wendell Holmes Jr., July 21, 1879, box 22, folder 28, seq. 1, OWHP.

23. Louis Menand, *The Metaphysical Club: A Story of Ideas in America* (New York: Farrar, Straus & Giroux, 2001), 338.

24. Oliver Wendell Holmes Jr., *The Common Law* (Boston: Little, Brown, 1881), 1.

25. Menand, *Metaphysical Club*, 338.

26. G. Edward White, *Oliver Wendell Holmes, Jr.*, 2nd ed. (New York: Oxford University Press, 2006), 41.

27. James Bradley Thayer to Oliver Wendell Holmes Jr., December 22, 1880, box 22, folder 28, seq. 5, OWHP.

28. Holmes, *Common Law*, iii.

29. James Bradley Thayer to Oliver Wendell Holmes Jr., December 22, 1880, box 22, folder 28, seq. 4, OWHP.

30. James Bradley Thayer to Oliver Wendell Holmes Jr., December 24, 1880, box 22, folder 28, seq. 7, OWHP. Those articles were the same two that Thayer had praised in his July 21, 1879, letter: "Possession" and "Common Carriers and the Common Law." Thayer's December 24, 1880, letter uses the phrase "the bailee + carrier articles," with "bailee" referring to the first article and "carrier" to the second.

31. James Bradley Thayer to Oliver Wendell Holmes Jr., March 6, 1881, box 22, folder 28, seq. 9, OWHP.

32. Holmes, *Common Law*, 1. Holmes lifted the opening from a book review he had published earlier; see "Book Notices," *American Law Review* 14 (March 1880): 234.

33. White, *Holmes: Law and the Inner Self*, 148–153, 170, 183–185; Brian Z. Tamanaha, "Understanding Legal Realism," *Texas Law Review* 87 (March 2009): 748; James E. Herget, *American Jurisprudence, 1870–1970: A History* (Houston, TX: Rice University Press, 1990), 46.

34. White, *Holmes: Law and the Inner Self*, 149.

35. James Bradley Thayer to Governor John Long, January 13, 1881, box 29, folder 17, seq. 27, OWHH.

36. Oliver Wendell Holmes Jr. to the Baroness Moncheur, January 9, 1915, box 20, folder 1, seq. 33–34, OWHH.

37. James Bradley Thayer, "Memorandum Book D," January 29, 1882, box 15, folder 29, seq. 32–37, OWHH.

38. "Governor Long Completes His Reorganization of the Supreme Court," *Boston Globe*, December 9, 1882.

39. Thayer, "Memorandum Book D," December 18, 1882.

40. Oliver Wendell Holmes Jr. to Charles William Eliot, November 1, 1881, in Mark DeWolfe Howe, *Justice Oliver Wendell Holmes*, vol. 2, *The Proving Years, 1870–1882* (Cambridge, MA: Harvard University Press, 1957), 261.

41. Thayer, "Memorandum Book D," December 18, 1882. The discussion of Thayer's role in Holmes's life ends with this episode in many biographies of Holmes. See Liva Baker, *The Justice from Beacon Hill: The Life and Times of Oliver Wendell Holmes* (New York: HarperCollins, 1991), 264; Howe, *Justice Oliver Wendell Holmes*, 2:269; White, *Holmes: Law and the Inner Self*, 200. In Novick's *Honorable Justice*, 149, the discussion of Thayer concludes with Kent's *Commentaries*.

42. Thayer, "Memorandum Book D," December 18, 1882.

43. Oliver Wendell Holmes Jr. to James Bradley Thayer, October 15, 1884, box 27, folder 15, JBT.

44. Thayer's letter is alluded to in Oliver Wendell Holmes Jr. to James Bradley Thayer, October 20, 1884, box 27, folder 15, JBT.

45. *Winthrop Delano v. Trustees of Smith Charities*, 138 Mass. 63, 64 (1884).

46. Holmes to Thayer, October 20, 1884.

47. Holmes, *Speeches,* 33.

48. *Commonwealth v. William B. Briant,* 142 Mass. 463, 464 (1886).

49. James Bradley Thayer, *A Preliminary Treatise on Evidence at the Common Law* (Boston: Little, Brown, 1898), 319.

50. *Briant,* 142 Mass. at 464.

51. James Bradley Thayer to Oliver Wendell Holmes Jr., January 13, 1888, box 22, folder 28, seq. 20, OWHP.

52. James Bradley Thayer to Oliver Wendell Holmes Jr., January 25, 1888, box 22, folder 28, seq. 23, OWHP.

53. James B. Thayer, "Presumptions and the Law of Evidence," *Harvard Law Review* 3 (November 1889): 149, 156n2; see also 147n4.

54. Oliver Wendell Holmes Jr. to James Bradley Thayer, November 23, 1889, box 24, folder 2, JBT.

55. Thayer, "Presumptions," 144.

56. Thayer, *Preliminary Treatise,* 265.

57. James B. Thayer, "'Law and Fact' in Jury Trials," *Harvard Law Review* 4 (November 1890): 147–148, 160–161, 169–170.

58. *Boston Daily Advertiser,* February 1, 1878, 1.

59. Oliver Wendell Holmes Jr. to James Bradley Thayer, December 3, 1890, box 18, folder 1, seq. 1–2, OWHH.

60. James Bradley Thayer to Oliver Wendell Holmes Jr., October 25, 1891, box 22, folder 29, seq. 1–2, OWHP.

61. *Commonwealth v. Josiah Perry,* 155 Mass. 117, 124 (1891) (Holmes, J., dissenting).

62. James Bradley Thayer to Oliver Wendell Holmes Jr., December 4, 1891, box 22, folder 29, seq. 6–7, OWHP.

63. Oliver Wendell Holmes Jr. to James Bradley Thayer, August 24, 1893, box 18, folder 1, seq. 11, OWHH.

64. *Hadley P. Hanson v. Globe Newspaper Company,* 159 Mass. 293, 300 (1893) (Holmes, J., dissenting).

65. *Hanson,* 159 Mass. at 301.

66. James Bradley Thayer to Oliver Wendell Holmes Jr., August 27, 1893, box 22, folder 29, seq. 19–20, OWHP.

67. Oliver Wendell Holmes Jr. to James Bradley Thayer, November 2, 1893, box 18, folder 1, seq. 16, OWHH.

68. Oliver Wendell Holmes Jr. to James Bradley Thayer, November 3, 1893, box 18, folder 1, seq. 17, OWHH.

69. Oliver Wendell Holmes Jr. to James Bradley Thayer, March 28, 1894, box 18, folder 1, seq. 20, OWHH.

70. Oliver Wendell Holmes Jr. to James Bradley Thayer, May 4, 1894, box 18, folder 1, seq. 21, OWHH.

71. Oliver Wendell Holmes Jr., "Privilege, Malice, and Intent," *Harvard Law Review* 8 (April 1894): 3.

72. Morton J. Horwitz, *The Transformation of American Law, 1870–1960: The Crisis of Legal Orthodoxy* (New York: Oxford University Press, 1992), 131.

73. Oliver Wendell Holmes Jr. to James Bradley Thayer, November 10, 1894, box 18, folder 1, seq. 24, OWHH.

74. Oliver Wendell Holmes Jr. to James Bradley Thayer, June 16, 1896, box 18, folder 1, seq. 25, OWHH.

75. Oliver Wendell Holmes, "The Path of the Law," *Harvard Law Review* 10 (March 1897): 469, 460–461, 466.

76. Holmes, 474.

77. James Bradley Thayer to Oliver Wendell Holmes Jr., January 11, 1897, box 22, folder 30, seq. 6–7, OWHP.

78. Oliver Wendell Holmes Jr. to James Bradley Thayer, January 12, 1897, box 18, folder 2, seq. 1, OWHH.

79. Oliver Wendell Holmes Jr. to James Bradley Thayer, February 11, 1897, box 18, folder 2, seq. 2, OWHH.

80. Oliver Wendell Holmes Jr. to James Bradley Thayer, November 23, 1898, box 18, folder 2, seq. 5, OWHH. For the law review article, see Oliver Wendell Holmes, "Law in Science and Science in Law," *Harvard Law Review* 12 (February 1899): 458.

81. Oliver Wendell Holmes Jr. to James Bradley Thayer, November 29, 1898, box 18, folder 2, seq. 6, OWHH.

82. Thayer, *Preliminary Treatise*, xiii.

83. Oliver Wendell Holmes Jr. to James Bradley Thayer, December 1, 1898, box 18, folder 2, seq. 9, OWHH.

84. F. Vaughan Hawkins, "On the Principles of Legal Interpretation," appendix C in Thayer, *Preliminary Treatise*, 580, 582.

85. Oliver Wendell Holmes Jr. to James Bradley Thayer, December 1, 1898, box 18, folder 2, seq. 8, OWHH.

86. Holmes, *Common Law*, 111.

87. Oliver Wendell Holmes Jr. to James Bradley Thayer, December 11, 1898, box 22, folder 30, seq. 18–19, OWHP.

88. James Bradley Thayer to Oliver Wendell Holmes Jr., December 12, 1898, box 22, folder 30, seq. 21–22, OWHP.

89. Oliver Wendell Holmes, "The Theory of Legal Interpretation," *Harvard Law Review* 12 (January 1899): 420, 417.

90. James Bradley Thayer to Oliver Wendell Holmes Jr., July 29, 1899, box 22, folder 30, seq. 24–25, OWHP.

91. James Bradley Thayer to Oliver Wendell Holmes Jr., July 22, 1900, box 22, folder 30, seq. 32–33, OWHP. See also James Bradley Thayer, *A Selection of Cases on Evidence at the Common Law: With Notes*, 2nd ed. (Cambridge, MA: Charles W. Sever, 1900), 1053.

92. Oliver Wendell Holmes Jr. to James Bradley Thayer, September 4, 1900, box 18, folder 2, seq. 23, OWHH.

93. "Justice Holmes Confirmed," *New York Times*, December 5, 1902.

94. *Lochner v. New York*, 198 U.S. 45, 56, 64 (1905).

95. *Lochner*, 198 U.S. at 75–76 (Holmes, J., dissenting). See Herbert Spencer, *Social Statics, or the Conditions Essential to Happiness Specified, and the First of Them Developed* (London: J. Chapman, 1851).

96. Horwitz, *Transformation of American Law*, 33.

97. William M. Wiecek, *The Lost World of Classical Legal Thought: Law and Ideology in America, 1886–1937* (New York: Oxford University Press: 1998), 152; Horwitz, *Transformation of American Law*, 33; Neil Duxbury, *Patterns of American Jurisprudence* (Oxford: Clarendon Press, 1995), 30–31; David E. Bernstein, "*Lochner* Era Revisionism, Revised: *Lochner* and the Origins of Fundamental Rights Constitutionalism," *Georgetown Law Journal* 92 (November 2003): 1. For scholarship that challenges the traditional view of *Lochner*, see Stephen A. Siegel, "*Lochner* Era Jurisprudence and the American Constitutional Tradition," *North Carolina Law Review* 70 (November 1991): 15–21; Brian Tamanaha, *Beyond the Formalist-Realist Divide: The Role of Politics in Judging* (Princeton, NJ: Princeton University Press, 2010), 36.

98. Tamanaha, *Beyond the Formalist-Realist Divide*, 101.

99. James Bradley Thayer to Oliver Wendell Holmes Jr., December 4, 1891, box 22, folder 29, seq. 6–7, OWHP.

100. Stephen Budiansky, *Oliver Wendell Holmes: A Life in War, Law, and Ideas* (New York: W. W. Norton, 2019), 293, acknowledges the relationship among *Lochner*, judicial deference, Thayer, and Holmes. Other biographers, including Novick (*Honorable Justice*, 306–307), White (*Holmes: Law and the Inner Self*, 326–327), and Baker (*Justice from Beacon Hill*, 416–417), do not explicitly link Thayer to Holmes's famous dissent.

101. Oliver Wendell Holmes Jr. to Frederick Pollock, April 23, 1910, in *The Pollock–Holmes Letters*, ed. Mark DeWolfe Howe (Cambridge: Cambridge University Press, 1942), 1:163.

102. *Abrams v. United States*, 250 U.S. 616, 617 (1919).

103. *Abrams*, 250 U.S. at 630 (Holmes, J., dissenting).

104. *Schenck v. United States*, 249 U.S. 47, 52 (1919).

105. For a discussion of how Holmes's dissent in *Abrams* ran to counter to his earlier approach in *Schenck* and *Lochner*, see Edward S. Corwin, *Liberty against Government: The Rise, Flowering and Decline of a Famous Juridical Concept* (Baton Rouge: Louisiana State University Press, 1948), 156n63.

106. Thomas Healy, *The Great Dissent: How Oliver Wendell Holmes Changed His Mind—and Changed the History of Free Speech in America* (New York: Metropolitan Books, 2013), 201–210, 214.

4. THAYER'S STUDENTS

1. Melvin I. Urofsky, *Louis D. Brandeis: A Life* (New York: Pantheon Books, 2009), 3, 4, 6, 8, 15, 11, 21, 23, 25.

2. Urofsky, 27–28.

3. Louis Brandeis to Alice Goldmark, October 13, 1890, in *Letters of Louis D. Brandeis*,

vol. 1 (1870–1907), *Urban Reformer,* ed. Melvin I. Urofsky and David W. Levy (Albany: State University of New York Press, 1971), 1:93.

4. Urofsky, *Brandeis: A Life,* 30.

5. Urofsky, 33, 31.

6. Quoted in Alpheus Thomas Mason, *Brandeis: A Free Man's Life* (New York: Viking Press, 1946), 43.

7. Quoted in Mason, 43.

8. Brandeis to Goldmark, October 13, 1890. Another luminary whom Thayer introduced to Brandeis was the celebrated English jurist Sir Frederick Pollock. See Urofsky, *Brandeis: A Life,* 83.

9. Urofsky, *Brandeis: A Life,* 38–40, 42–44.

10. Louis Brandeis to Walter Bond Douglas, July 6, 1879, in *Letters of Brandeis,* 1:36. For Douglas and Brandeis as roommates, see *Letters of Brandeis,* 1:18. For the salary from part-time work, see Urofsky, *Brandeis: A Life,* 44. See also Philippa Strum, *Louis D. Brandeis: Justice for the People* (Cambridge, MA: Harvard University Press, 1984), 28.

11. Brandeis to Goldmark, October 13, 1890.

12. Mason, *Brandeis,* 65.

13. Urofsky, *Brandeis: A Life,* 78–79.

14. James Bradley Thayer, "Memorandum Book D," January 29, 1882, box 15, folder 29, seq. 33, OWHH.

15. Thayer, "Memorandum Book D," January 29, 1882. For the grandfather's profession as a shipbuilder, see Mason, *Brandeis,* 65.

16. Thayer, "Memorandum Book D," January 29, 1882.

17. Thayer, "Memorandum Book D," January 29, 1882.

18. Louis Brandeis to Oliver Wendell Holmes Jr., December 9, 1882, in *Letters of Brandeis,* 1:65.

19. James Parker Hall, "James Bradley Thayer," in *Great American Lawyers,* ed. William D. Lewis (Philadelphia: John C. Winston, 1909), 8:345; Daniel R. Coquillette and Bruce A. Kimball, *On the Battlefield of Merit: Harvard Law School, the First Century* (Cambridge, MA: Harvard University Press, 2015), 625.

20. Thayer, "Memorandum Book D," January 29, 1882.

21. Bruce Kimball, *The Inception of Modern Professional Education: C. C. Langdell, 1826–1906* (Chapel Hill: University of North Carolina Press, 2009), 229–230.

22. Quoted in Mason, *Brandeis,* 65.

23. Kimball, *Inception,* 84, 168, 207–208, 349.

24. Quoted in Mason, *Brandeis,* 66. For Brandeis's health issues, see Urofsky, *Brandeis: A Life,* 33–35. See also Strum, *Brandeis,* 35–36.

25. Thayer's close relationship with Brandeis suggests that he was free of the antisemitism that was still common in elite circles. Still, one letter in the Thayer Papers raises questions. In 1872 a relative of Thayer's in New York complained to him about a twenty-two-year-old Jew who worked in a family-run baking business and was active in ward politics in Brooklyn. "Meyer is a German Jew," the relative wrote, "a Greedy man as are all the Jews." Thayer forwarded the letter to Ralph Waldo Emerson, along with a note of

his own that read, "Meyer is evidently no infant in politics." Thayer's note neither endorsed nor denounced his relative's blunt antisemitism, and his mentorship of Brandeis would not necessarily preclude him from harboring negative views of "the Jews" as an abstraction. Still, there is no known comment in Thayer's hand expressing prejudice toward Jews, and his support for abolitionism and Native American rights, long before they became mainstream causes, makes the prospect of Thayer's bigotry toward Jews that much less likely. See Henry Poor to James Bradley Thayer, September 30, 1872, box 15, folder 7, JBT; James Bradley Thayer to Ralph Waldo Emerson, October 4, 1872, box 15, folder 7, JBT. Thayer's son, Ezra, once described someone as "a rather stupid, tho' industrious, Jew," despite knowing that his father had an amiable relationship with the Jew in question, perhaps another indication that Thayer was relatively enlightened toward Jewry. See Ezra Ripley Thayer to James Bradley Thayer, n.d., box 18, folder 19, JBT.

26. Louis Brandeis to Adolph Brandeis, May 30, 1883, in *Letters of Brandeis*, 1:65, 65–66n2.

27. Urofsky, *Brandeis: A Life*, 81–83; Kimball, *Inception*, 231.

28. Urofsky, *Brandeis: A Life*, 82.

29. Louis Brandeis to Charles William Eliot, April 25, 1893, in *Letters of Brandeis*, 1:113–116.

30. Louis Brandeis to James Bradley Thayer, November 24, 1889, box 2, folder 24, JBT.

31. Quoted in David S. Schwartz, *The Spirit of the Constitution: John Marshall and the 200-Year Odyssey of* McCulloch v. Maryland (New York: Oxford University Press, 2019), 285n38.

32. Alice G. Brandeis to Mrs. Thayer, February 17, [1902], box 25, folder 9, JBT.

33. Felix Frankfurter, "Mr. Justice Brandeis and the Constitution," *Harvard Law Review* 45 (November 1931): 38. See also Strum, *Brandeis*, 335.

34. Melvin I. Urofsky, *Louis D. Brandeis and the Progressive Tradition* (Boston: Little, Brown, 1981), 51–53.

35. Quoted in Urofsky, *Brandeis: A Life*, 221.

36. *Jay Burns Baking Co. v. Bryan*, 264 U.S. 504, 534 (1924) (Brandeis, J., dissenting).

37. A rare instance of Brandeis citing Thayer was *Great Northern Railway Co. et al. v. Merchants' Elevator Co.* 259 U.S. 285, 292n1 (1922).

38. Urofsky, *Brandeis: A Life*, 477.

39. *Abrams v. United States*, 250 U.S. 616, 630 (1919) (Holmes, J., dissenting).

40. *Gilbert v. Minnesota*, 254 U.S. 325, 336, 337 (1920) (Brandeis, J., dissenting).

41. Beatrice Wigmore Hunter, Recollections, 2–3, box 17, folder 11, JHW.

42. William R. Roalfe, *John Henry Wigmore: Scholar and Reformer* (Evanston, IL: Northwestern University Press, 1977), 19–20, 71.

43. Hunter, Recollections, 3.

44. Roalfe, *Wigmore*, 10–11.

45. James Bradley Thayer to John Henry Wigmore, January 3, 1889, box 108, folder 27, JHW.

46. James Bradley Thayer to John Henry Wigmore, August 2, 1889, box 108, folder 27, JHW.

47. James Bradley Thayer to John Henry Wigmore, September 3, 1893, box 108, folder 27, JHW.

48. John Henry Wigmore to James Bradley Thayer, May 31, 1896, box 19, folder 6, JBT; John Henry Wigmore to James Bradley Thayer, October 17, 1897, box 19, folder 6, JBT; John Henry Wigmore to James Bradley Thayer, January 13, 1902, box 19, folder 6, JBT.

49. John Henry Wigmore to James Bradley Thayer, November 3, 1895, box 19, folder 6, JBT. See also John Henry Wigmore to James Bradley Thayer, December 30, 1894, box 19, folder 6, JBT.

50. John Henry Wigmore to James Bradley Thayer, May 6, 1894, box 19, folder 6, JBT; John Henry Wigmore to James Bradley Thayer, March 4, 1895, box 19, folder 6, JBT; James Bradley Thayer to John Henry Wigmore, February 28, 1895, box 108, folder 27, JHW; James Bradley Thayer to John Henry Wigmore, May 30, 1895, box 108, folder 27, JHW.

51. John Henry Wigmore to Mrs. Thayer, February 16, 1902, box 25, folder 9, JBT.

52. John Henry Wigmore to James Bradley Thayer, December 30, 1894, box 19, folder 6, JBT. He was referring to James Bradley Thayer, *Select Cases on Evidence at Common Law* (Cambridge, MA: Charles W. Sever, 1892).

53. John Henry Wigmore to James Bradley Thayer, September 23, 1900, box 19, folder 6, JBT.

54. For Wigmore's citation of Thayer's *Select Cases on Evidence*, see John Henry Wigmore, *A Treatise on the System of Evidence in Trials at Common Law*, 4 vols. (Boston: Little, Brown, 1904–1905), 2:1879n1, 2:1940n4.

55. James Bradley Thayer to John Henry Wigmore, September 23, 1899, box 108, folder 27, JHW.

56. Simon Greenleaf, *A Treatise on the Law of Evidence*, 16th ed., rev. John Henry Wigmore (Boston: Little, Brown, 1899), 1:vi–ix. Wigmore's original chapters were 4, 5, and 11.

57. Roalfe, *Wigmore*, 43.

58. James Bradley Thayer to John Henry Wigmore, September 28, 1899, box 108, folder 27, JHW.

59. James Bradley Thayer to John Henry Wigmore, February 8, 1900, box 108, folder 27, JHW.

60. James Bradley Thayer, *A Selection of Cases on Evidence at the Common Law*, 2nd ed. (Cambridge, MA: Charles W. Sever, 1900), 728.

61. John Henry Wigmore to James Bradley Thayer, September 23, 1900, box 19, folder 6, JBT.

62. Wigmore to Thayer, September 23, 1900.

63. John Henry Wigmore to James Bradley Thayer, November 30, 1901, box 19, folder 6, JBT.

64. John Henry Wigmore to James Bradley Thayer, November 23, 1898, box 19, folder 6, JBT.

65. Wigmore to Thayer, November 23, 1898.

66. John Henry Wigmore to James Bradley Thayer, May 9, 1900, box 19, folder 6, JBT.

67. James Bradley Thayer to John Henry Wigmore, May 13, 1900, box 108, folder 27, JHW.

68. James Bradley Thayer to John Henry Wigmore, September 19, 1900, box 108, folder 27, JHW.

69. John Henry Wigmore to James Bradley Thayer, January 23, 1902, box 19, folder 6, JBT.

70. John Henry Wigmore to Mrs. Thayer, February 16, 1902, box 25, folder 9, JBT. On Wigmore's strained relationship with his family, see Roalfe, *Wigmore*, 20.

71. Robert Wyness Millar, Recollections, 1, box 18, folder 1, JHW.

72. Joseph Henry Beale, "Book Reviews," *Harvard Law Review* 18 (April 1905): 478.

73. Louis Brandeis to John Henry Wigmore, August 1, 1904, box 38, folder 33, JHW.

74. "What Is Thought of Wigmore on Evidence," circa 1905, 1, box 228, folder 6, JHW.

75. James Bradley Thayer, *A Preliminary Treatise on Evidence at the Common Law* (Boston: Little, Brown, 1898), 264–265.

76. Wigmore, *Treatise*, 1:31–35. Note that Wigmore quotes Thayer's articles that were aggregated into the *Preliminary Treatise*. It is unclear why Wigmore chose to cite the original articles and not the *Preliminary Treatise*, but Thayer's language remained the same.

77. See Andrew Porwancher, *John Henry Wigmore and the Rules of Evidence: The Hidden Origins of Modern Law* (Columbia: University of Missouri Press, 2016).

78. Thayer, *Preliminary Treatise*, 428–429.

79. Wigmore, *Treatise*, 4:3481.

80. Wigmore, 2:1657.

81. Wigmore, 2:1672.

82. Thayer, *Preliminary Treatise*, 528.

83. Wigmore, *Treatise*, 2:1117.

84. Thayer, *Preliminary Treatise*, 309. For Wigmore's citation of Thayer, see Wigmore, *Treatise*, 4:3601.

85. Thayer had done legwork in preparation for the next volume; see box 11, folders 2–4, JBT.

86. Porwancher, *Wigmore*, 97–99.

87. Porwancher, 87–90.

88. Quoted in *Law Book Bulletin* 67 (October 1924): 2, 3, 4, box 228, folder 6, JHW.

89. For the dedication, see Wigmore, *Treatise*, 1:v. For the reference to Thayer as "the great master," see Wigmore, *Treatise*, 1:31. The *Treatise* was also dedicated to Charles Doe, onetime chief justice of the New Hampshire Supreme Court. Holmes was surprised by Wigmore's affection for Doe. "I thought there was not a great deal of brandy in his water," Holmes remarked. See Holmes to Wigmore, January 14, 1910, reel 39, frame 20, Oliver Wendell Holmes Jr. Papers, microfilm edition.

90. David Wigdor, *Roscoe Pound: Philosopher of Law* (Westport, CT: Greenwood Press, 1974), 3, 7–9, 18, 24, 31, 32; quotations appear on 31, 32.

91. Roscoe Pound, "Edward Henry Warren," *Harvard Law Review* 58 (October 1945): 1124–1125.

92. Roscoe Pound, "Law in Books and Law in Action," *American Law Review* 44 (January–February 1910): 12–36.

93. Wigdor, *Pound*, 46.

94. Wigdor, 71, 103, 106–109; N. E. H. Hull, *Roscoe Pound and Karl Llewellyn: Searching for an American Jurisprudence* (Chicago: University of Chicago Press, 1997), 7–8.

95. Roscoe Pound to John Henry Wigmore, April 11, 1907, box 98, folder 7, JHW.

96. Porwancher, *Wigmore*, 138, 140–143.

97. Louis Brandeis to John Henry Wigmore, May 8, 1912, box 38, folder 33, JHW.

98. Porwancher, *Wigmore*, 138.

99. Quoted in Wigdor, *Pound*, 204.

100. James Bradley Thayer, "Our New Possessions," *Harvard Law Review* 12 (February 1899): 468, 469.

101. Roscoe Pound, "Common Law and Legislation," *Harvard Law Review* 21 (April 1908): 385.

102. James Bradley Thayer, "A People without Law," in *Legal Essays* (Boston: Boston Book Company, 1908), 138.

103. Roscoe Pound, "Justice According to Law," *Columbia Law Review* 13 (December 1913): 703, 703n26.

104. Thayer, *Preliminary Treatise*, 198–199.

105. Roscoe Pound, "Some Principles of Procedural Reform," *Illinois Law Review* 4 (January 1910): 395. Note that Pound's footnote mistakenly cites page 299 rather than page 199 in the *Preliminary Treatise*.

106. Roscoe Pound, "President's Address—Taught Law," *American Law School Review* 3 (November 1912): 167–168.

107. Roscoe Pound, "Toward a Better Criminal Law," *Annual Report of the American Bar Association* 58 (1935): 326–327.

108. Roscoe Pound, "The End of Law as Developed in Legal Rules and Doctrines," *Harvard Law Review* 27 (January 1914): 195–198, 201–202, 202n29; Thayer, *Preliminary Treatise*, 9–10.

109. Roscoe Pound, *Outlines of Lectures on Jurisprudence*, 5th ed. (Cambridge, MA: Harvard University Press, 1943), 40–41.

110. "Speech of James B. Thayer," in *A Record of the Commemoration, November Fifth to the Eighth, 1886, on the Two Hundred and Fiftieth Anniversary of the Founding of Harvard College* (Cambridge, MA: John Wilson & Son, 1887), 323, 320.

111. Roscoe Pound, "The Lay Tradition as to the Lawyer," *Michigan Law Review* 12 (June 1914): 634–635, 638. Note that Pound cited page 321 of Thayer's address, but the quotation actually appears on page 320.

112. Roscoe Pound, *Readings on the History and System of the Common Law*, 2nd ed. (Boston: Boston Book Company, 1913), iii, 123–124, 151.

113. Pound, 145n1, 348n1.

114. James Bradley Thayer, "Advisory Opinions," in *Legal Essays*, 59.

115. The second edition of Pound's *Readings on History and System* was more fulsome than the first in its use of Thayer's body of work.

116. Roscoe Pound, "The Revival of Personal Government," *Proceedings of the Twenty-Third Annual Session of the Bar Association of Kansas* (1920): 138.

117. Roscoe Pound, "Do We Need a Philosophy of Law?" *Columbia Law Review* 5 (May 1905): 346.

118. Roscoe Pound, "The Place of Judge Story in the Making of American Law," *American Law Review* 48 (September–October 1914): 694.

119. Gerald Gunther, *Learned Hand: The Man and the Judge* (Cambridge, MA: Harvard University Press, 1994), 3, 5, 6, 13, 21.

120. Gunther, 40, 42–43, 13, 54.

121. Gunther, 44–45.

122. Gunther, 50.

123. Jerome N. Frank, "Some Reflections on Judge Learned Hand," *University of Chicago Law Review* 24 (1957): 684–685.

124. Learned Hand, "Samuel Williston—1861–1963," *New York State Bar Journal* 35 (April 1963): 105.

125. Quoted in Gunther, *Hand*, 50.

126. Learned Hand, "Chief Justice Stone's Conception of the Judicial Function," *Columbia Law Review* 46 (September 1946): 697.

127. Learned Hand, "Discussion of the Improvement of Technical Rules of Evidence," *Proceedings of the Academy of Political Science* 10 (July 1923): 101.

128. Law School Note-book (6) Evidence (Prof. J. B. Thayer), 1, Paige box 12, LH.

129. Hand, "Discussion," 101.

130. Law School Note-book (6), 10.

131. Law School Note-book (6), 29–37.

132. Hand, "Samuel Williston," 105.

133. Law School Note-book (6), 72.

134. Law School Note-book (6), 32.

135. Learned Hand to Edmund Morris Morgan, March 25, 1941, box 76, folder 31, LH.

136. Learned Hand, "Three Letters from Alumni," *Harvard Law School Bulletin* 4 (January 1949): 7. Louis Menand credits Thayer with imparting to Hand an anti-universalist ethic. Louis Menand, *The Metaphysical Club* (New York: Farrar, Straus & Giroux, 2001), 425.

137. Hand, "Three Letters," 7.

138. Gunther, *Hand*, 45, 54.

139. Quoted in Gunther, 687n207.

140. James Bradley Thayer, "The Presumption of Innocence in Criminal Cases," *Yale Law Journal* 6 (March 1897): 199, 211.

141. Learned Hand to James Bradley Thayer, April 12, 1897, box 16, folder 6, JBT; Gunther, *Hand*, 55.

142. Marginal notes by Learned Hand in James B. Thayer, *Selected Cases on Evidence*, 1892, Paige box 4, LH.

143. James Bradley Thayer to Learned Hand, June 24, 1897, box 10, folder 16, LH.

144. James Bradley Thayer to Learned Hand, June 29, 1897, box 10, folder 16, LH.

145. Gunther, *Hand*, 57.

146. James Bradley Thayer to Learned Hand, February 14, 1898, box 10, folder 16, LH.

147. Learned Hand, "Historical and Practical Considerations Regarding Expert Testimony," *Albany Medical Annals* 21 (November 1900): 599–617; Learned Hand, "Historical and Practical Considerations Regarding Expert Testimony," *Harvard Law Review* 15 (May 1901): 40–58.

148. Tal Golan, "Revisiting the History of Scientific Expert Testimony," *Brooklyn Law Review* 73 (Spring 2008): 913, 915–916.

149. Hand, "Historical and Practical Considerations Regarding Expert Testimony" (1901), 54–56.

150. Hand, 40n1.

151. James Bradley Thayer to Learned Hand, January 21, 1900, box 10, folder 16, LH.

152. James Bradley Thayer to Learned Hand, September 18, 1898, box 10, folder 16, LH.

153. Quoted in Gunther, *Hand*, 52.

154. Learned Hand, "Due Process of Law and the Eight-Hour Day," *Harvard Law Review* 21 (May 1908): 500.

155. Frank, "Some Reflections on Hand," 688.

156. Learned Hand, "The Speech of Justice," *Harvard Law Review* 29 (April 1916): 620–621.

157. Frank, "Some Reflections on Hand," 690.

158. *Coppage v. Kansas*, 236 U.S. 1 (1915).

159. Learned Hand, "Normal Inequalities of Fortune," *New Republic*, February 6, 1915, 5.

160. Gunther, *Hand*, 248, 252.

161. Gunther, 151–158. Quoted in *Masses Publishing Co. v. Patten* 244 F. 535, 540, 543 (S.D.N.Y. 1917).

162. Gunther, *Hand*, 162–167.

163. *United States v. Dennis et al.*, 183 F.2d 201 (2d Cir. 1950).

164. Gunther, *Hand*, 599, 601, 604, 605.

165. Quoted in Gunther, 653.

166. Learned Hand, *The Bill of Rights: The Oliver Wendell Holmes Lectures, 1958* (Cambridge, MA: Harvard University Press, 1958), 56, 69.

167. Hand's biographer tries to reconcile this inconsistency, arguing that Hand was making a policy argument rather than a constitutional argument—heightened judicial scrutiny of speech regulations was "a matter of desirability and statecraft, not constitutional interpretation." Gunther, *Hand*, 658.

168. Hand, *Bill of Rights*, 70, 71, 73.

169. Quoted in Gunther, *Hand*, 52.

5. THAYER'S HEIR

1. H. N. Hirsch, *The Enigma of Felix Frankfurter* (New York: Basic Books, 1981), 12.

2. Quoted in Sanford V. Levinson, "The Democratic Faith of Felix Frankfurter," *Stanford Law Review* 25 (February 1973): 446.

3. Helen Shirley Thomas, *Felix Frankfurter: Scholar on the Bench* (Baltimore: Johns Hopkins University Press, 1960), 3.

4. Quoted in Levinson, "Democratic Faith," 447.

5. Hirsch, *Enigma*, 12; Michael Parrish, *Felix Frankfurter and His Times: The Reform Years* (New York: Free Press, 1982), 8.

6. Harlan B. Phillips, ed., *Felix Frankfurter Reminisces* (New York: Reynal, 1960), 290; Thomas, *Frankfurter*, 3. Although he eschewed the devotional aspects of Judaism in his adulthood, at the twilight of his life he requested that a Jewish prayer known as the Kaddish be recited at his funeral, explaining, "I came into the world a Jew and I want to leave it as a Jew." Quoted in Paul A. Freund, "Felix Frankfurter (1882–1965)," *American Jewish Year Book* 67 (1966): 36.

7. Quoted in Melvin Urofsky, *Dissent and the Supreme Court: Its Role in the Court's History and the Nation's Constitutional Dialogue* (2015; reprint, New York: Vintage Books, 2017), 241.

8. Felix Frankfurter, "Law and the Law Schools," *American Bar Association Journal* 1 (October 1915): 539.

9. Felix Frankfurter, "John Marshall and the Judicial Function," *Harvard Law Review* 69 (December 1955): 231.

10. *AFL v. American Sash and Door Co.*, 335 U.S. 538, 557 (1949) (Frankfurter, J., concurring).

11. Thomas, *Frankfurter*, 4.

12. Quoted in Noah Feldman, *Scorpions: The Battles and Triumphs of FDR's Great Supreme Court Justices* (New York: Twelve, 2010), 6. See also Hirsch, *Enigma*, 20; Parrish, *Frankfurter and His Times*, 18.

13. Hirsch, *Enigma*, 19. Hirsch quotes Frankfurter reflecting on Coney Island: "The whole course of my life was changed by that diversion."

14. Hirsch, 128.

15. Quoted in Melvin I. Urofsky, *Felix Frankfurter: Judicial Restraint and Individual Liberties* (Boston: Twayne, 1991), 31. Frankfurter referred to Thayer as the jurist "who through his writings has influenced me most as to public law." Quoted in Hirsch, *Enigma*, 128.

16. Quoted in Jay Hook, "A Brief Life of James Bradley Thayer," *Northwestern University Law Review* 88 (1993): 8. Feldman writes, "Joining the diverse trinity of Brandeis, Holmes, and Thayer—progressivism, nihilism, and historicism—into a single godhead of judicial restraint was Frankfurter's most important intellectual accomplishment during his years as a professor." Feldman, *Scorpions*, 31–32. See also Thomas, *Frankfurter*, viii; Hirsch, *Enigma*, 129.

17. Quoted in Hirsch, *Enigma*, 129.

18. Felix Frankfurter, "Joseph Henry Beale," *Harvard Law Review* 56 (March 1943): 702.

19. Felix Frankfurter, "Samuel Williston: An Inadequate Tribute to a Beloved Teacher," *Harvard Law Review* 76 (May 1963): 1322.

20. Frankfurter, "John Marshall," 225.

21. Felix Frankfurter, "Edmund M. Morgan," *Vanderbilt Law Review* 14 (June 1961): 706–707.

22. Felix Frankfurter, "Eugene Wambaugh," *Harvard Law Review* 54 (November 1940): 7.

23. Urofsky, *Frankfurter: Judicial Restraint*, 2.

24. Leonard Baker, *Brandeis and Frankfurter: A Dual Biography* (New York: Harper & Row, 1984), 70.

25. Phillips, *Frankfurter Reminisces*, 78.

26. Felix Frankfurter, *Of Law and Life & Other Things that Matter* (Cambridge, MA: Harvard University Press, 1965), 59–60. Thayer's *Cases on Constitutional Law* also subscribed to a living constitutionalist approach that met with Frankfurter's approval. See James Bradley Thayer, *Cases on Constitutional Law: With Notes* (Cambridge, MA: Charles W. Sever, 1894), 1:vi; Felix Frankfurter and James M. Landis, "The Compact Clause of the Constitution—A Study in Interstate Adjustments," *Yale Law Journal* 34 (May 1925): 720n133.

27. Frankfurter, "Law and the Law Schools," 533.

28. Frankfurter, 533.

29. For a discussion of the differences between Holmes and Frankfurter, see Levinson, "Democratic Faith," 431–432; Feldman, *Scorpions*, 233; Urofsky, *Frankfurter: Judicial Restraint*, 32.

30. Phillips, *Frankfurter Reminisces*, 299–301.

31. Frankfurter, "John Marshall," 225.

32. Felix Frankfurter, "A Note on Advisory Opinions," *Harvard Law Review* 37 (June 1924): 1003–1004.

33. As Richard A. Posner puts it, "Frankfurter advocated Thayerism with a noisy passion unequaled by any other Thayerian." Richard A. Posner, "The Rise and Fall of Judicial Self-Restraint," *California Law Review* 100 (June 2012): 530. Urofsky goes even further, claiming that Frankfurter became "a prisoner of an idea—judicial restraint." Melvin I. Urofsky, "William O. Douglas and Felix Frankfurter: Ideology and Personality on the Supreme Court," *History Teacher* 24 (November 1990): 14.

34. James Bradley Thayer, *John Marshall* (Boston: Houghton, Mifflin, 1901), 103–110.

35. Frankfurter, "Note on Advisory Opinions," 1007.

36. Felix Frankfurter, "The Present Approach to Constitutional Decisions on the Bill of Rights," *Harvard Law Review* 28 (June 1915): 792–793.

37. James B. Thayer, "The Origin and Scope of the American Doctrine of Constitutional Law," *Harvard Law Review* 7 (October 1893): 156.

38. *AFL*, 335 U.S. at 556 (Frankfurter, J., concurring).

39. Thayer, "Origin and Scope," 155.

40. Frankfurter, "John Marshall," 232.

41. Thayer, *John Marshall*, 108–109.

42. Frankfurter, "Note on Advisory Opinions," 1007, 1004, 1008.

43. James Bradley Thayer, "Advisory Opinions," in *Legal Essays* (Boston: Boston Book Company, 1908), 53–54.

44. Felix Frankfurter and Adrian S. Fisher, "The Business of the Supreme Court at the October Terms, 1935 and 1936," *Harvard Law Review* 51 (1938): 620, 620n76.

45. *AFL*, 335 U.S. at 557 (Frankfurter, J., concurring).

46. Thomas, *Frankfurter*, 281.

47. Felix Frankfurter, "The Supreme Court in the Mirror of Justices," *University of Pennsylvania Law Review* 105 (April 1957): 794.

48. Thayer, *Cases on Constitutional Law*, 2:2190.

49. Frankfurter and Landis, "Compact Clause," 728–729.

50. Thayer, *John Marshall*, 83, 85.

51. Frankfurter, "John Marshall," 219.

52. Thayer, *John Marshall*, 89.

53. Frankfurter, "John Marshall," 219.

54. *Minersville School District v. Gobitis*, 310 U.S. 586 (1940).

55. Feldman, *Scorpions*, 181; Baker, *Brandeis and Frankfurter*, 400.

56. Quoted in Urofsky, *Dissent and the Supreme Court*, 241.

57. Thayer, "Origin and Scope," 156.

58. *Gobitis*, 310 U.S. at 599. Frankfurter also wrote in the same vein: "The wisdom of training children in patriotic impulses by those compulsions which necessarily pervade so much of the educational process is not for our independent judgment. Even were we convinced of the folly of such a measure, such belief would be no proof of its unconstitutionality" (598).

59. *Gobitis*, 310 U.S. at 600.

60. Feldman, *Scorpions*, 185–186, 228.

61. Quoted in Baker, *Brandeis and Frankfurter*, 405–406.

62. *West Virginia State Board of Education v. Barnette*, 319 U.S. 624, 666, 667, 651, 648 (1943) (Frankfurter, J., dissenting). Urofsky writes that *Barnette* "nearly denied the Court any role in enforcing the Bill of Rights." Melvin I. Urofsky, "The Flag Salute Case," *OAH Magazine of History* 9 (Winter 1995): 31.

63. *Barnette*, 319 U.S. at 667–670 (Frankfurter, J., dissenting).

64. Thayer, *John Marshall*, 104–110; quotation appears on 106.

65. Quoted in Baker, *Brandeis and Frankfurter*, 445. For Frankfurter's summer cottage, see Feldman, *Scorpions*, 25, who notes, "The attorney general of Massachusetts was so worried about these efforts that he ordered a wiretap on Frankfurter's telephone."

66. Other scholars have commented on Frankfurter's inconsistency. See Thomas, *Frankfurter*, 62–63; Urofsky, *Frankfurter: Judicial Restraint*, 166; Hirsch, *Enigma*, 193.

67. *Everson v. Board of Education of the Township of Ewing*, 330 U.S. 1, 18 (1947).

68. *Illinois ex rel. McCollum v. Board of Education of School District*, 333 U.S. 203, 216–217, 231 (Frankfurter, J., separate opinion).

69. *Illinois ex rel. McCollum*, 333 U.S. at 238–256 (Reed, J., dissenting).

70. *Zorach v. Clauson*, 343 U.S. 306, 320–323 (1952) (Frankfurter, J., dissenting).

71. Quoted in Levinson, "Democratic Faith," 447.

72. William H. Manz, "Cardozo's Use of Authority: An Empirical Study," *California Western Law Review* 32 (Fall 1995): 39.

73. Alexander Bickel, *The Least Dangerous Branch*, 2nd ed. (New Haven, CT: Yale University Press, 1986), 35.

74. Theodore Roosevelt, *Theodore Roosevelt: An Autobiography* (New York: Macmillan, 1913), 61.

75. "Appendix A" in *Proceedings of Sixth National Conference: American Society for Judicial Settlement of International Disputes, December 8–9, 1916, Washington, DC* (Baltimore: Williams & Wilkins, 1917), 252–253; Andrew C. Pavord, "The Gamble for Power: Theodore Roosevelt's Decision to Run for the Presidency in 1912," *Presidential Studies Quarterly* 26 (Summer 1996): 643n7.

CONCLUSION

1. Learned Hand, "Three Letters from Alumni," *Harvard Law School Bulletin* 4 (January 1949): 7.

2. Jerome N. Frank, "Some Reflections on Judge Learned Hand," *University of Chicago Law Review* 24 (1957): 680.

3. Felix Frankfurter, "Hours of Labor and Realism in Constitutional Law," *Harvard Law Review* 29 (February 1916): 364, 362, 365.

4. Frankfurter, 362n30. Frankfurter was more on the mark in identifying Holmes as a forerunner of sociological jurisprudence. It is curious, however, that Frankfurter cited the *Perry* dissent, which did not advance sociological jurisprudence. A more obvious reference might have been made to "The Path of the Law," the pioneering article in which Holmes famously predicted: "For the rational study of the law the black-letter man may be the man of the present, but the man of the future is the man of statistics and the master of economics." Oliver Wendell Holmes, "The Path of the Law," *Harvard Law Review* 10 (March 1897): 469.

5. Jerome Frank, *Law and the Modern Mind* (New York: Brentano's, 1930).

6. Frank, "Some Reflections on Hand," 686, 687.

Index

Page numbers in italics refer to figures.

AALS (Association of American Law
  Schools), 55-56
Abrams v. United States (1919), 85–87, 97, 122
advisory opinions
  Frankfurter on, 131–132
  Thayer on, 32–33, 38, 112, 131–132
American Social Science Association
  (ASSA), founding of, 19
Ames, James Barr, 25–26
ASSA, founding of, 19
Association of American Law Schools
  (AALS), 55–56

balancing tests
  Holmes and, 77
  Pound and, 112–113
  Thayer and, 5–6
Boston Brahmin culture, Thayer and, 5,
  11, 16
Brandeis, Louis, 88–98, *89*
  Abrams v. United States (1919), 97
  appointed to US Supreme Court, 96
  background, 88
  and Brewster's Harvard course on
    Massachusetts law, 94–95
  and civil liberties protections, 97–98
  correspondence with Thayer, 95
  and death of Thayer, 95–96
  as disciple of Thayer, 1, 2, 88
  and economic legislation, views on,
    97–98
  failure to cite Thayer in later work, 97
  friendship with Thayer, 89, 90–91,
    165n25
  and fundraising for Harvard, 91–92
  Gilbert v. Minnesota (1920), 97
  on Harvard faculty, 93
  and *Harvard Law Review,* founding of, 94

and Harvard Law School, close ties after
    graduation, 93–95
  and Harvard Law School Association,
    93–94
  and hiring of Holmes at Harvard, 68,
    91–92
  Jay Burns Baking Co. v. Bryan (1924),
    96–97
  and judicial restraint, 96–98
  legal career, 90, 93, 96
  and the living constitution, 96
  Muller v. Oregon (1908), and Brandeis
    brief, 96, 142
  as one of greatest federal judges, 88
  on Pound, 108
  and progressivism, support for, 98
  as student at Harvard Law School,
    88–90
  support for fundamental liberties, 97–98
  on *Wigmore on Evidence,* 103
Brewster, Frank, 94–95

Carter, James C., 53–54
case method, introduction at Harvard Law
    School, 1, 20–21, 26, 33–34, 35, 88–89
Cases on Constitutional Law (Thayer)
  Holmes on, 77, 81–82
  Pound and, 112
  privileging of practicality over universal
    maxims, 132–133
  reviews of, 43–44
civil liberties
  Brandeis and, 97
  and judicial restraint, 41–42, 134–136
  See also freedom of speech
collectivism
  Frankfurter's embrace of, 129
  Pound's embrace of, 113

Commentaries on American Law (Kent),
    Holmes and Thayer's editing of,
    62–65
Commonwealth v. Josiah Perry (1891), 75,
    84–85
Commonwealth v. William B. Briant (1886),
    71–72
constitutionality of legislation, as distinct
        from prudence or wisdom
    Brandeis on, 96
    Frankfurter on, 130–131, 135
    Thayer on, 34, 42
constitutionality of legislation,
        presumption of
    Frankfurter on, 129–130, 134
    Hand on, 120, 121
    Holmes on, 75, 83–84
    Thayer on, 2, 3–4, 30–31, 36–40
    Wigmore on, 104–105
    See also judicial restraint; judicial
        review
constitutions, in legal realism
    allowability of actions not explicitly
        prohibited in, 34–35, 56–57, 76–77
    judges' deference to legislature's
        interpretation, 2, 3–4, 30–31,
        36–40
    as living documents requiring modern
        reinterpretation, 2, 4, 34–35, 56–57,
        108–109, 128
Coppage v. Kansas (1915), 121
court system, pyramidal nature of, 3

deference to legislature. *See*
        constitutionality of legislation,
        presumption of; judicial restraint
democracy, meritorious law-making
        as legislature's and voter's
        responsibility in
    Frankfurter on, 129–130, 134, 135
    Hand on, 123
    Thayer on, 37, 58–59
    Wigmore on, 104
Dicey, A. V., 55
Dillon, John F., 54–55

disciples of Thayer, 1
    characterization of Thayer as prophet,
        3, 115, 143–144
    differing relationships with Thayer, 124
    exaggeration of Thayer's uniqueness
        and prescience, 141–143
    and legal realism's rise to dominance,
        2–3, 88
    other influences on, 5
    overemphasis of continuity of their
        thought with Thayer's, 142–143
    prominence and influence of, 1, 2, 8, 88,
        140
    quasi-religious devotion to Thayer, 3,
        144
    and second-generation Thayerites, 125
    and spread of Thayerism, 139
    on Thayer's putative radicalism, 5,
        116–117, 141–142
disqualification by interest, 47
due process clause, and laissez-faire
        economic policy
    Hand on, 120
    Holmes on, 83–85

Eliot, Charles William
    Brandeis and, 89, 93
    and course on Massachusetts law, 94–95
    and hiring of Holmes at Harvard, 68, 91
    and Septem Club, 19, 27
    transformation of Harvard into modern
        research university, 19–20
Emerson, Ralph Waldo
    as advocate for generalist knowledge,
        18–19
    Brandeis and, 90
    contribution to Anne Lyman memoir, 9
    "Self-Reliance," 18
    Thayer and, 17–19
    as uncle of Thayer's wife, 17–18
Espionage Act
    Hand's ruling on, 121–122
    Holmes on, 85–87
establishment clause, Frankfurter on,
        137–139

Everson v. Board of Education (1947), 137
evidence law
  Holmes and Thayer's discussion of,
    70–74, 78, 80
  and judicial review, Wigmore on,
    104–105
  Thayer's publications on, 28–30, 35–36,
    72–73, 95
  See also *A Preliminary Treatise on
    Evidence at the Common Law*
    (Thayer); *Wigmore on Evidence*
    (Wigmore)
expert testimony, Hand on, 118–120

fact *vs.* opinion in evidence, Thayer on,
  115–116
formalism
 , definition of, 2
  Hand's rejection of, 121
  Holmes's rejection of, 67, 71, 76
  Lochner and, 84
  Pound's rejection of, 109–110, 111
  Thayer's rejection of, 2, 6, 38, 48–49,
    103–104, 109, 111, 116, 141
  Wigmore's rejection of, 103–104
framer's intentions. *See* originalism
Francis, Willie, 136–137
Frank, Jerome, 114, 120, 141–144
Frankfurter, Felix, 125–139, *127*
  abandonment of Jewish faith, 125–126,
    139, 172n6
  as adviser to Franklin Delano Roosevelt,
    128
  on advisory opinions, 131–132
  and American Civil Liberties Union, 128
  appointment to Supreme Court, 128
  background, 125
  on Brandeis, 96
  and capital punishment, 136–137
  causes supported by, 128
  on constitutionality of law *vs.* prudence
    or wisdom, 130–131, 135
  early legal career, 128
  on establishment clause, 137–139
  Everson v. Board of Education (1947), 137

  on Harvard Law faculty, 108, 128
  as Harvard Law student, 126, 127, 128
  on Holmes and sociological
    jurisprudence, 142, 175n4
  influence of Thayer and disciples on,
    126–128, 172n16
  on judicial restraint, 129–137, 174n58
  and legal realism, 128, 132–133
  on legislatures, prophetic judgment of,
    126, 132
  and living constitutionalism, 128
  on Marshall's fallibility, 133
  McCollum v. Board of Education (1948),
    137–138
  Minersville School District v. Gobitis
    (1940), 134–135, 174n58
  and modernity, embrace of, 128–129
  on new age replacing individualism
    with collectivism, 129
  privileging of practicality over universal
    maxims, 132–133
  on public schools as tool for unifying
    diverse population, 138
  on regulation of electrical power, 133
  religious attachment to American
    democracy, 126, 139
  on sociological jurisprudence as
    Thayer's invention, 142
  West Virginia v. Barnette (1943),
    135–136
  Zorach v. Clauson (1952), 138–139
freedom of speech
  Abrams v. United States (1919), 85–87,
    97, 122
  Espionage Act and, 85–87, 121–122
  Hand on, 121–124, 171n167
  Holmes on, 86–87
  as issue before World War I, 154n48
  Masses Publishing Co. v. Patten (1917),
    121–122
  Schenck v. United States (1919), 86–87,
    122
  standard of judicial restraint in cases
    implicating, 42
  United States v. Dennis (1950), 122

Gilbert v. Minnesota (1920), 97–98
Greenleaf, Simon and his treatise, 16,
    46–48, 100–101, 110

Hall, James Parker, 11, 17
Hand, Learned, 113–124, *114*
    background, 113–114
    correspondence with Thayer, 117–118,
        120
    as disciple of Thayer, 1, 2, 88, 114–115
    early law career, 117–118
    as federal district judge, 121, 122
    and freedom of speech, 121–123, 171n167
    at Harvard Law School, 114–117
    "Historical and Practical
        Considerations Regarding Expert
        Testimony," 118–120
    Holmes and, 122
    Holmes Lectures at Harvard Law
        School (1958), 123–124
    on judicial restraint, 120–124
    on liberty of contract, 120
    Masses Publishing Co. v. Patten (1917),
        121–122
    as one of greatest federal judges, 88, 123
    on Pound, 108
    support for social welfare legislation, 121
    on Thayer, 117, 119, 120, 141, 144
    Thayer's influence on, 115–117, 123–124
    United States v. Dennis (1950), 122
Hanson v. Globe Newspaper Co. (1893), 76
Harvard Law Review
    founding of, 94
    Hand and, 114
    Wigmore and, 99
Harvard Law School
    admission requirements, in 1850s, 14
    building used by, *15*
    course on Massachusetts law, 94–95
    gender, race, and anti-Catholic bias at,
        46
    as model for other law schools, 45–46
    Pow Wow Club, 89, 114
    professionalization of, 20, 24, 92
    Thayer as student at, 14–16, 22

Harvard Law School, Thayer as professor
    at
    and Brewster's course of Massachusetts
        law, 94–95
    and case method, 21, 26, 33–34, 35
    constitutional law course, 116–117
    early difficulties with teaching, 25
    efforts to expand law library, 24, 92
    excellence as teacher, 25–26
    first address as Royall Chair, 21–24
    and fundraising, 24, 91–92
    Hand's account of classes, 115–117
    hiring of, 19
    and hiring of Holmes, 68, 91–92
    influence on students, 88
    length of teaching career, 88
    and moot courts, 26–27
    as Royall Chair in Law, 19
    stature and credibility of position, 5,
        141–142
    teaching style, 26
    and Weld Professorship, 92
Harvard Law School Association, 93–94
Harvard University
    Eliot's transformation into modern
        research university, 19–20
    Thayer's undergraduate education at, 9,
        11–12
    and town of Cambridge, 10, 57
Hawkins, F. Vaughan, 81–82
historical legal science school of
        jurisprudence, Thayer and, 147n23
history in study of law
    Holmes and Thayer debate on, 79
    as key to reform, Thayer on, 59, 111
    Thayer on historical contingency of
        law, 2, 22
    Thayer's emphasis on, 116
Holmes, Oliver Wendell, Jr., 62–87, *63*
    Abrams v. United States (1919), 85–87,
        97, 122
    abrupt departure from Harvard faculty,
        68–69, 92
    address for Harvard's 250th
        anniversary, 71

at *American Law Review,* 64, 66
as apprentice in Thayer's law firm, 62
background and education, 62
as Civil War soldier, 62
The Common Law, 66–67, 81
Commonwealth v. Josiah Perry (1891),
    75, 84–85, 142, 175n4
Commonwealth v. William B. Briant
    (1886), 71–72
consultation with Thayer on a pending
    case, 70–71
correspondence with Thayer, 66–67,
    70–83
on deference to legislature, 75, 83–85
as disciple of Thayer, 1, 2
dissents, famous, 83–87
and economic legislation, views on,
    97–98
editing of Kent's *Commentaries,* 62–65
on experience, not logic, as life of law,
    48, 67
on freedom of speech, 86–87
friends' influence on legal doctrine of,
    87
Gilbert v. Minnesota (1920), 97
Hand and, 122
Hanson v. Globe Newspaper Co. (1893),
    76
on Harvard Law faculty, 68–69, 91–92
on history in study of law, 78–79
Jay Burns Baking Co. v. Bryan (1924),
    96–97
on judicial decisions as legislating from
    bench, 77–78
and judicial restraint, 75, 83–85, 86
on law as man-made, 78
law practice with brother, 64
and legal realism, 67, 76, 77–78, 82
Lochner v. United States (1905), 83–85
Lowell Institute lecture series, 66, 68
and Massachusetts Supreme Judicial
    Court, 67–69
nomination to US Supreme Court, 83
"The Path of the Law," 78–79, 175n4
Pound and, 108

"Privilege, Malice and Intent," 77–78
and progressivism, views on, 98
relationship with Thayer, 70, 74–75
rise to chief justiceship of
    Massachusetts Supreme Judicial
    Court, 82
Schenck v. United States (1919), 86–87.
at Shattuck, Holmes, & Monroe, 65–66
and sociological jurisprudence, 175n4
Speeches, 74–75
and Thayer, consonance of views, 71, 82
Thayer on selfishness of, 69
Thayer's aid to career of, 67–68
"The Theory of Legal Interpretation,"
    82
*Winthrop Delano v. Trustees of Smith
    Charities* (1884), 70–83
Hubbard, William J., 16, 17

Jay Burns Baking Co. v. Bryan (1924), 96–97
Jehovah's Witnesses' refusal to salute
    US flag, Supreme Court cases on,
    134–136
John Marshall (Thayer), 57–60
on abuses of judicial review, 57–59
on advisory opinions, 131
Frankfurter's quoting of, in *Barnette*
    dissent, 136
on judicial restraint, 129–130, 136
on Marshall and judicial review, 57–59
on Marshall's fallibility, 133
reviews of, 60
judicial discretion
    Hand on, 121–123
    Holmes on, 74, 77
    Wigmore on, 105
judicial discretion, Thayer on
    and distinguishing substantive from
        procedural law, 51
    in evidence, 105
    and legislating from the bench, 2, 49,
        115
    and need for judicial restraint, 2
    and privileging of practicality over
        universal maxims, 132–133

judicial impartiality as façade
Hand on, 121, 123
Holmes on, 78
Thayer on, 6, 38, 48–49
judicial overreach, Holmes on, 77
judicial overreach, Thayer on
negative effects on legislators and
citizens, 30–31, 38–39, 58–59, 130–131,
136
judicial restraint
Brandeis and, 96–98
and civil liberties protections, 41–42,
134–137
in evidence law, Wigmore on, 104–105
Frankfurter on, 129–130, 134–137,
174n58
Hand on, 120–121, 122–123
Holmes and, 75, 83–85
Pound on, 112
progressivism and, 4, 84, 85
Wigmore on, 104–105
judicial restraint, Thayer on
early work on, 16
as his most enduring contribution, 16
and modernization, 39
and potential for abuse of judicial
review, 57–58
and presumption of constitutionality, 2,
3–4, 30–31, 36–40
presumption of legislature's decency
and competence underlying, 37
as principled rather than partisan
position, 85
and psychoanalytic jurisprudence, 143
"reasonable doubt" standard for, 30, 36
teaching to students, 116
See also "The Origin and Scope
of the American Doctrine of
Constitutional Law" (Thayer)
judicial review
and evidence law, Wigmore on, 104–105
other critics of, in 1880s, 31
judicial review, Thayer on
potential for abuse of, 57–58
rationale for limits on, 4

Thayer's "Origin and Scope" on, 3–4
jury-judge division of labor, Thayer and
Holmes on, 73–74
jury system, Thayer on, 29, 50

Kent, James, 62–63
Kent, James, Jr., 63, 65

Langdell, Christopher Columbus
background of, 20
and case method, 20–21
Cases on Contracts, 26
as dean of Harvard Law School, 20
as legal realist, 158n111
personality of, 20
and professionalization of Harvard Law
School, 20, 24–25
relationship with Thayer, 20, 24–25
teaching style, 26
vision for legal education, 45
language, interpretation *vs.* intent,
Holmes and Thayer's discussion of,
81–83
law, Thayer on
general principles of, 115
lack of coherence in, 115–116
principles in, as merely guidelines, 2,
22
Law and the Modern Mind (Frank), 143
law career, Thayer on
early views, 13–14
knowledge required for, 23
law career in mid-nineteenth century
law degree unnecessary for, 14–15
and professional specialization, 18
law career of Thayer
choice of, 14
early work, 16
forming of own law firm, 17
Holmes as apprentice in Thayer's firm,
62
and intellect not suited to litigation,
17
passing of bar exam, 16
rise to master of chancery, 17

law reviews, and modernization of legal
  academia, 94
legal education, Thayer and, 1, 44–45,
  55–56
legal history, bias in field of, 7
legal realism
  contemporaries of Thayer advocating
    for, 5, 53–55
  diversity within movement, 6
  Frankfurter and, 128, 132–133
  Holmes and, 67, 76, 77–79, 82
  on judicial impartiality as façade, 6, 38,
    48–49
  in nineteenth century, current debate
    on prevalence of, 55, 157–158n111
  Pound and, 112–113
  rise to dominance, due to Thayer's
    disciples, 2–3, 88
  as term, 6
  Wigmore and, 103–104, 105–106
legal realism of Thayer
  in first lecture at Harvard Law, 22–23
  interdependence of law and society in,
    2, 23
  law as historically contingent in, 2, 22
  on law as socially constructed, 2, 22
  legal principles as merely guidelines in,
    2, 22
  vs. modern legal realism, 5–6
  as more farsighted than his peers, 55
  in *Preliminary Treatise on Evidence*,
    48–51
  as response to modernization, 1–2, 22,
    57, 141
  teaching of, 115–116
legal system of nineteenth century, absence
  of organizing philosophy, 6
legal thought of Thayer
  elements other than legal realism in,
    147n23
  as innovative but not radical, 5, 116–117,
    141–142
  summarization of, in first lecture at
    Harvard Law, 21–23
legislating from the bench

contemporaries of Thayer on, 54–55
  Holmes on, 77–78
  as unavoidable, in Thayer's view, 2, 49,
    115
legislative errors, correction as prerogative
  of legislature and voting public
  Frankfurter on, 130
  Thayer on, 4, 59, 130, 136
liberty of contract
  Hand on, 120, 121
  Holmes on, 83–84
  Pound on, 110–111
  Supreme Court on, 83, 84
living constitutionalism
  Frankfurter and, 128
  Pound and, 108–109
  Thayer on, 2, 4, 34–35, 56–57, 108
Lochner v. United States (1905), 83–85
logic, Holmes *vs.* Thayer's definition of,
  73
Lyman, Anne, 9, 12, 14

Maitland, F. W., 52–53
Marbury v. Madison (1803), 57–58
Marshall, John, 39, 133. See also *John
  Marshall* (Thayer)
Masses Publishing Co. v. Patten (1917),
  121–122
McCollum v. Board of Education (1948),
  137–138
McCulloch v. Maryland (1819), 133
Meigs, William, 31–32, 40–41
Minersville School District v. Gobitis (1940),
  134–135
money, paper, Thayer on constitutionality
  of, 34–35, 56
Muller v. Oregon (1908), and Brandeis
  brief, 96, 142

Native Americans, Thayer on legal equality
  for, 109
negligence, Holmes-Thayer debate on, 74,
  80
"normal speaker of English" standard,
  82–83

originalism, Thayer on, 34–35, 56–57
"The Origin and Scope of the American
    Doctrine of Constitutional Law"
    (Thayer), 36–43
    "Constitutionality of Legislation" as
        prequel to, 30–31, 42
    Holmes on, 76–77
    influence of, 3, 4, 36, 43, 129–130, 134,
        139–140
    on judicial impartiality as façade, 38
    on judicial presumption of
        constitutionality, 36–40
    on judicial review, 3–4
    original delivery as address at World's
        Fair (1893), 36, 39
    Pound and, 112
    reprinting and distribution of, 36, 40
    reviews and reactions, 5, 40–43
    on state conflicts with federal
        government, 42–43
    and Thayer's teaching, 116

parol evidence rule, 48, 103–104
Philippines, constitutionality of US
    conquest of, 56
Pollock, Frederick, 52–53
Pound, Roscoe, 106–113, *107*
    on administration of justice without
        law, 109
    background, 106
    as dean of Harvard Law School, 108
    as disciple of Thayer, 2, 88
    as distinct from Thayer, 112–113
    and formalism, rejection of, 109–110, 111
    on Greenleaf, 110
    at Harvard Law School, 106–107
    influence of, 108
    on judicial restraint, 112
    on law as balancing of interests, 112–113
    "Law in Books and Law in Action," 107
    on law's obligation to the collective
        rather than to individuals, 113
    legal and academic career, 107–108
    and legal realism, 112–113
    and living constitutionalism, 108–109

more-distant relationship with Thayer,
    113
and progressive agenda, support for,
    112
as prolific scholar, 7, 108
*Readings on the History and System of
    the Common Law,* 112
on reasons for public's contempt for
    lawyers, 111–112
and sociological approaches to law,
    107–108, 110–111, 112–113
and Thayerites as close-knit group, 108
Thayer's influence on, 107–112
on three stages of law, 110
"Toward a Better Criminal Law," 110
*A Preliminary Treatise on Evidence at the
    Common Law* (Thayer), 46–53
    appendices in, 80–81, 82
    on artificiality of legal categories, 50
    as distinct from *Wigmore on Evidence,*
        105
    on evidence law as product of
        experience rather than logic, 48–49
    on formalism, 109
    on fundamental tenets of evidence law,
        103
    Hand and, 116
    Holmes and, 78, 79–81, 82
    influence of, 51–53, 103–104, 105, 111, 139
    on judicial activism, 51
    on judicial discretion in evidence, 105
    on judicial impartiality as façade, 48–49
    on law as part of social fabric, 49–50
    legal realism in, 48–51
    on necessary flexibility of legal
        principles, 49
    and need for evidence law reform,
        46–47
    on need for simple and flexible
        evidence doctrine, 51
    on outcome-based reasoning, 50–51
    planned sequel to, 47–48, 51
    on practical aims of law, 50
    publication of, 48
    reviews of, 51–53, 157n99

on substantive *vs.* procedural law, 51
Wigmore and, 101, 103–104
presumption
vs. evidence to overcome presumption,
Thayer on, 117
of law *vs.* fact, Holmes and Thayer's
debate on, 71–73
"Privilege, Malice and Intent" (Holmes),
77–78
progressives, and judicial restraint, 4, 84, 85
psychoanalytic jurisprudence, Thayer and,
143
publications by Thayer
article on Fisher Ames (1854), 13
"Bedingfield's Case—Declarations as a
Part of the *Res Gesta*," 28–30
"Constitutionality of Legislation: The
Precise Question for a Court,"
30–31, 42
contribution to Lyman memoir, 9
early variety in, 17
influence of, 3, 28, 146n14
"'Law and Fact' in Jury Trials," 73–74
"Legal Tender," 34–35, 56
magazine articles and reviews, 17
modest number of, 3, 28, 60–61
other priorities taking precedence over,
7–8, 28
"Our New Possessions," 56–57
"Presumptions and the Law of
Evidence," 72–73, 95
"The Teaching of English Law at
Universities" (Thayer), 44–45, 99
Thayer's perfectionism and, 28, 60–61
See also *Cases on Constitutional
Law* (Thayer); *John Marshall*
(Thayer); "The Origin and Scope
of the American Doctrine of
Constitutional Law" (Thayer); *A
Preliminary Treatise on Evidence at
the Common Law* (Thayer); *Select
Cases on Evidence at the Common
Law* (Thayer)
public schools as tool for unifying
population, Frankfurter on, 138

Rabban, David M., 147n23, 154n48
railroads
and modernization of US, 13
Thayer's reporting on, as journalist, 13
real-world consequences, Thayer's interest
in, 13
reasonableness, as standard, 49, 81
Reed, Stanley, 138
Roosevelt, Franklin D., 128
Roosevelt, Theodore, Jr. "Teddy," 139–140
Ross, Edward A., 107–108

Schenck v. United States (1919), 86–87, 122
*Select Cases on Evidence at the Common
Law* (Thayer), 35–36
Brandeis on, 95
Holmes and, 82–83
reviews of, 35–36
second edition of, 118
Wigmore and, 100, 101–102
Septem Club, 16–17, 19, 20, 27
Smith Act, 122
sociological jurisprudence, Frankfurter's
claim for Thayer as originator of, 142
spontaneous exclamations (*res gesta*),
Thayer on, 28–29
Sumner, Charles, 17–18

Taft, William Howard, 45–46
Tamanaha, Brian Z, 157–158n111
Thayer, James Bradley, *12, 21, 33*
American Social Science Association
founding, 19
and antisemitism, 165–166n25
and Boston Brahmin culture, 5, 11, 16
Boston's Septem Club membership,
16–17, 19, 20
character of, as factor in his influence,
141
death of, 1, 61, 83, 95–96, 102, 120
as eulogist, 61
evidence treatise unfinished at death,
102, 105–106
family and early life, 9
funeral of, 1, 61

Thayer, James Bradley, *continued*
  genteel values of, 5
  on history as key to legal reform, 111
  and ideal of gentleman-scholar, 5, 13, 16
  influence of, 3, 5, 7–8, 88, 125, 139–140
  and Langdell's professionalization of
    Harvard Law School, 24
  on laws of evidence, inclusion of
    substantive law in, 48, 115
  marriage, 17
  modernizing world and, 1–2, 5, 10–11, 12,
    13, 18–19, 23, 24, 34, 39, 40, 45, 56, 57,
    92, 141
  rise from lowly background, 27
  scholarship on, 7
  as teacher, after college, 12–13
  on teaching methods, 35
  Unitarianism of, 14, 23
  work as journalist, 13, 44, 141
  See also Harvard Law School; judicial
    discretion, Thayer on; law career of
    Thayer; publications by Thayer
Thayer, Sophia Ripley (wife), 17, 18
A Treatise on the Law of Evidence
  (Greenleaf), 46–47, 100–101

University of Cincinnati law school,
  founding of, 45–46

variance doctrine, 47

Warren Court, activist approach to
  personal liberties, 123
Weld, W. F., 68, 91–92
West Virginia v. Barnette (1943), 135–136
Wigmore, John Henry, 98–106, 99
  acknowledgments of Thayer's
    influence, 103, 106, 124
  and Ames Prize for contribution to
    legal scholarship, 100

background and education, 98–99
Confessions, 100
correspondence with Thayer on
  pedagogical issues, 99–100
on deference to legislature, 104–105
as disciple of Thayer, 102
early teaching career, 99
editing of Greenleaf's *Treatise on the
  Law of Evidence*, 100–101
and formalism, rejection of, 103–104
and *Harvard Law Review* board, 99
Harvard Law School success, 99
legal disagreements with Thayer,
  101–102
and legal realism, 103–104, 106
as Northwestern Law School dean, 99
Pound and, 108, 110
as prolific scholar, 7
specialization in evidence law, 99–100
Thayer's classroom use of works by,
  100
Wigmore on Evidence (Wigmore), 102–106
dedication to Thayer and Doe, 106,
  168n89
influence of, 106
on judicial discretion in evidence, 105
on judicial restraint in evidence law,
  104–105
and legal realism, 103–104, 106
review of, 102–103
Thayer's influence on, 103–104, 105,
  106
writing of, 102
*Winthrop Delano v. Trustees of Smith
  Charities* (1884), 70
Wright, Chauncey, 11, 16, 20

Young, Brigham, 22–23

Zorach v. Clauson (1952), 138–139